THE LIFE OF HUNTING AND GATHERING TRIBE IN THE EASTERN GHATS

THE LIFE OF HUNTING AND GATHERING TRIBE IN THE EASTERN GHATS

Dr. C. Subba Reddy

KALPAZ

The Life of Hunting and Gathering Tribe in the Eastern Ghats

Rs. 750

ISBN : 81-7835-691-0

Published in 2010 in India by
Kalpaz Publications,
C-30, Satyawati Nagar,
Delhi-110 052
Phone: 9212729499
E-mail : kalpaz@hotmail.com

Laser Type setting by: Isas System, Delhi
Printed at: G. Print Process, Delhi

Contents

List of Table

List of Charts

List of Figures

Preface

The life of hunting and gathering communities is altogether distinct from that of the agrarian and industrial communities. The former communities dwell in the forests and they eke-out all the substance for their subsistence from the forest whereas the latter live in plain areas, majority depend on agriculture, industry and other livelihood activities.

The forest and hunting - gathering tribes are traditionally linked with each other and each one's survival is metaphorically attributed to the other. Tribals and forest have become two inseparable words *vanavasi, vanajathi, girijan* etc. are synonyms for tribals which means the forest dwellers, forest race and hill people respectively. The tribal relationship with forest is sentimental, symbolic and symbiotic.

The prejudice that the rural agricultural and urban industrial based communities hold that the hunting and gathering tribes are 'uncivilized' and 'inferiors'. Such extreme negative validation carry implicitly developmental paradigms of breaking the bond between "nature" an culture as an essential pre requisite to ameliorate the lot of these tribal people.

The resource base of the hunting and gathering communities' i.e. forest is declining on alarming rate. The destruction of forest for construction of dams, power plants, ammunition factories, establishing of police / military training camps, etc., is justified in the name of greater common good. The forest dwellers are facing the shortage of food providing vegetation. The grazing grounds and medicinal resource are gradually declining. Large scale industrialization, immigration of non tribal into the tribal lands have brought the radical changes in the tribe -forest relationship. The present day forest - dwelling tribals are increasingly subjected to a forced separation from their natural environment. Their economy, traditional resource management practices, customary rights and property rights regimes, traditional political arrangements, social institutions, resource sharing have been largely changed. The life of the forest dweller is at cross- roads and they are unable to survive in the changing circumstances.

The present book's emphasis is on eliciting the Chenchu (hunting - gathering tribe) relationship with forest focusing on territorial, instrumental, sentimental and symbolic dimensions. The Chenchus is the most primitive hunting and gathering tribe in Andhra Pradesh, is dwelling in Nallamalai, the middle section of the Eastern Ghats in India.

The entire book is organized into seven chapters. The background of the problem in perspective, review of literature, need of the present work on the hunting and gathering tribe, field work among the Chenchus in Nallamalai are discussed in chapter-1 Chapter- 2 is devoted to portraying the ethnographic account of the Chenchus including the geographical distribution, dress, settlements pattern, social organization, family, marriage, kinship system, economic organization, literacy status, political organization and religion and its changes due to tribe-caste continuum.

Chapter- 3 gives an account of the natural resources availability and distribution, seasonality, utilization of various types of floral and faunal resource for various purposes like food, fodder, fuel, medicine, commercial, magico-religious, liquor etc. An emphasis is also given on describing the traditional way of categorization of the forests as per the Chenchu , usage of floral resources based on their type. i.e. tree, plant, shrub, herb, etc. and based on parts used etc.

An attempt has been made in chapter 4 to estimate quantity of the flow of Non -Timber Forest Produce (NTFP) at the household level for various uses and converting them into monetary values. The ecological implication of the exploitation of NTFP is also attempted.

Chapter - 5 is devoted to describing the cultural perception of the forest, the traditional beliefs and knowledge systems of the Chenchus regarding the environment and floral, faunal and water resources. Chapter-6 deals with the various institutional aspects pertaining to utilization, management and conservation of forest resource as practised among the Chenchus traditionally. Specifically, it addresses the notions of property, rules pertained to defining and maintenance of resource boundaries, social organization of the village community, authority structure and conflict resolution mechanisms in respect of utilization and conservation of forest resource. The last chapter (7th) gives the summary and conclusions based on the empirical study.

Dr. C. Subba Reddy

their livelihood, ... plant ... birds harvested, and forest on ... [illegible] etc.

Acknowledgements

I wish to express my deep sense of gratitude, profound reverence, and heartfelt thanks to my teacher and Research Supervisor Dr. V. Gangadharam, Associate Professor, Department of Anthropology, Sri Venkateswara University, for suggesting a novel and fascinating problem for execution and also for his invaluable, scholarly guidance, constant encouragement, help and cooperation all through this task, which enabled me for successful completion of the thesis. His thorough discussions, scholarly guidance and critical analysis are responsible for the present form of the thesis. My mere words may not suffice to express my gratitude for all that I have learnt from him.

I would like to express my thanks to Prof. G. Prakash Reddy, Prof. M. Suryanarayana, Dr. P. Sudhakara Reddy, Dr. K. Vishwanadha Reddy, Dr. K. Nirmalananda Reddy and other teaching staff of the Department of Anthropology for their suggestions and help in successful completion of the thesis. My sincere thanks are due to Prof. A. Papa Rao, Head of the Department for his cooperation.

I am very grateful to Prof. Gurumurthi, Prof. D.R. Raju, E. Shobhan Balu, Research Scholar and Narasimha Reddy watchman, Telugu University, Srisailam, for providing accommodation during my stay at Srisailam.

My thanks are also due to following personnel of the ITDA, Srisailam: Mr. Sasthry, Mr. Chinna Veera

Badhrudu, Project Officers ; Subba Reddy, Agriculture officer, for providing data and accommodation in Ashram Schools ; Mr. Koti Veeraiah, Medical Assistant, for accompanying me in visiting Chenchu settlements ; Pothuluraiah, Warden, Polamma, Cook and Pothuraju watchman, Ashram School Palutla for providing accommodation and helping me in the collection of data.

I wish to express my gratitude to my friends B. Saikrishna, P. Bala Krishna Reddy, N. Tippe Swamy, V. Surya Narayana, P. Dilli, U. Harinath, M. Jeevaraj for their kind help in finalising the thesis.

I must express my deep sense of gratitude and great reverence to the following Chenchu members : Kudumula Bodeiah and Pothamma (who treated me with affection as if I was their child) and Bhumani Veeraiah, Earamma and Pothuraju of Palutla settlement, who provide boarding with a big heart and treated me as a member of their family throughout my stay in the field. Apart from them I am bound to express my gratefulness to Chevula Pothamma, Kudumula Pothuraju, Chigulla Pothaiah, Damsani Veerathatha, Chevula Anjaiah, Kudumula Anjaiah and Baigadu (Bailu) of Palutla settlement, Seelam Muthaiah, Kudumula Errapothadu, Chinna Pothuraju, Bujju, Polaiah, Damsani Pulla Guravadu, Bayyamma of Guttalachenu settlement, Kudumula Venkatesam, Eadhamma and Thikkalankadu of Alatam settlement, Kudamula Reddi Ankanna and Peddankulu of Ponnalabailu, Chevula Siddaiah and Nadipothadu of Nekkanti, Dasari Pothanna (teacher), and Muganna of Chinthala and Kudumula Gaddam Bayanna, Pedda Pothadu of Marripalem settlement for providing valuable data for my work and accompanying me in touring the forest area of their respective settlement. I am bound to pay tributes and profounded thanks to all my Chenchu friends who welcomed me as a member into their society and for their constant help during my stay in the field.

My emotional thanks are due to my parents, my wife and other members of my family without whose constant cooperation and immense encouragement this book would not have come into the present form.

Dr. C. Subba Reddy

1
Introduction

In India the tribes constitute an important socio-political segment, quite distinct from the other social segments such as castes. Tribal people are considered to be autochthonous and autocephalous. Their culture and history goes back to times immemorial. One chief feature of these people is their habitation in the forest. A majority of the tribal population (92.16 per cent of the total Indian tribal population) lives in the forest/rural areas (Mahapatra, 1994).

The relationship between tribes and forest is perceived, by and large in generalized terms for a long time. Tribals have always been seen sentimentally attached to the forest and considered them as the nature's gift. There is a symbolic relationship between the tribal social organization and forest economy. Tribals are not only forest dwellers but also for centuries they have evolved a way of life which on one hand, is woven around forest ecology and forest resources and on the other, ensures that the forest is protected against degradation.

Sinha (1957) and Vidyarthi (1963) have made analytical contribution in visualizing and delineating cultural matrix of Indian tribes vis-a-vis the forest in a spiritual domain. The tribal communities have developed a vast knowledge system and they have evolved several cultural practices to preserve the biodiversity. Anthropological studies indicate that the tribal people have strong ethically and spiritually doused and sustainable linkages with the forest. We find umpteen statements reflecting an inseparable and interdependent, tangible and intangible connotations concerning the ever-lasting bondage between the forest and the tribal people. "The tribes and forests are interdependent and each one's survival is metaphorically attributed to the other" (Deeney and Fernandes, 1992).

This major and sometimes the sole purport is conjured on the basis of fragmented details. The most obviously given picture is that the tribal population depends on the forest for all the subsistence needs. In turn the tribal people are beholden to the nature; it is respected, supplicated and nurtured. Linkenbach (1998) criticises that prior generalizations dominate these discourses and descriptions of the tribal relation to the forest. Typically the forest is conceptualized under the dominant stereotype of very cordial and perfect sustainable relationship.

There are various versions of thought as to the question of how the tribals have come to make forest as their habitat. One school of thought Haimendorf (1982) is that the tribals were gradually pushed back into the harsh environments. Some archaeologists Murthy (1985; 2000) argue that there is evidence suggesting human occupation of the present tribal habitats from prehistoric times. In the dominant 'elitist' Indian culture, such as *Sanskritic* tradition, and the modernist outlook, forest is visualized mostly as inauspicious and unfit for human habitation as seen in the former case and instrumental that too as a commercial resource as in the latter view point. Forest dwellers have been considered as people who are 'inferiors' and 'outlaws' as an oppositional category to those inhabitants in the rural areas and cities.

In certain gross estimates of the development planners, forest is seen evidently as an impediment primarily unsuitable to human existence. Further in extension of the same perspective a life in the forest such as those of tribals do not deserve the qualification of a life that is worth living. Such extreme negative validations carry implicitly developmental paradigms of breaking the bond between 'nature' and 'culture' as essential prerequisite to ameliorate the lot of these tribal people.

The latest satellite picture shows that over 19 per cent of India's landmass is covered by forests but the same imagery also shows that dense coverage amounts to less than 12 per cent. Even in the dense forest, considerable portion is either under monoculture plantation or devoid of the rich ground vegetation that it once had. Very little of India's land today retains good natural forest or pristine biodiversity (Kothari, 1995). India's biological diversity is rapidly eroding. More than half of its forest has vanished. Habitat destruction, hunting, over exploitation and pollution has caused a decline in many species. Of what remain, 10 per cent of flowering plants, 21 per cent of animals and 5 per cent of birds are believed to be under threat (Kothari, 1996).

In the past few decades, the tribe-forest linkages have assumed a specialized importance particularly in the event of degraded environment and problems of changes in climate, irregular rains that do not synchronize with the existing cycles of agriculture etc. The issue of conserving bio-diversity has received highest importance and the role of indigenous communities' in protecting the bio-diversity has been increasingly recognized. There is also a growing recognition that cultural variations manifest in different constructions of the forest (Eder, 1996; Bruun and Kalland, 1995). Escobar (1996) argued that in the invention of sustainable development, nature is reinvented as environment by post-modern capitalism through a discursive process. Thus, there is a 'reinvention' of the tribe-forest relationship.

Until recently, resource management based on local practices or traditional practices did not carry any significance in the views of bureaucracy, developmental experts and scientists. Now there is a growing concern to investigate the ecological sense of traditional practices. Modern resource management practices are based on explicitly stated rationale; they are implemented on the basis of written prescriptions, rules and regulations. These rules can be supported by explanations that are scientifically developed through research and experimentation. Traditional resource management practices are largely standardized over years through experience, trial and error. The traditional resource management practices, hence, are difficult to be supported by scientific explanations. A particular resource management practice such as exhibition of restraint on the use of a certain resource in a traditional community may be at best intended not to offend a deity or simply a matter of violation that would attract social sanctions. It is unlikely that the community members explicitly recognize that such practices yield an ecosystem service. It has, therefore, often been argued that the conservation consequences of traditional resource utilization practices are totally unintended or merely incidental coincidence (Diamond, 1993). It is quite likely that much of the resource management traditions among the indigenous communities may be simply rules of thumb which might have been institutionalized, that is, agreed upon to observe the rule(s) at least as a matter of convention by a majority.

However, conservation consequences of the inter-relationship between tribal culture and the forest have been challenged (Kalam, 1998; Freeman, 1998). The nature of tribe-forest relationship, at least in Indian context, is not much researched. Not much information exists regarding four important issues crucial in explicating the nature of tribe-forest relationship: (1) ecological understanding of the physical setting, particularly to know the constraints imposed by the environment that the community has to negotiate in order to gain subsistence and realize other needs (the nature and pattern of availability of various types of resources); (2) quantitative flow of Non-timber Forest Produce (NTFP) at the household level; (3) cultural conception and traditional knowledge about various floral and faunal resources and their utilization and (4) institutional mechanisms and social organizational arrangements in the management of resources. These issues will throw a better idea about the nature of forest-tribe relationship.

Even though it is well known that tribal people depend upon forests, adequate attention seems to be lacking with regard to the nature, range and extent of dependence on various types of forest resources. Food resources and medicinal herbs were given greater importance in the studies. Information on the number of plant species utilized, the quantities collected, and the end-uses has become extremely important in view of the recent, dramatic twist given in the management of natural resources. Further, we do not have data that reflect temporal trends in the demand for and supply of various forest resources.

An Overview of the Tribe-Forest Linkage

Man's relationship with the nature has attracted the attention of several anthropologists. The forests and tribals are traditionally linked with each other. The socio-economic life of the tribals is intimately interrelated and intermingled with the forests. Tribals and forests have become two inseparable words. *Vanabasi, Vanaputra,*

Vanajati, Girijan, etc., are synonyms for tribals, which mean the forest dwellers, forest sons, forest 'race', hill people respectively. They have developed a symbiotic relationship with each other. The tribals draw their sustenance from the forests. About ninety per cent of forest dwellers are tribals essentially depending on forest resources (Fernandes, 1983). The forest provides various types of food resources like fruits, flowers, tubers, mushrooms, honey, nuts, etc. The food habits, procuring methods, technology and sharing systems of food, band organization among the hunter-gatherer society attracted the attention of many anthropologists worldwide (Haimendorf, 1943; Berndt, 1972; Clastres, 1972; Damas, 1972; Gardner, 1972; Lee, 1972; Rogers, 1972; Silberbauer, 1972; Trindale, 1972; Adhikary, 1984). They conducted studies among hunters and gatherers in various parts of the world and portrayed how they procure food resource, the hunting methods, sharing the game among the local groups, etc.

In India, the studies focussing on the above issues in understanding tribe-forest relationship are very scanty. Most of the existing anthropological literature does not address these issues cohesively and directly. Notable exceptions that are Reddy, Sudersen and Patnaik (1987); Shukla, et al, (1990); Malhotra, et al (n.d) ; Bhanu (1982); Dash (1998); Gardner (1972); Bird-David (1990).

The literature directly addressing the tribe-forest relationship may be scanty in the Indian context, but anthropologists (Bhanu, 1992; Misra and Bhanu, 1980; Roy, 1994; Fernandes, 1984; Reddy, 1984; Kumari, 1990) have made significant contribution to this aspect in their studies on tribal people. Their works are related to boundary organization, territoriality, social organization and nomadism, rituals and belief systems concerning the flora and fauna, world view and economic organization etc., help in gaining insights into the stated problem of tribe-forest relationship. Karuppaiyan (1990) has brought forth the perspective that segmental division among the upland *Kallars* is territorial-based and having political functions.

Vidyarthi (1963) studied the relationship of man with the nature and spirit among the *Maler* - a hill tribe in Bihar. Chandra (1981) studied the ecological implications on the religion and belief systems of the *Kinner* - the mountain dwellers of northwestern Himalayas. Gupta (1981) analysed the relationship of nature-man-spirit complex. Mann (1981) used the cultural-ecological approach in his study among the *Bhils,* and the *Nigrito* hunters and gatherers. Morab (1981) attempted to elicit the relationship between ecology, society and religion among the *Soliga* - a hill tribe in south India. Prasad (1981) elicited nature-man-spirit complex relationship among the *Parahaiys.* Sahay (1981) portrayed the relationship of Nicobarese with the nature. Sinha (1981) attempted to elicit the nature-man-spirit complex among *Pando* tribe. Bhanu (1992) brings out clearly how *Cholanaickan* identity is intimately established by means of ecological regions subdivided into well-demarcated territories.

Bose (1964) depicted the dependence of the *Onges* on the nature for their survival. The availability of various types of food resource, methods of exploitation, and redistribution system among the *Onges* are also analysed. Reddy (1984) elicited the pattern of availability and utilization of food resources among the Andaman and Nicobar Islanders. Hart and Hart (1986) portrayed how the hunter-gatherers depend on forest for food resources. They analyzed the ecological basis of subsistence among the *Mbuti* of eastern Zaire in African rain forest. Most of the studies cited above focussed their attention only on food resources and not paid adequate attention to other non-timber forest produce (NTFP) used for various purposes like fodder, fuel, medicine, magico-religious purposes, etc. The Kalahari Bushmen project (Lee and DeVore, 1968) brings out various dimensions of the Kung Bushmen with their environment and resources.

The hunter-gatherers and other forest dwelling people seem to have developed institutions, rules and regulations in order to manage the natural resources in a sustainable manner. The indigenous organizational mechanisms like band, group and task group organization and rules regarding territoriality etc., attracted the attention of the anthropologists (Haimendorf, 1941; Turnbul, 1968; Helm, 1968; Sinha, 1972; Sarkar, 1986; Bhanu 1992; Andrews, 1993; Gangadharam, 1997).

Forest is a chief source of herbal medicine which, the tribes utilize for healing various ailments. In fact, the forest dwelling people have been surviving on these medicinal plants for centuries. "Even the commercial medicine depends on forest to a great extent. It is estimated that over forty per cent of all drugs have a natural base" (Fernandes, 1983:12). There are several studies concerning herbal medicine among several tribal communities, (Husain, 1950; Aneeta, 1974; Tarafdar, 1984; Roy and Chaturvedi, 1986; Pal and Sen, 1986; Shukla and Brij, 1991; Arora, 1993; Patnaik, 2000). Many of these studies have not appraised the resource base of herbal medicine, patterns of exploitation, depletion, conservation practices, etc.

Besides providing food, fodder, medicine, fuel etc., the forest is the major source of income to most of the forest dwelling tribals. They collect non-timber forest produce for commercial purpose. The sale of Commercial Non-Timber Forest Produce (CNTFP) like tamarind, soap-nuts, wax, honey, seeds and nuts, *tendu* leaves etc., is the most important source of income for them. Even when the forest dwelling tribals are shifting from their traditional occupation, the collection of forest produce continues to be the most important source of cash earning (Roy, 1990). Many scholars attempted to estimate the dependence of the forest dwellers on the CNTFP. (Geelani, 1986; Malhotra, et al, n.d.; Kant and Mehta, 1993; Kant, et al, 1996; Kant, 1997; Behara, 2000). The above studies attempted to estimate the income generated by sale of various forest produce and the problems faced by the forest dwellers in its collection and sale. Malhotra, et al, (n.d,) attempted to estimate the flow of NTFP at household level among the forest dwellers of Midnapur district in West Bengal.

The forests satisfy not only the instrumental and economic needs of the tribals but also their sentimental needs. The tribal beliefs, religion, rituals, folklore, dance, games etc., are evolved around the forests and its various resources. The cultural and emotional dependence of the tribals on the forests can clearly be seen in the institution like *sarna,* a sacred grove where the village deities are venerated (Gupta, Banerji and Guleria, 1981: 9). Chaudhuri, Rai and Pal (1975); Gadgil and Vartak (1976); Malhotra, Komne and Gadgil (1983); Das (2000); Jena (2000) have worked to elicit how the forest-dwellers, protect the forests by associating with spiritual and divine qualities. The totemic plants, animals and the sacred groves are highly revered by the tribals.

The policies made by the state regarding the management of forests have gradually marginalized the indigenous communities, particularly the forest-dwelling tribes. Before the advent of the British, there were only customary regulations on the forests. The situation gradually changed as the British exercised control over the forests in order to realize the commercial value of the forests and to augment the revenue to the state. Many scholars have examined the impact of the Forest Policies on the forest-dwellers (Reddy, 1982; Baxi, 1983;

Fernandes, 1983; 1990; Joshi, 1983; Kulkarni, 1983; Chakrabarthi, 1989; Gangwar, 1990; Aree Parampil, 1992; Mahapathra, 1994). They also made an attempt to understand causes for deforestation and the changes in tribal behaviour and attitude towards the forest.

The Indian Forest Act 1878 divided the Indian forests into three categories viz, (1) reserved forest, (2) protected forest and (3) village forest. Trespassing and grazing were prohibited in the reserved forest. The local governments were empowered to notify any forestland as protected forest.

Even after Independence there is not much change in the Forest Policy. The first National Forest Policy after Independence was issued in 1952 which laid paramount importance to the national needs (Kulkarni, 1983). This laid down that the claims of communities living in and near forest should not override national interests. The destruction of forest for construction of roads, irrigation dams, agriculture etc. was justified in the name of national interest. The *adivasis* (tribals) were discouraged from using forest resources. The government tried to obtain more and more revenue from the forests and treated the tribals as enemies of the forest (Kulkarni, *ibid*). In 1976 the National Commission on Agriculture (NCA) stated that, free supply of forest produce to the rural/ tribal population and their rights and privileges brought destruction to the forest, and so it was necessary to reverse the process. The commission did not take into account the needs of the tribals, and recommended stringent regulations to keep out the tribals from exploiting the forest resources (NCA quoted in Kulkarni, *ibid*).

The major objectives of the National Forest Policy, 1988 are: environmental stability, conservation of nature heritage, checking of soil erosion, increase the tree cover, meeting people's fuel wood, timber and minor forest produce (MFP) requirements, effective use of forest produce, creating a massive peoples' movement around afforestation (Fernandes, 1990). Though the policy consists of people-oriented statements, it mentions industrial requirements as national needs and seems to create a contradiction between national needs and peoples' needs.

Industrialization and modernization have displaced many forest dwellers by acquiring their land for building the infrastructure such as dams, roads, and industry. A major dam may irrigate large tracts of land belonging mostly to large and medium farmers, but the tribals are uprooted and little concern is given for their rehabilitation. Studies show that only 25 per cent of the families displaced in 1950-60s have been rehabilitated till now (Fernandes, 1990).

On account of these policies, programmes and developmental projects, the tribals have lost their resource base. The forest resources on which the tribals depend started shrinking. They are facing shortage of food providing plant species. The grazing grounds and medicinal resources are gradually disappearing. They have to walk for long distance for collection of firewood. The life of the forest-dwellers is at cross roads and unable to survive in the changing circumstances.

Expansion of agriculture, large-scale commercialization, penetration of market forces, immigration of non-tribal communities into the areas traditionally inhabited by tribes have brought a radical change in the tribe-forest relation. The present day tribal communities are increasingly subjected to a forced separation from their natural environment. Their economy, resource-management practices, customary rights and property rights regimes, traditional political arrangements and social relations, customary resource sharing and distribution have not remained what they were, though the traditional ethos in these aspects are still seen. The above review of literature indicates that there is an urgent necessity to launch studies on tribe-forest relationship in India.

In the light of the above background the present study is envisaged. The major aim is to elicit the tribe-forest relationship analytically focussing on territorial, instrumental, sentimental and symbolic dimensions. For this purpose, the Chenchu - a well-known tribe of Andhra Pradesh is chosen for the present study. Very few studies (Haimendorf, 1941; 1943; Sekhar, 1965; Reddy, 1972; Pratap, 1973; Bhowmick, 1989; Rao, 1993; Sastry,1993 ; Gangadharam, 1999) are conducted on the Chenchus. In Andhra Pradesh, there are about 33 tribes, which are known as Scheduled Tribes, promulgated according to the Indian Constitution. The Chenchu is the only tribe traditionally lived a life of hunting and gathering, depending directly on the forest resources. Though several changes are taking place, forest continues to be the central focus to the life and culture of the Chenchus. For all other tribes agriculture, horticulture, swidden cultivation and other artisanal occupations form the main stay though forest resources are no less important. However, agricultural production is central to the life and culture of the many tribes such as the *Koya*, the *Bhagatha*, the *Khond*, the *Savara*, the *Gond*, the *Bhil* etc. Agriculture is neither new nor totally absent among the Chenchus. But majority of the Chenchus is not adept in agriculture. Further, agriculture being an alien occupation has not been integrated into the socio-cultural life of the Chenchus. On the other hand, the forest has been a home to the Chenchus of the Nallamalai since times immemorial and as such their socio-cultural and religious life is intertwined with the forest.

Objectives

The main objectives of the present study are :

(1) to understand analytically the critical features of the physical environment, pattern of distribution and seasonal availability of the floral and faunal resources and to bring out the constraints imposed by the physical environment in the Nallamalai region on the Chenchus;

(2) to record various uses of non-timber forest produce (NTFP) and to quantify the flow of NTFP at the household level in the sample Chenchu settlements;

(3) to understand the cultural perception and traditional knowledge of the Chenchus concerning the forest and its resources and to elicit symbolic and sentimental dimensions the Chenchus have with the environment, more particularly with the forest; and

(4) to understand the institutional arrangements (in terms of rules and regulations concerning conservation, utilization of NTFP, property rights, social organization, etc.) devised by the Chenchus in the governance and management of NTFP.

METHODOLOGY

Area of the Study

The present study is conducted among the Chenchu-a hunting and gathering tribe of Nallamalai forest of Andhra Pradesh. The Chenchu is one of the twelve Primitive Tribal Groups (PTG) identified in the state. Most of the Chenchu population inhabits in the Nallamalai forest, which is their original ancestral land. "Seventy three per cent of their population is found in the districts of Kurnool, Prakasam, Guntur and Mahboobnagar which adjoin the ancestral land of the Chenchus (Gangadharam, 1999:19).

However, the area of the present study is confined to the Chenchus of the Nallamalai in Prakasam district of Andhra Pradesh. The Chenchus of hill areas in Prakasam district are leading their life in a more traditional manner than the Chenchus of the other neighbouring districts of the Nallamalai. Their dependence on the forests is also high. The infiltration of the non-Chenchus in the Chenchu settlements in hilly areas is almost absent due to their relative isolation and lack of transport facilities. "Relative inaccessibility and isolation of the Chenchu habitations, non-availability of cultivable fields to the peasants and relatively harsh conditions of the environment from the point of view of the peasants, stringent regulations of the Forest Department are some of the reasons which plugged infiltration" (Gangadharam, *Ibid*: 10). Owing to these reasons the present study is confined to the Chenchu settlements in the Nallamalai of Prakasam District.

Sample Selection

In order to select sample settlements for the present study, the author consulted various resource persons and agencies. He held discussions with the Research Officer of the Tribal Cultural Research and Training Institute, Hyderabad - a Research Organ of Tribal Welfare, Government of Andhra Pradesh, the Project Officer, Integrated Tribal Development Authority, of Primitive Tribal Group Chenchu (ITDA, PTG, Chenchu) Srisailam, the Field Director, Nagarjuna Sagar - Srisailam Tiger Reserve, Srisailam, and some of the Chenchus. The researcher prepared a list of thirteen Chenchu settlements in the Prakasam district. Pilot study was conducted in the Chenchu settlements like Chinthala, Marripalem, Thummalabailu, Chinnarutla, Panthanala,

Nekkanti, Palutla, Guttalachenu, Alatam, Ponnalabailu, Nadathadikala, Burugundala, and Chama in Prakasam District.

Eight sample settlements are selected for the present study based on the following criteria :

1. Greater dependence on forest resources for food, fodder, fuel, structural, medicinal and other purposes;
2. The practice of agriculture and other occupations should be very less;
3. Persistence of hunting and gathering way of life at least for a significant extent;
4. Absence or insignificant influence of the 'out siders'; and
5. Relative isolation from the plain area.

This type of purposive sample has become necessary in view of the objective of studying the dependence of forest-dwelling hunting-gathering community on the forest resources for subsistence and to elicit the traditional knowledge, indigenous institutional practices in management of natural resources. The selected sample settlements are Alatam, Chinthala, Guttalachenu, Marripalem, Nekkanti, Palutla, Panthanala and Ponnalabailu. All the households in all the selected villages were covered for collection of the data.

Alatam, Guttalachenu, Nekkanti, Palutla and Ponnalabailu fall in the jurisdiction of Yerragondapalem Mandal. Chinthala, Marripalem and Panthanala fall under the jurisdiction of Dornala Mandal. Except Chinthala, all the remaining settlements are to be reached on foot. Chinthala is located at the 35th km from Srisailam shrine towards Dornala by the roadside. Marripalem is located 5 kms south of Chinthala. Panthanala, Nekkanti, Palutla, Guttalachenu, Alatam and Ponnalabailu are located in the eastern side of Srisailam shrine at the distance of 8, 18, 25, 30, 35 and

Map 1.1

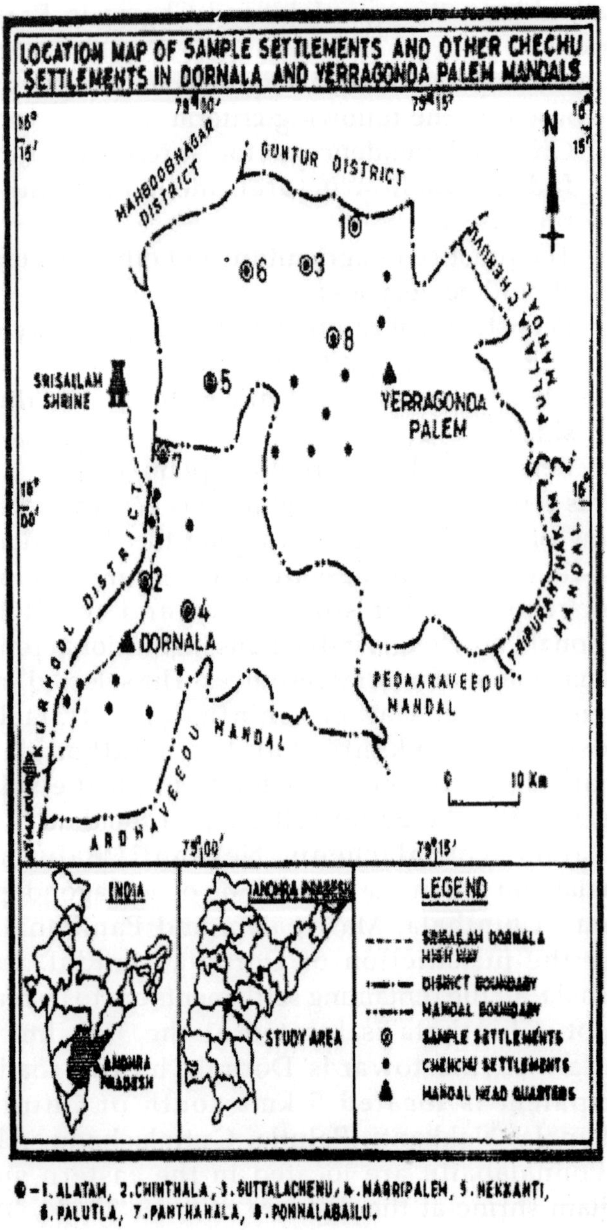

◎ – 1. ALATAM, 2. CHINTHALA, 3. GUTTALACHENU, 4. NARRIPALEM, 5. NEKKANTI, 6. PALUTLA, 7. PANTHAHALA, 8. PONNALABAILU.

30 kms., respectively. All these settlements are to be reached only on foot. The map 1.1 shows the sample settlements along with other Chenchu settlements in Dornala and Yerragondapalem mandals of Prakasam district.

FIELD-WORK

The field-work was conducted for two years during 1997 and '98. It was carried out in five phases: (1) January to April, (2) July and August, (3) November and December of 1997 and (4) May and June, (5) September and October of 1998. The field-work was chalked out to cover all the seasons in the year.

Techniques Used for Collection of Data

Data collection among the Chenchus is an extremely difficult job. The people are very much suspicious of 'outsiders' and are quite timid in the presence of outsiders. A great deal of reservedness seems to be the chief feature of the Chenchus. They speak very less and do not participate in conversation with enthusiasm. If pestered, they tend to express their displeasure, or simply disappear. Many of them are fond of consuming locally made liquor. In general, there is a sense of aloofness, alienation vis-a-vis outsiders.

Hence, establishing confidence and their acceptance of the researcher's presence among them became essential. The researcher entered each settlement through the Chenchus, whom he met at Srisailam market or introduced to him by many of his friends in Telugu University, Integrated Tribal Development Authority (ITDA) and the Forest Department. The Chenchu teachers were much helpful; they not only provided necessary background about the informants but also helped in 'validating' (cross-checking) information collected.

Rapport building involved working with the Chenchus in the forest, accompanying them during their hunting trips, seasonal migration, sharing food, spending time with the elderly, advocacy on their behalf with the interventionists and Development Agencies.

The chief method employed for data collection was participant observation. The researcher lived in a hut located at vantage point in each settlement. The option of living among them is a good starting point in the field-work though there were subtle objections which were overcome by means of explaining the need and necessity (much of the information could be collected without distracting them from the work they indulged in). The researcher mingled with the people and participated in their daily chores, which naturally attracted the attention of others. He took special care to move with the persons who had relatives in other sample settlements, so that, a sort of continuity is maintained. (The researcher's experience in one village is transcended into other sample villages). This was done particularly by two means. He used to take an informant of one settlement into the next settlement and made him to stay on for a few days (maximum of eight days), thereby this informant acted as a 'spokesman'. He always quoted the details from the first village such that he got feedback besides making a good beginning to draw their attention to get answers to the queries. The Table 1.1 shows the various tools used for the collection of data.

Table - 1.1 Techniques used for Collection of Data

Sl. No.	*Techniques*	*Data Collected*
1	Participant observation	Organization, values, norms, ceremonies, practices, belief systems of the Chenchu society, hunting,

		distribution ot the game, collection of food, honey and minor forest produce, grazing.
2	Schedules	Household data like: number of members in the family, age, sex, marital status endogamous, exogamous, monogamy or polygamy, literacy levels, migration, occupation, live-stock, agricultural land, income, consumption of NTFP, seasonal camps.
3	Structured interview	Data regarding flora and fauna and their utilization.
4	Interview guide	Village territoriality, clashes between villages, seasonal camps, indigenous conservative practices, sacred groves, rituals etc. Indigenous view on forest, availability and utilization of flora and fauna, traditional medicinal practices, animal behaviour etc. History and origin of the Chenchus and other ethnographic information.
5	Case Study	Conflicts in collection of CNTFP, seasonal camps, hunting and sharing the game, rituals, sacred groves, conflicts between the settlements, etc.
6	Documents	Secondary data regarding the Chenchu tribe like origin of the tribe, racial relations with others, population etc. Data on environment that is Nallamalais, Forest types, Forest policies etc and developmental programmes implemented by ITDA and tribal welfare agencies, etc.
7	Ecological survey	Sample sites consisting the size of 10 mtrs by 10 mtrs are selected in different areas and the number of species and plants were counted to know the spatial distribution of floral resources.

Apart from these tools, group discussions, interviewing the key-informants were also carried out.

Further details of methods of data collection are given in respective places in the following chapters.

Analysis of Data and Interpretation

Data analysis was carried out manually by using the scientific calculator. The data were first edited and grouped into various categories. The frequency tables were made out of the household census schedules. Frequency distribution of household according to clans, type of marriages, occupation, quantitative aspects of NTFP are tabulated.

The data collected regarding the flora and fauna of the Nallamalai in the studied area were classified into various groups like habitat of floral and fauna, end-use, parts used, season of availability etc., and were tabulated. The main aim of this study is to understand the dependence of the Chenchus on the available natural resources. To estimate this dependence various intermediate aspects were studied. For instance, to understand the dependence of Chenchus for food on the floral resources, aspects like habitation of the plant or animal, technology, group activity, seasonality, sharing rules, ownership rights etc., were studied. Regarding animal resource, the habitation, season of reproduction, food, and their utilization to the Chenchus, and the animal behaviour were also analysed. The methods of quantitative estimation of the NTFP consumed or utilized at the household level are discussed in chapter four.

Presentation of the Thesis

The study is presented in seven chapters. The first chapter discusses the problem in the perspective, the review of literature and research methodology. An ethnographic account of the Chenchus reflecting their present and past culture is presented in the second chapter. The availability and the utilization of the flora and faunal resources, the types of flora and fauna utilized, the seasonal changes of the resources, the end-uses etc., are discussed in the third chapter. The fourth chapter deals with the consumption of biomass at household level. The details on the estimated quantitative flow of non-timber forest produce (NTFP) for various purposes like food, fodder, fuel, structural etc., are given in this chapter. The fifth chapter is devoted to elicit cultural perceptions of the forest, the traditional beliefs and knowledge systems of the Chenchus regarding the flora and fauna and their utilization. The sixth chapter discusses the institutions developed by the Chenchus regarding the management of the natural resources and the recent changes occurring in the tribe-forest relationship. The seventh chapter gives the summary and conclusions based on the empirical study.

2
Ethnography of the People

The state of Andhra Pradesh is the traditional homeland of thirty three tribal groups. Rao (1993) proposed a five fold classification of tribal areas of Andhra Pradesh: (1) the Gond-Kolam region, (2) the Koya-Konda dora region (3) the Khond-Savara region, (4) the Chenchu region and (5) the Plain areas. Among the prominent tribal groups mention may be made of: the Gonds and the Kolams (Adilabad district); the Koya and the Konda Reddy (East Godavari, Khammam and Warangal districts); the Savara, the Khond and the Bagatha (Visakhapatnam district); the Chenchu (Prakasam, Kurnool, Mahboobnagar and Guntur); and the Yanadi and the Yerukala (Nellore and Cuddapah districts).

Most of the tribal groups inhabit the mountainous areas along the Eastern Ghats starting from Cuddapah district to Visakhapatnam and Srikakulam and a spectrum of occupations is seen in the tribal economy. While agriculture is the most predominant occupation for many tribal groups, occupations like shifting cultivation, animal husbandry, horticulture, fishing and food gathering are also reported (Rao, *ibid*).

THE CHENCHU

The Chenchu is an ancient tribe traditionally known to have led a life of food gathering and hunting.

Haimendorf (1943) singles out the Chenchus as the most simple tribe leading a life of food gathering and hunting. The Government of Andhra Pradesh has categorized the Chenchus as the Primitive Tribal Group (PTG) along with eleven other groups. The total population of the Chenchus is 31,000 in Andhra Pradesh (1991 census quoted in Rao, *Ibid*).

Very little is known about the history of the Chenchus. The epics *(Manusmrithi)* and other popular stories revealed that the Chenchus are the first dwellers of the Andhra region, much earlier than the Dravidian stock. Thurston (1909) quotes different accounts (Buchanan, 1807; New Bold, 1846; Mechanjee, 1862; Kurnool District Manual, 1885) to delineate ethnic affinity with the *Irulas*, the *Sugalis* and the *Yanadis*. However, the Chenchus of Nallamalai hold no such connection with these tribes.

Thurston (1909) and Guha (1931) described the physical features of the Chenchus. According to them the Chenchus are of medium height and stature with slightly lengthy limbs, dark but bright sunken eyes, weavy hair, receding chin with a beard resembling a tuft, short nose with blunt and prominent cheek bones. The people are usually lean, well proportioned and black to brown in complexion.

Geographical Distribution of the Chenchu Tribe

The Chenchus are distributed throughout Andhra Pradesh. However, the Nallamalai forest is said to be their ancestral homeland. Nearly 75 per cent of their total population is found in the Nallamalai adjoining four districts viz., Kurnool, Prakasam, Guntur and Mahboobnagar. Even in these districts the Chenchus are predominantly concentrated in a few Mandals. Nandhyal, Velugodu and Athmakur Mandals of Kurnool district, Dornala and Yerragondapalem Mandals of

Prakasam district, Mannanur and Amrabad Mandals of Mahboobnagar district and Vinugonda Mandal of Guntur district are the most concentrated areas of the Chenchus.

Origin of the Chenchus

The popular mythology that expounds the origin of the Chenchus centres on a theme that Lord *Maha Vishnu,* in the incarnation of *Nrusimha,* after killing the *asura* (demon) king *Hiranyakashyapa* was cooled down by a damsel who is said to belong to the Chenchus. This Chenchu girl is called *Chenchu Lakshmi* who is the incarnation of Goddess *Lakshmi,* the consort of *Sri Maha Vishnu. Nrusimha* fell in love and married *Chenchu Lakshmi.* This myth neither explains the origin of the Chenchus nor why Goddess *Lakshmi* was born in the Chenchu group. The Chenchus simply narrate this myth to proclaim that their 'girl' was married to Lord *Maha Vishnu.*

The Name and Identity

Various explanations are in vogue regarding the meaning and origin of the name Chenchu (Census, 1961). These interpretations are shown in the Table 2.1.

Table-2.1 Explanation of the Meaning and Origin of the Name of the Chenchus

Sl. No.	*Dimension/ Interpretation*	*Explanatory Meaning*
1.	Ecological	Habit of living under a *chettu* (tree)
2.	Economical	Habit of *chanch* (wandering-seasonal nomadism) for collection of food resource.
3.	Racial	Chenchu hair was like *chendu* (ball)
4.	Cultural	Habit of eating *chunchu elaka* (a kind of rat)

Note : The racial interpretation seems to be not valid because many Chenchus do not have curly hair.

Dress and Ornaments

Traditionally the Chenchu men used to wear only a loin cloth to cover gènitals and a waist cloth. They left their hair untrimmed and made a knot at the back of the head. The women used to wear a blouse and a cloth wrapped around waist. They used to wear several ornaments like ear-rings, nose-rings, bangles, armlets etc., which they used to purchase from the neighbouring plain areas or vendors. Tattoo marks adorned their face and forearms.

In the last thirty years radical changes have taken place in their dress pattern. The young Chenchu men wear trousers or knickers and shirts. Women wear blouse and full sari. However, the old men and women still retain their traditional dress pattern.

Settlement Pattern

The earliest reports (Newbold, 1846; Haimendorf, 1943) observed that the Chenchus lived in settlements of small huts erected in cleared spots amidst the jungle. In Scott's Ferista, the Chenchu are said to have lived in caves or under the shade of trees (quoted Gangadharam, 1999). Haimendorf (*ibid*) recorded the peoples' memory of the days during which their ancestors roamed in the jungle living under trees or rock shelters without any hut. Today the Chenchus live in 'permanent' settlements and have 'sufficiently' and 'solidly' built huts.

The Chenchus generally live in small settlements locally called *gudems* or *pentas*. It was mentioned in the Census of India (1961) that their habitations fixed at one place, bearing a proper name of the place must be a later development. The Chenchu settlements in the Nallamalai are widely dispersed. It is rarely seen that any two *gudems* are built closely. Usually, there is a minimum distance of about 5-6 kms between any two adjacent *gudems*. While a few of them are located at the edge of forest or nearby the roadways, many are nestled in the picturesque localities inside the forest. The settlements chosen for the present study are located in the interior forest.

Each Chenchu settlement comprises two categories of individuals: *mirasidars* and *punnapollu*. *Mirasidars* are the descendants of the original settlers belonging to single *kulam* (surname group/clan). *Punnapollu* are the immigrants and their descendants. They belong to different *kulams/clans* migrated from different settlements. The huts belonging to the *mirasidars* or *punnapollu* do not huddle together to signify distinctiveness. On the other hand the huts of the *mirasidars* and *punnapollu* are dispersed throughout the settlement mixing up together.

Usually the Chenchu settlements are located one or two furlongs far away from the natural water source, as the wild animals will be visiting these water bodies. Generally the huts are constructed on elevated places and forest clearings dotted by several trees. The Table 2.2 gives the brief account of topographical features of the sample settlements.

Table - 2.2 Topographical Features of Sample Settlements

Sl. No.	*Name of the Settlement*	*Topographical features*
1.	Alatam	Gentle slope with rocky terrain on the right bank of Krishna river
2.	Chinthala	Foot hills
3.	Guttalachenu	Level ground on Palutla plateau
4.	Marripalem	Foot hills
5.	Nekkanti	Hill top on Palutla plateau
6.	Palutla	Basin on Palutla plateau
7.	Panthanala	Level ground on Palutla plateau
8.	Ponnlabailu	Plateau

Settlement sites are not permanently pitched to a site. Whenever, the Chenchus feel inconvenient due to suspicion of the wandering of evil spirits in the settlement, or occurrence of frequent deaths, they shift the settlement to a new place. For instance, the Nekkanti settlement was shifted from old place to the new place in 1990 upon the occurrence of frequent deaths within a short span of time. Even within the settlement, the individuals shift their huts from one place to another due to the clashes with neighbours, death of a member in the family and frequent illness to the members of the family.

Each Chenchu settlement may be divided spatially into two or more divisions. Each division is separated from the other by a distance of 100 to 200 metres. Each division is also known by a specific name particularly reflecting the topography. For instance, in Palutla settlement, three sub-divisions are seen: (1) *Jenkula banda gudem;* (2) *Marri chettu gudem;* and (3) *Peddha gudem.* These sub-divisions have developed due to population growth and subsequent separation from the parent group and conflicts. A more conspicuous feature of the Chenchu settlements is that they comprise several clusters of huts separated from each other by a reasonal distance. The huts in each cluster belong to a group of kin, which may be designated as kindred. Each cluster may comprise 5 to 8 huts. Figure 2.1 shows the settlement pattern of the Chenchus in Palutla settlement.

The huts in the settlements are solidly built with bamboo wattle walls. There are three types of huts (Fig. 2.2) in the Chenchu settlements: (1) *Chuttu gudfsa* (round hut) (2) *Mula gudisa* (square hut) and (3) *Kottamu* (rectangular hut). The types and measurements of huts are shown in the Table 2.3.

Table - 2.3 Types of Huts in Chenchu Settlement

Sl. No.	*Name/Type of huts*	*Total area (Mtrs)²*	*Length (Mtrs)*	*Breadth (Mtrs)*	*Height (Mtrs)*
1.	Chuttu gudisa	2.16	Perimeter[1]	3.60	4
2.	Mulagudisa	16	4	4	4
3.	Kottamu	26	6.50	4	4

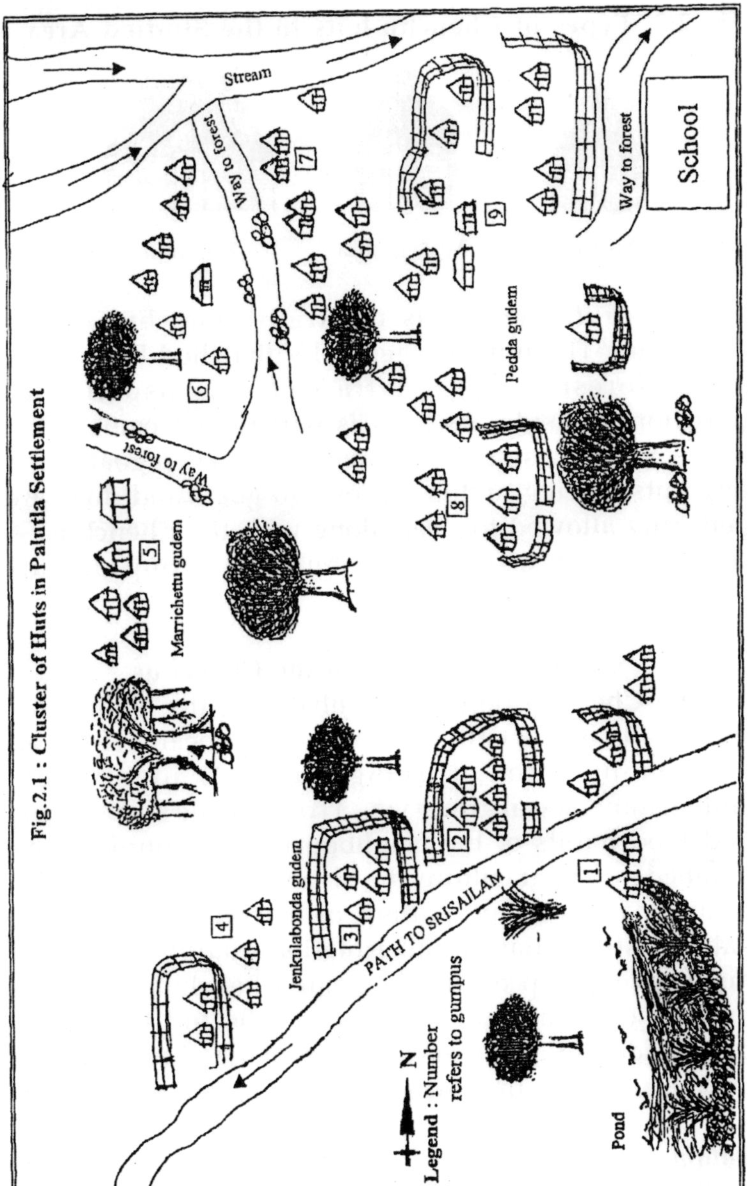

Fig.2.1 : Cluster of Huts in Palutla Settlement

Fig 2.2. Types of Chenchu huts in the Studied Area

Chuttu gudisa Mula gudisa Kottamu

The *chuttu gudisa* is the traditional hut of the Chenchus. The huts are generally thatched by *katterra gaddi* (forest grass). *Chuttu gudisa* is usually not partitioned inside. *Kottamu* is partitioned comprising rooms for food storage, kitchen and to keep goats. In a few huts, during nights one or two goats and dogs are generally allowed to sleep along with the Chenchus. A fence may enclose a single hut or a group of huts together.

Social Organization of the Chenchus

The Chenchu population inhabiting the Nallamalai forest falls into a culturally and linguistically (with an indigenous form of Telugu dialect) identifiable endogamous social group viz., a tribe. While some rituals and food habits of the neighbouring communities are imbibed into their culture, the distinctive features of their traditional economy, pattern of marriage and family, value system, dialect and isolation qualify them as a distinctive group of people. Some Chenchus point out proudly of their habit of living in hills and forest as a distinct identity. The principal units of the Chenchu social organization are the *kulam,* the *gumpu* and the family.

Kulam

The Chenchu tribe comprises several exogamous groups locally known as *kulams.* These groups are also known as *intiperu* (surname). The members belonging to the same *kulam* are known as *kulapollu*. The *kulam* can be equated with the clan. The main characteristic feature of the *kulam* among the Chenchus is exogamy. The members of the same *kulam* are considered as the descendants of an unknown and unnamed ancestor. Hence, the marital relationship among the members of the same *kulam* is strictly prohibited.

To the question of the origin and etimological meaning of the *kulams*, the Chenchus are obscure in their explanations. Some of the names indicate rough equivalent Telugu meanings, which need not be true meanings. To cite an example the *Nimmala kulam* can be deemed as either a lime plant or *nemali* (a peacock). In the same way the *Nallapothula kulam* may mean either a black he-goat or a nilgai. The origin of few clans is narrated by the Chenchus. According to Kudumula Pothamma (60) of Palutla, the *Chevula kulam* has originated from a woman called *Chevula Daravva* who was said to have longer *chevulu* (ears).

According to the Chenchus, there are 64 *kulams* but they are unable to reveal all the names. The 1961 Census (1966:8) identified only 26 *kulams* among the Chenchus. These *kulams* are widely distributed throughout the Nallamalai. Each settlement comprises several *kulams*. Of these, only two or three *kulams* are numerically predominant over the other *kulams*. It appears, as a few *kulams* are concentrated in different localities. For instance, the *Chevula Kulam* is predominant in Palutla and Nekkanti but is absent in Chinthala basin. The *Kudumula* and *Bhumani kulams* are widely found in Marripalem and Chinthaia region. Haimendorf (1943:89) opines "that the clans were once regional units and in possession of clearly defined tracts of land". However, several other *kulams*, each represented by a meagre number of households are seen in almost all the Chenchu settlements. Table 2.4 gives *Kulam* wise distribution of households in the sample settlements.

Table - 2.4 Number of Households of Various Kulams in the Sample Settlements

Sl. No	*Name of Kulams*	*Sample Settlements*								
		Alatam	*Chintala*	*Guttalachenu*	*Marripalem*	*Nekkanti*	*Palutla*	*Panthanla*	*Ponnalabailu*	*Total*
1.	Arthi		2							2
2.	Bhumani		19	1	8		1			29
3.	Chevula					7	20		1	28
4.	Chevuri			1						1
5.	Chigulla			2	2		5	3		12
6.	Damsam				3					3
7.	Damsani			4		1	12		1	18
8.	Dasari		6		3					9
9.	Gulla				2					2
10.	Jalla		3		5		1			9
11.	Kudumula	6	10	10	24	2	20	1	8	81
12.	Mandli					1	6			7
13.	Nimmala						1			1
14.	Pitta						2			2
15.	Pulicherla				3					3
16.	Seelam			2						2
17.	Udathala						2			2
	Total households	6	40	20	50	11	70	4	10	211

Note: Average number of *kulams* per settlement is 5.

Each sample settlement in the present study comprises several *kulams* excepting Alatam which has only one *kulam* namely *Kudumula.*

In some settlements the households of the *Kulams* of immigrants are numerically predominant than the households of *kulam* of the original settlers. The Table 2.5 gives details of *kulams,* numerically preponderant vis-a-vis original *kulams* in sample settlements.

Table - 2.5 Distribution of *Kulams, Kulam* of Original Settlers, and Numerically Predominant *Kulams* in Sample Settlements

Sl. No.	*Name of the settlement*	*No. of kulams*	*Kulam of First settlers*	*Present numerically predominant kulam*
1.	Alatam	01	Kudumala	Kudumala
2.	Chinthala	05	Arthi	Bhumani
3.	Guttalachenu	06	Kudumala	Kudumala
4.	Marripalem	08	Kudumala	Kudumala
5.	Nekkanti	04	Chevula	Chevula
6.	Palutla	10	Chevula	Kudumala and Chevula
7.	Panthanala	02	Chigulla	Chigulla
8.	Ponnalabailu	03	Kudumala	Kudumala

It seems in the remote past, there might not have been as many *kulams* as seen at present in each settlement. Each settlement might have been inhabited by one *kulam*. Haimendorf (1943: 88) writes each tract of the country is mainly inhabited by one or two clans, although individual families of other clans may live in their midst.

The *kulams* in each *gudem* can be categorized under a group of consanguineous and a group of affines. The former is called *annadammula varasa kulalu* and the latter group is called *bammardhula varasa kulalu*. Marital relations are prohibited between the members of the former group but permitted with the members of latter group.

Gumpu

Apart from the exogamous group the *kulam*, the Chenchu social organization is characterized by the existence of the egocentric groups. Each group is referred to by a blanket term called *gumpu*, which means a group. This *gumpu* comprises five to ten families of both the affinal, agnatic and uterine relatives of the ego. All the members need not be closely related. Usually all the families in the *gumpu* live together in a cluster of huts. The *gumpu* is referred to by the name of the 'ego' around whom the *gumpu* is formed. Haimendorf (1943:97) recognised the presence of these groups and termed them as local groups "whose cohesion is based on common interest and more or less identical activities".

The *gumpu* is a cooperative unit. The members assist one another in such activities, which require additional labour, more than one's own family labour. Some of these activities are hut construction, agricultural works like ploughing, sowing, threshing, honey collection, group-hunting. The transactions among the *gumpu* are based on reciprocity and cooperation. Usually members of the *gumpu* unitedly exploit the food resources in one area. The hunted game is invariably shared among the members of a *gumpu*. Further details of the *gumpu* are given in Chapter-VI. The members of a *gumpu* generally do have relationship with the ego in one way or the other. However, the non-relative also can join with the *gumpu* by establishing friendship with the ego or any other member in the *gumpu*.

Family

The family is the most important and basic institution in the Chenchu society. It is a well-defined and conspicuous unit in the social structure of the Chenchus. As a viable social unit the family possesses relatively permanent and clearly perceivable composition and provides customary opportunity for sexual relations and division of labour.

A majority of the Chenchu families are nuclear, constituting wife, husband and unmarried children. Sometimes, relatives of either the husband or the wife are also seen residing under the same roof. Generally the married sons leave their parents and establish their own house. The married girl leaves her parents' home and lives with her husband. Sometimes the parents also live with their married son. Residence in the bride's place of origin is also fairly common.

The Chenchu family is a fitting example of the definition given by Murdock (1965). All the four functions enunciated by him can be seen: mutual sexual rights; division of labour; reproduction; and socialization. The Chenchu family, however, is under a serious obligation to lead a cooperative life in conjunction with other families. Though a primary responsibility is vested with the wife and the husband who constitute the chief actors in the family, the process in the actual realization of these four functions depends to a large extent by the active cooperation, linkages and participation by individuals living in other families.

Within the family sphere, the wife and the husband perform various roles, which are sometimes mutually exclusive and sometimes mutually interchangeable. For instance, baby-sitting is a job of both male and female; hunting is the domain of males; food gathering is the pre-occupation of women even though men sometimes also take part in this.

Sexual rights are mutually exercised and sexual loyalties and fidelity are jealously guarded. Sexual incompatibility is resolved by recourse to separation. Wife and husband enjoy equal status. Both are equally responsible for the maintenance of the family. A spirit of competitiveness exists between them.

The Chenchu family operates through interfamilial linkages, so that it gains sustenance rather than to face hardships. This can be exemplified by the fact that the Chenchu prefer to live in *gumpu* rather than leading an isolated and independent life. Haimendorf (1943) observes "there are times in the life of practically every family when without the assistance of outsiders its very existence would be endangered". Each family has to depend on other neighbouring families for assistance in such issues like providing security to the children while the parents are working away from the settlement, at the time of illness and old age, during the periods of food scarcity, seasonal camps, etc.

Kinship System

Kinship plays a vital role in the Chenchu society. The kinship system of the Chenchus can be labeled as bilateral and is based on shallow depth, wherein the common ancestors who were dead long back are ignored. They rarely trace the relationship beyond that of the oldest people who are alive.

A Chenchu individual (ego) conceives his kinsmen into eleven categories based on generation and relationship: (1) *thatha-mutthathalu* (grand and great grand fathers), (2) *manamallu-manamarallu* (grand sons and grand daughters) (3) *avvagarlu* (Mother's mother and father's mother) (4) *chinnayya-peddayyalu* (father's brothers and husband of mother's sister) (5) *chinnamma-peddammalu* (wife of father's brother and mother's sisters) (6) *attha-mamalu* (mother's brother and his wife or father's sister and her husband) (7) *anna-dhammulu* (Brothers) (8) *akka-chellellu* (sisters) (9) *vadina-maradallu* (brother's wife, wife's sister and husband's sister) (10) *bava-bammardi* (sister's husband and wife's brother or father's sister's son or mother's brother's son (11) *allullu-kodallu* (a group of sons-in-law and daughters-in-law), Apart from these categories of relatives the Chenchus also conceive another set of persons with whom relationship is reckoned through *Mam;* a person belonging to one's own affinal *kulam* is treated as an affinal relative of classificatory order.

Marriage

Marriage is universal among the Chenchus. Normally everybody gets married. There are certain clearly defined rules and regulations regarding the marriage in Chenchu society. But these rules and regulations assume certain degree of relaxation. Marriage between individuals belonging to same *kulam* is treated as incestuous and hence prohibited. Further marriage between the members of few other *kulams* which stand in consanguinial relation to each other is also prohibited. Alliance is to be contracted with the members of a *kulam,* which stands in the group of *kulams* called *bammardula kulam.* It is also difficult to group all the *kulams,* under the two groups of *kulams,* uniformly for all the Chenchus in the Nallamalai. The connubium of each *kulam* differs from settlement to settlement. Depending upon marital connections existing between the *kulams,* in each Chenchu settlement, the consanguinity and affinity between the *kulams,* are decided. Discrepancy can be observed in the marital connections between *kulams* of sample settlements. The Table 2.6 shows the existing connections of alliance between *kulams* grouped together for all the sample villages.

There is another term called *kulabammardulu,* which means the members of a particular *kulam* can marry in any *kulam* irrespective of the relationship (brotherly/ affinal) with that *kulam.* For example, in Palutla tract, Damsani and Pitta *kulam* members are treated as *kulabammardulu.* They can marry in *Kudumula, Chigulla* and *Chevula kulam* but *Kudumula, Chigulla* and *Chevula kulams* are not brotherly *kulams,* and they are affinal *kulams.* The *kulabammardula kulam* is not one and the same to entire Chenchu tribe. It differs from settlement to settlement.

Table - 2.6 Affinal Clans (Kulams) in the Region Studied

Sl. No.	Kulams	*Arthi*	*Bhumani*	*Chevula*	*Cheruri*	*Chigulla*	*Damsam*	*Damsani*	*Dasari*	*Gulla*	*Jalla*	*Kudumula*	*Mandii*	*Nimmala*	*Pitta*	*Pulicherla*	*Seelam*	*Udathala*
1.	Arthi		√			√			√									
2.	Bhumani	√							√			√						
3.	Chevula							√				√	√		√			√
4.	Chevuri											√						
5.	Chigulla	√						√				√						
6.	Damsam		√															
7.	Damsani					√						√						
8.	Dasari										√	√						
9.	Gulla						√					√	√					
10.	Jalla								√			√						
11.	Kudumula	√	√	√	√	√	√	√	√	√	√			√	√	√	√	√
12.	Mandli			√		√	√	√										
13.	Nimmala		√									√	√					
14.	Pitta			√								√						
15.	Pulicheria					√	√	√	√									
16.	Seelam											√	√					
17.	Udathala											√	√					

Note : The tick mark indicates that the *kulams* coinciding at the respective boxes enter into alliances.

As a custom, the Chenchus prefer mother's brother's daughter as the most preferential and potential mate. However, paternal cross-cousin marriages do occur. Mother's brothers have the exclusive rights on the marriage of their first niece. The Table 2.7 gives the details of the relationship of wife and husband before marriage.

Table-2.7 Relationship of the Husband with Wife Before Marriage in the Sample Settlements

Sl. No.	Relationship	Total Unions
1.	Daughter of father's father's brother's daughter. *(Attha kuthuru)*	8
2.	Daughter of father's sister. *(Menattha kuthuru)*	20
3.	Daughter of mother's father's brother's son. *(Mama kuthuru)*	15

4.	Daughter of mother's brother. *(Menamama kuthuru)*	32
5.	Daughter of father's brothers daughter. *(Akka kuthuru)*	13
6.	Daughter of mother's sister's daughter. *(Akka kuthuru)*	2
7.	Sister's daughter. *(Sontha akka kuthuru)*	15
8.	Daughter of father's father's brother's *(Attharjala)**	2
9.	Daughter of step mother's brothers. *(Mama kuthuru)*	2
10.	Levirate *(Vadhina)*	5
11.	Sororate *(Maradhalu)*	10
12.	Outer *(Kotha sambandham)*	104
	Total number of unions	228

Note: * Rare marriage type.

Monogamous unions are very common. If the spouse dies or divorces remarriage usually takes place. There is no prescription as to the number of times a male or female is permitted to marry.

In the Chenchu tribe three types of mate selections are in vogue: (1) *Peddalu chesina pelli* (negotiation/arranged marriage): In this type, the parents or guardians of the boy and the girl negotiate with each other through the village eldermen. If parents of both sides agree for marriage the eldermen will decide the marriage date; (2) *Theesukupovadam* (love and elopement marriages): If both the boy and the girl like each other they elope and return to *gudem* after few days. The village people recognise them as legitimate spouses. Some time the married woman elopes with other man. Then the second husband has to pay *thappu* (compensation) to the first husband. This compensation is decided in the *kulapanchayathi* by the village eldermen. Then the new couple is treated as legitimate spouses; and (3) *Kalusukovadam* (mutual agreement) : Individuals who are bereaved or divorced may form a union with the other individual by mutual acceptance and start living together by the informal consent of the respective relatives and sometime the *kulapanchayathi*. The Table 2.8 gives the frequency of various types of mate selection in the sample settlements.

Table - 2.8 Frequency of Types of Mate Selection in the Sample Settlements

Sl. No.	*Types of mate selection*	*Frequency of marriages*		
		First marriage	*Second marriage*	*Third marriage*
1.	Peddalu chesina pendli	146	16	3
2.	Theesukupovadam	33	13	-
3.	Kalusukovadam	8	9	-

The rule of village exogamy is observed. Generally, the Chenchus prefer to select a bride from outside of their *gudem*. In the studied area, a majority of the marriages are village-exogamous unions wherein the bride and bridegroom hail from different villages. The Table 2.9 gives the details of the village exogamous and endogamous marriages.

Table - 2.9 Village Exogamous and Endogamous Unions

Sl.No.	*Name of the village*	*Total No. of unions*	*Village exogamy*	*Village endogamy*
1.	Alatam	8	8	-
2.	Chinthala	45	31	14
3.	Guttalachenu	26	19	7
4.	Marripalem	51	28	23
5.	Nekkanti	12	11	1
6.	Palutla	69	42	27
7.	Panthanala	5	5	-
8.	Ponnalabailu	12	9	3
Number of total unions		228	153	75

The above Table 2.9 shows that 2/3 of the marital unions are village exagamous marriages. Each village has marital relation with many settlements. The following Table 2.10 shows the number of settlements with which each sample Chenchu settlement has marital relations.

Table-2.10 Marital Connections of Each Sample Settlement with Other Settlement

Sl. No.	*Sample settlement*	*Number of settlement*	*Maximum Distance (kms)*	*Minimum Distance (kms)*	*Average Distance (kms)*
1.	Alatam	6	20	8	14
2.	Chinthala	11	15	3	12
3.	Guttalachenu	10	30	4	18
4.	Marripalem	14	25	5	17
5.	Nekkanti	5	15	7	12
6.	Palutla	16	25	4	16
7.	Panthanala	4	35	15	25
8.	Ponnalabailu	7	12	6	9

The number of settlements with which the sample settlements have marital connections vary. On an average, each sample settlement has marital connections with ten settlements. This proliferates kin connections over a wide area. The village exogamy facilitates wide choice of accessibility to individuals for resources exploitation in the regions other than their own catchment territory at the time of resource scarcity.

Marriage among the Chenchus is an institution, which helps proliferating kin connection over a wide area. Post-marital residence in the bride's native place is considered an unavoidable obligation. The cultural ideal is that the son-in-law should arrive with his wife to stay along with his father-in-law whenever an opportunity arises. In the same way he can also reside at other places where the relatives of his father-in-law are residing. In effect, marriage enhances one's circle of relatives, thereby one's accessibility to a number of settlement becomes possible.

Divorce

Divorce is permitted and its incidence seems to be rather high. Either of the spouses can freely initiate the divorce. The major reasons for divorce are: adultery, non-cooperation due to lack of interest between the spouses, impotence, frigidity, barrenness, husband's laziness or excessive drunkenness and suspicion on the partner regarding sexual life, ill-health, incompatible temperament etc. In case of adultery the guilty are assembled before the *kulapanchayathi* and the culprits are fined. If divorce is initiated on account of wife's fault, the wife's father or guardian is required to pay *thappu* (compensation/penalty) levied by the *kulapanchayathi* to the husband. Remarriage to the woman is not permissible till divorce with the husband is resolved. Generally the husband initiates divorce due to the misbehaviour and maltreatment of his wife. Whenever she dislikes her husband, she either develops a love affair with other man and elopes with him or she leaves for her parents' home. Then the aggrieved husband calls upon the *kulapanchayathi* and demands for compensation either from the wife's parents or wife's next husband. Once compensation is paid, divorce is said to have come into effect and socially recognised.

Economic Organization

Occupational Pattern

The traditional occupation of the Chenchus is food-gathering and hunting. Now-a-days each Chenchu household relies on several occupations - a combination of both traditional and modern occupations like agriculture, forest-labour, employment in government service etc. Most of the Chenchu households are engaged in collection of commercial non-timber forest produce (CNTFP). Many of the occupations are seasonal. The

Table 2.11 shows the number of households practicing various occupations.

Table-2.11 Occupational Pattern of the Chenchus in the Studied Area

Sl. No.	*Occupations*	*No. of house-holds*
1.	Collection of CNTFP	31
2.	Agriculture and collection of CNTFP	70
3.	Collection of CNTFP, agriculture and cattle rearing	20
4.	Employment	10
5.	Agriculture	20
6.	Collection of CNTFP and wage labour	30
7.	Arrack brewing, herding* and wage labour	24
8.	Collection of CNTFP and cattle rearing	6
	Total Number of households	211

Note: (1)* Grazing the cattle of peasants of plain areas for wages.
(2) Food gathering, hunting and fishing is common occupation to all households apart from the occupations mentioned above.

Food gathering and hunting is a cherished occupation to all the households, and the Chenchus recede to forest as and when a chance comes and is convenient for it. Most of the Chenchus collect commercial non-timber forest produce (CNTFP) like *Sugandapala* roots*, soap-nuts, honey, seeds of *musti**, *kanuga** (pongamia) etc., and sell them in the Girijan Cooperative Store (GCC). CNTFP collection gives substantial income to the Chenchus. The Chenchus practice agriculture at very small scale only. Traditionally they are not much interested in agriculture. They cultivate crops like bajra, jowar, *korra, variga* (food grains) etc. The Chenchu agriculture is seasonal and rain-fed. The yield of food grains is not sufficient to support the Chenchus for the year. They have to buy the food grains and essential

* Name of flora and fauna are mentioned in Italics. Unfortunately for many plants and animals the botanical names are not available.

commodities from the Girijan Cooperative Store (GCC) or private shop holders. Forest Department and forest contractors engage the Chenchus as labourers for daily wage in the activities such as bamboo cutting, splintering, thinning the forest, nursery work, etc. This work is seasonal, lasting for two to three months in a year.

Some households of the Chenchus of roadside settlements like Chinthala, secretly sell timber to the plain people. Arrack brewing is also practiced by some families in these *gudems*. The Chenchus graze the cattle belonging to the peasants living in the plain areas. They collect Rs. 10/- per cattle per month.

Resorting to multiple occupations is an adaptive response to the forest policy over the years, which, by and large, either marginalised or discouraged the Chenchus from relying on their traditional livelihood. Further, the Government is implementing various programmes. As a result multiple occupations are emerging in the Chenchu economy.

Seasonal Activities

The Nallamalai forest is characterized by three distinctive seasons: the hot summer season (March to June); the rainy season (July to October); and the winter season (November to February). Largely the presence and absence of green foliage closely follows the onset of rainy and summer. Because of the deciduous character of the forest, the behaviour of the plants, (flowering, fruit and leaf formation, tuber formation) and their regenerative properties are the most important ecological determinants of the Chenchu subsistence. The seasonality of various stages in the life cycle of various plants differs, giving an opportunity for the Chenchus to design diet selectivity accordingly.

Hunting possibilities are to a certain extent influenced by the seasonal variation. For instance, hunting of iguana is possible only during early monsoon season. Hunting of the spotted deer, nilgai, Indian-elk is successful when tender green grass blades carpet the ground. Hunting of birds and other arboreal animals is possible during summer.

Not only food gathering and hunting pursuits but also other major occupations like the collection of commercial non-timber forest produce (CNTFP), wage labour and cultivation are also influenced by the seasonal variation. The following Chart 2.1 shows the seasonal economic activities of the Chenchus.

Chart 2.1 Seasonal Economic Activities of the Chenchus

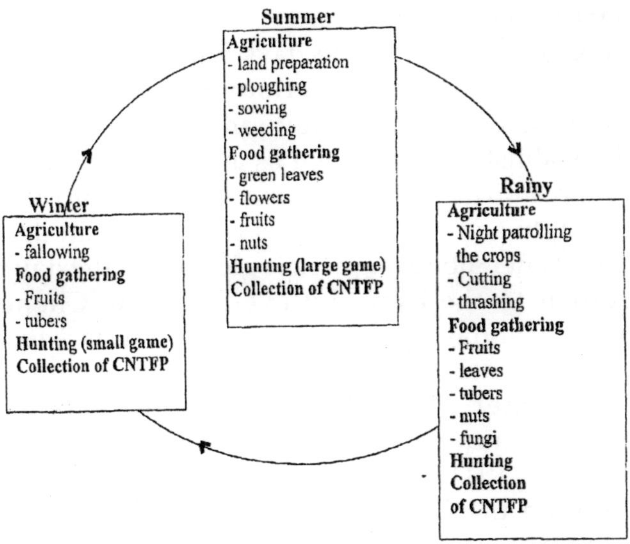

Though hunting is not confined to a particular season, hunting success rate is high in summer and early rainy season. In summer the undergrowth is cleared by setting fire. The trees shed their leaves and offer no shade. The small water bodies get dried. Hence the game particularly large game move to the *selas* (ravines) where small evergreen patches and perennial water bodies are available. The Chenchus execute hunting camps in these areas in summer. In early rainy season, the land is carpeted with green grass and water is available in plenty. The animals move to the plain lands. The Chenchu go for night hunting. In later part of rainy and winter the land is covered with heavy grass. The identification of the game is difficult hence the hunting of large game is difficult. They hunt only the birds and rabbits. The traditional calendar and the availability of floral resource is discussed in the Chapter 3.

Seasonal Camps

The Chenchus recall the days when their ancestors roamed in the forest without any permanent shelter. Presently the Chenchus exhibit radiating mobility from a 'well-established' settlement as a base. They glean the area surrounding the settlement till resources are exhausted. In summer, a camp is established in definite sites and its neighbouring area is gleaned in the day time and return to the camp by evening. The Chenchus conduct seasonal camps locally known as *kandava/ nidrapolam*. Generally it is executed in late winter and whole summer season for collection of food and commercial non-timber forest products (CNTFP). Haimendorf (1941) reported this type of movement in his study on the Chenchus of Mahboobnagar district. These camps are made at certain named localities within the catchment territory of each permanent settlement. Usually the members of same *gumpu* go unitedly to the camps. Generally the camp consists of 5 to 10 families. Many campsites are identified in the catchment area of sample settlements. For instance, Palutla people go to the places like *Thota, Kantrevumadalu, Gajji banda, Malla gundam, Korasamani banda, Kuntalabodu* etc., and Guttalachenu people go to *Sankella gundam, Thavisichettu, Sulluti, Birruti* etc. At the campsites they built temporary huts. Campsites are changed from one place to another as the resources in one locality are exhausted.

Temporary settlements are also established for carrying out coupe-cutting activity conducted by the Forest Department. Even for hunting purpose they go for a short camp for three to four days but they do not erect huts. Further details regarding the seasonal camps, residential shifts and nomadic movements are discussed in Chapter 4.

Division of Labour

In the Chenchu society most of the activities are undertaken interchangeably by male and female. Both wife and husband act as purveyors in the house. Generally speaking, division of labour is based on age and sex. Individuals aged 18 years and above get themselves trained in almost all activities. Sexual division of labour becomes apparent gradually from the age of 10 years. Till then boys and girls move closely getting acquainted in various works. Children below the age of 12 years are usually let free and are not entrusted with any work. They generally lend helping hand in cooking, water fetching, childcare, grazing, collection of fuel, green leaves etc., to a limited extent.

Boys and girls grow up together. They start associating with their father and mother or other relatives and friends respectively only when they advance in age (usually around the age of maturation). Children of different age combine together to form play groups and learn different skills by imitating their elders. Due to this kind of socialization the male and the female acquire various skills needed in both the domestic front and in

Chart 2.2 Major Activities and Division of Labour Based on Sex

Exclusive male's activities	*Exclusive Female's activities*	*Equal participation by male and female*	*Male's activities with unequal participation by female*	*Female's activities with unequal participation by male*
- Honey collection - Hunting camps for large game - Making and setting the traps - Making of hunting instruments like bow, arrow, trap etc. - Butchery and redistribution of meat. - Ploughing - Making agriculture implements - Dealing with the contractors and government officials. - Passing judgement and solving disputes. - Political control - Music playing	- Collection of roots, tubers, fruits, green leaves for domestic consumption. - Fire wood collection - Water fetching - Cleaning utensils - Sweeping the house and cleaning surroundings. - Husking grain - Broadcasting of seeds - Weeding	- Fishing - Liquor preparation - CNTFP collection - Procuring material for hut construction - Hut construction - Harvesting - Threshing - Bamboo cutting - Plantation work - Decision making in the household matters - Baby sitting - Recreation	- Hunting - Manufacture mending and repairs of household implements - Participation in religious sphere - Making hay-stacks	- Grazing - Cooking - Weeding - CNTFP processing - Milking the cows

economic sphere. Division of work based on sex is shown in Chart 2.2.

Property and Inheritance

The property of the Chenchus can broadly be divided into two categories viz (1) individual property; and (2) common property. The individual property comprises material equipment like bow and arrows, axe, *pesikabbi* (a small knife) agricultural implements, household utensils, agriculture land, live-stock etc. The most basic implements are a digging stick, a hatchet, knife and bow and arrow which are possessed by almost all adults, the first one usually belongs to women. These are the traditional implements. Of late, the Chenchus also keep live-stock, especially goats and cows. Only a few households have agricultural implements. The Chenchus know how to make and repair traditional implements, but not the agricultural implements.

Crop cultivation is not new to the Chenchus, even though they themselves have not evinced much interest in it. Backyard horticulture, dibbling cultivation is practiced by them for the past several years. For the last two decades, the Chenchus themselves have been involved in small-scale rain-fed cultivation. The Forest Department has permitted the Chenchus to clear a defined forest area to convert into agricultural fields. For a long time agricultural fields were not treated as a property. In the recent past the Chenchus have learnt the art of cultivation or leasing out their lands to the neighbouring peasants or other tribals. This has regularly fetched them some grains. Now-a-days, the Chenchus see the full importance of the agricultural fields and treat them as a property. Possession of agricultural land also fetches them other benefits from the Integrated Tribal Development Authority (ITDA) - a government of Andhra Pradesh organization created for implementing the developmental programmes for the Chenchus such as agricultural subsidy, free oxen, agricultural implements, seeds, fertilizers, irrigation facilities etc. However, agriculture is not yet picked up in full swing. Culturally the Chenchus are tied down to the forest and forest based foodstuff is most cherished.

Landholding is not evenly distributed among the Chenchus in the sample settlements. The table 2.12 gives the details of the land holdings at household level in the studied settlements.

Table - 2.12 Distribution of Households Based on the Size of Land Holding in the Sample Settlements

Sl. No.	*Settlements*	*Size of land holding (acres)*						
		1-3	*4-6*	*7-9*	*10-13*	*14-above*	*Land less*	*Total*
1.	Alatam	3	1	-	-	-	2	6
2.	Chinthala	12	9	2	1	-	16	40
3.	Guttalachenu	5	8	1	-	-	7	21
4.	Marripalem	12	18	1	2	-	17	50
5.	Nekkanti	2	-	1	2	-	5	10
6.	Palutla	16	26	2	3	1	22	70
7.	Panthanala	2	-	-	-	-	2	4
8.	Ponnalabailu	3	2	-	1	-	4	10
	Total number of households	55	64	7	9	1	75	211

It can be seen from the Table that 1/4th of the total households have less than 3 acres of land and 1/3rd of the Chenchu households are landless. Possession of large size of land holding does not entail a Chenchu to be classified as a good cultivator. Quite a few do not till their lands. And equally quite a few, who cultivate, leave their lands fallow for 2 to 3 years. One reason behind this comportment is that, the Chenchus have an intrinsic inclination towards relying upon the forest resources as gatherers and hunters rather than food-producers.

The corporeal property is usually owned by the individuals. Husband and wife are the proprietors, but each when separated, becomes the owner of a thing, which he or she acquired. After the death of their parents, the property is shared equally by the sons. The daughters usually get their share of a goat or a hen or a calf and a few utensils at the time of her marriage. The gifts given to the daughters are locally called *aranam*. Daughters are not entitled to inherit agricultural land and other household property of their parents. It seems on the whole, the Chenchus have not evolved a definite code in the distribution of the cattle and lands.

There are several incorporeal properties which, exist in the form of rights over the resources. The common property consists of hunting and grazing-grounds, food resources, water holes, streams, wild animals, birds etc. All the residents have a right to exploit these resources for their survival. Resources are in essence, are common property. But the community access to and exploitation of specific resources like honey, tamarind, soap-nuts, gum trees etc., are subjected to certain conditions and normative observances. These are discussed in Chapter 6.

Originally inheritance at the household level was not an important issue to the Chenchus. Even though the Chenchu society was clearly a patrilineal society, the authority was not strictly succeeded in line of the father. Males on the mother's side also succeeded authority in order to bring up sister's children. The traditional norm was not to distinguish the male and female lines of authority. It was oriented towards expanding networks cutting across the male-female lines.

Income and Expenditure

The major sources of income for the Chenchus are : the sale of Commercial Non-timber Forest Produce

(CNTFP), wage labour, live-stock rearing and agriculture. Most of the Chenchus collect CNTFP and sell them either to GCC store or private merchants. CNTFP selling is the major source of income generation to the Chenchus. The Chenchus generally go for wage labour for bamboo cutting, and other works like thinning, watering the nurseries etc., organised by Forest Department. The wage rates are not equal for both men and women. The male gets Rs. 30/- and female gets Rs. 20/- per day. The male children below the age of 18 years also get Rs. 20/-. On an average there may be maximum of thirty to forty working days. But the income from wage labour is erratic as the bamboo coups are not organized every year and the non-Chenchus are also indulged in bamboo cutting. The Chenchus sell the live-stock in the case of need of money. A few Chenchu households who possess land near the streams cultivate cash crops like chillies, groundnuts and cotton. But the yield is very less. Hence, the income from agriculture is a meager amount.

The expenditure of the Chenchu household is classified into seven categories like expenditure on food, cosmetics, ornaments, intoxicant items (tobacco, liquor), amusements, clothes, household items and miscellaneous purposes like medical, rituals etc. The average income and expenditure of a Chenchu household per annum is shown in the Table 2.13.

Table-2.13 Average Income and Expenditure at Chenchu Household Level Per Annum

Sl. No.	*Income Sources*	*Amount (Rs.)*	*Sl. No.*	*Expenditure*	*Amount (Rs.)*
1.	Sale of CNTFP	5,400/-	1.	Food	1,850
2.	Agriculture	450/-	2.	Cosmetics and ornaments	300
3.	Live-stock	300/-	3.	Intoxicants	1,500
4.	Wage labour	300/-	4.	Amusement	1,000
			5.	Clothes	1,000
			6.	Household	300

			utensils	
		7.	Miscellaneous	500
Total	6,450/-		Total	6,450

It is observed that the expenditure on liquor and amusement together is more than the expenditure on food. This indicates the dependence of the Chenchus on forest foods. Generally the Chenchus are fond of drinking arrack. They consume local made liquor twice or thrice per week. On an average Rs. 125/- is spent on liquor and *beedis* per month. Regarding amusement the Chenchus do not have cinemas or videos in the studied area. They have to go to either Yerragondapalem or Srisailam (near by towns) for amusement. Once the Chenchu comes to the town he stays at least four days to one week in the town. He stays in the hostels of the tribal schools or in the ITDA office. They rarely use cosmetics like soap and other creams. Regarding ornaments the Chenchu women wear only ear-rings, nose-rings made of brass and the bangles.

Education and Literacy

The literacy level in the Chenchu tribe is very low. Table 2.14 shows the literacy level of the Chenchus as found in the sample settlements.

Table-2.14 Class Wise Literacy Level in Sample Settlements

Sl. No.	*Class studied*	*No. of males*	*No. of females*	*Total literates*
1.	1-3	124	98	222
2.	4-5	74	27	101
3.	6-9	18	3	21
4.	10-12	19	-	19
5.	Illiterates	150	300	450
	Total	385	428	813

Note: The members who crossed the age of six years are taken into consideration.

A majority of the literates have studied upto 5th class and from then onwards literacy rate drastically decreases. Almost all Chenchu settlements have schools upto elementary level that is from the first standard to the fifth standard. High schools are located only in a few settlements located near roads. The Chenchus do not have any motivation in getting themselves educated in the schools as the syllabus is something which alienates them from their own environment and culture. However, the Chenchus admit their children in the school to avail of the benefits of boarding and other incentives. Dropouts and absenteeism are very rampant. Two reasons behind poor literacy are: (1) lack of interest, and (2) opportunity cost. The children participate in activities like grazing, fruit collection, baby-sitting etc., from the age of 10 years. Generally they dropout from the school soon after the fifth class. The child usually does not seek for higher education either due to lack of school facility with in the *gudem* or disinclination towards education. Besides the Chenchus get married at the early age at 15 to 18 years. A few people complete their high school education. Males are more in number than females. This is because the Chenchu girls are not allowed to stay out of their own *gudem* till she gets married.

It is seen that in the studied area the literacy rate is very less in the age group of 30 and above. The female literacy is almost nil. It seems the literacy rate has been gradually increasing in the Chenchu *gudems* only for the last thirty years since late 1970s.

Political Organization

The traditional political institution at the village level is locally called as *kulapanchayathi* or *panchayathi* (the council of village elder men). This *kulapanchayathi* institution is an independent body, which gives judgement on the matters relating to the village people. The *kulapanchayathi's* resolutions are confined to the respective *gudems* only. There is no wider political institution beyond the *gudem.*

The *kulapanchayathi* comprises representatives of each *Kulam* or a bunch of eldermen locally called *peddamanushulu.* All the adult members of both sexes can participate in the proceedings of the *kulapanchayathi.*

The *kulapanchayathi* is headed by one individual called *raju* or *peddhamanishi* (headman). He is assisted by other members called *manthri* (secretary) and *kolegadu* (messenger). Generally, these three members are chosen unanimously based on their age, experience and their skills in articulating and solving the problems. The common rule is that *raju* must hail from the *kulam* of original settlers of the *gudem. Manthri* and *kolegadu* hail from *kulams,* which are numerically preponderant over the other *kulams.* The *kulams* of the office bearers are not one and the same in all the *gudems.* They change from *gudem to gudem* based on original settlers and the numerical strength of the *kulam.* For instance, in Palutla *gudem, raju* belongs to *Chevula kulam, manthri* and *kolegadu* hail from *Kudumula* and *Damsani kulams* respectively. But in Guttalachenu settlement, *raju* hails from *Kudumula kulam. Manthri* and *kolegadu* belong to *Damsani* and *Seelam kulams* respectively. In Alatam all the *raju, manthri* and *kolegadu* belong to *Kudumula kulam* only because there are no other *kulams.*

Kolegadu is a messenger. He informs all the households about the *kulapanchayathi* meeting. *Manthri* generally articulates the problem in the *kulapanchayathi.* Then any member in the *kulapanchayathi* can speak about the problem. Ultimately the *peddamanusulu* (village eldermen) in the *panchayathi* unanimously pass the verdict. The *raju* will read the verdict. *Raju* cannot pass resolution or give punishment to the culprit on his own.

He must abide by the advice of all the members of the *panchayathi*.

Apart from settling the disputes, the *peddamanusulu* (village eldermen) offer mediation to individuals in matters relating to mate selection, marriage celebration, elopement, adultery, refusal of the wife to live with her husband, incompatibility, non-cooperation between spouses, stealing, life cycle rituals, rituals of worship, etc.

The members of the council do not enjoy any special rights in their day-to-day life. The only privilege the *peddamanchi (raju)* seems to enjoy is that of eating and drinking first on ceremonial occasions. But his share in the food and drinks is not greater than that of the other men.

The *kulapanchayathi* solves the cases on the spot. However, some cases, which need some evidences are adjourned for further hearing. The food and drink to the members of the *panchayathi* are provided by the client. But ultimately the culprit must pay this expenditure to the victim.

If the dispute involves the residents of two neighbouring *gudems,* then the eldermen of both the *gudems* assemble at a place between the two *gudems* and settle the dispute. The culprit is asked to pay compensation to the victim. For instance, in 1995 *Chevula Letha Eadaiah* of Palutla has stolen the soap-nuts in Guttalachenu territory. Guttalachenu people called on the eldermen of Palutla. Both Palutla and Guttalachenu eldermen assembled at a place called *Erravagu* - a boundary place between two *gudems.* The *Panchayathi* men scolded Eadaiah and asked him to hand over the booty to Guttalachenu people.

However, in some Chenchu *gudems* the traditional *kulapanchayathi* institution is surpassed by the Peoples War Group (PWG) Naxalites or the Forest Officials. The

Chenchus resort to Forest Officials or PWG leaders for Justice. Further details on leadership and conflict resolution are given in Chapter 6.

Religion

The Chenchu pantheon consists of many gods and goddesses mostly known and worshipped by the neighbouring Hindu caste people. The different names of the deities are vaguely significant. They have a scanty conception of functions and origin of the deities. Almost all deities excepting a few have no shrine or abodes at all. The image of most of these deities are neither anthropomorphic nor zoomorphic but simply represented by a stone slab. The ritual specialists are not found but in a few cases certain individuals undertake the priestly activities.

Chenchus believe in the life after death and rebirth. Dead people are believed to join the stock of ancestors. The Chenchus worship all their ancestors belonging to male and female lines lest they will be subjected to the wrath of their ancestors. Any misfortune is attributed to the wrong action of the people such as forgetting to worship, not fulfilling the promise or oath that has been taken on the name of ancestors, or gods, failing to give the names of ancestors or gods to the children etc. A few of the deities are believed to be associated with certain diseases (vomits, small pox, diarrhea, fever, paralysis, chronic pains, weakness and loss of physical growth and body weight and epidemics), mortality of domestic animals (cattle, goats), abortion and miscarriage etc. They are not however very sure of which deity is actually responsible.

The Chenchus attribute supernatural connotations to the Sun and the Moon and even to air and water. They hold that the nature is of mystic quality and that the natural phenomenon of rain, wind, day light and darkness are associated with spiritual power and supernatural forces. They believe that certain localities like *serries* (honey deposits), waterholes, streams, ponds, burial grounds, hunting area, certain big-dried up trees, and deserted huts and time periods especially nights are associated with spirits and deities. They also have a belief that ghosts and spirits wander during nights and hence they do not come out of their huts alone during the nights. These places are sacred to them and they won't allow polluting or disturbing these places. If these places are polluted it is believed that the associated deities would become irritated and create problems to them. There are many named places associated with deities in the study region: (1) *Challapidathala revu dona* and *Sankella gundam* in *Guttlachenu* territory; (2) *Thota kolanu* in Palutla territory; and (3) *Darabaiti vaagu* in Nekkanti territory. The *serries* (honey comb deposits to a cliff in a gorge or steep ravine are also associated with deities especially goddess *Malalamma* (the goddess of honey). Apart from *Malalamma* there are *Bayanna, Veerulu, Pothuraju, Peddamma, Lingamaiah* etc., are also associated with the *serri*. The Chenchus prepare *naivedhyam* (sacred food consisting of rice and jaggery) and keep it before the goddess *Malalamma* and the other gods before climbing down to the *serries*. They also offer honey of first *pera* (honeycomb) to the deities before they eat.

Hunting grounds and the hunting activity are also associated with the deity, whom they call *devara* (deity) and a share in the game is given. Generally the Chenchus believe that deity *Nalla maisamma* is associated with hunting. Periods of stress are interpreted as the wrath of the deity. Some times she alerts the game and evades them from the line of hunters. Before setting out for hunting, the deity is prayed for providing some game to fill the stomach.

The Chenchus celebrate almost all Hindu festivals. *Sivarathri* is an important festival for them. They worship all Hindu gods along with their local deities. Every year they celebrate a communal festival to goddess *Porlamma*.

Chenchus believe in witchcraft and magic. If a person is suffering from diseases or series of death of animals, he will go to the person called *gadde cheppevadu* (divinator). He detects the causes of the problem and performs a ritual function called *datimpu* to cure the problems.

Contact with the plains' peoples especially caste-cultivators is not new to the Chenchus of the sample settlements. Even though, the Chenchu settlements are located quite for away from the plain peasant villages, the Chenchus used to visit these places to exchange forest produce for certain essential items like salt, chillies, rice, jowar, iron, etc. But these visits were very rare. After the emergence of township at *Sunnipenta* near Srisailam the Chenchus visits to this place has increased gradually. Establishing various government institutions have further brought the Chenchus contact with wider society to merchants, contractors, wage labours have also started visiting the Nallamai. The settlements situated on the road side are exposed to outside contact much more than the settlement located interior and quite far away from the road. However, the developmental programmes are now taken to and implemented in remote settlements too. Owing to these interventions, certain changes are taking place among the Chenchus.

The most conspicuous change is seen in the sphere of economy. New occupations are adopted, and money is the medium of economic transaction. Their economy is now linked to the market economy of the neighbouring townships and marketing centres, with contractors, Forest Department and Girijan Cooperative Society. Religious and political system are also now linked to the neighbouring peasant villages and *panchayathiraj*. These are the new linkages which the people have established in order to cope up with the changing circumstances.

However, the Chenchus seem to have retained the basic qualities of their social relations. There is not variation in the family, marriage and kinship relations, descent rules, the nature and function of the exogamous group, described by Haimendorf (1943) about 60 years ago. Their property relations, association with the forest reciprocal selection, dependence on forest produce have not envisaged radical changes. Their attitudes towards the forest, its resources, and various natural features are almost intact.

In future also they may protect their distinction in their socio-cultural life from the influence of the plain people. They may not mingle immediately with plains' people. However, as a rule of nature the change may come slowly in the Chenchu society and till then they live in the forest as hunters and gatherers with minor changes in their living pattern.

3
The Environment and Forest Resources

This chapter gives an account of the natural resources available in the Nallamalai in general and the catchment territories of the sample Chenchu settlements in particular. The major aim of this chapter is to capture climatic and edaphic features, distribution and seasonality of the floral resources, and to present an inventory of various natural resources and their utilization by the Chenchus. It is intended to find out the ecological conditions and constraints having implications for the social arrangement for the exploitation and management of resources. The data regarding the floral and faunal resources are collected from the Chenchus themselves. As such there would be some difference between the resources that are physically existing and the resources that are recognized by the Chenchus.

THE NALLAMALAI

The middle section of the Eastern Ghats falling almost in the middle line of south Andhra Pradesh is known as the Nallamalai. The Nallamalai constitute the most impressive chain of rolling hills laid in north to south and south-west direction in tune with the western coastal belt of Bay of Bengal. Geographically these hill ranges are located roughly between 15° 10' and 16° 30' Northern latitude and 78° 30' and 80°10' Eastern longitude. The northern most boundary of the Nallamalai lies in the Palnadu basins of Guntur district and the southern boundary lies in Tirupati hills.

The total length of the Nallamalai from the northern edge to the south is 430 kms. The average width from east to west is 30 kms. The elevation of the Nallamalai ranges between 275 mtrs to 915 mtrs with an average of 750 mtrs. The altitude thus varies considerably within the Nallamalai. The total area of the Nallamalai forest is 5161 sq kms with 39 per cent of the forest seen on flat and rolling hills and 61 percent on hill ranges (Parthasarathy, 1978: 91). The terrain of the Nallamalai is undulated comprising stretches of rolling hills, plateaux, interspersed by valleys, gorges, ravines, basins, perennial deep streams etc.

The Nallamalai are divided into two blocks by the river Krishna: northern block and southern block. The northern block encompasses parts of Mahboobnagar and Nalgonda districts. The southern block comprises parts of Kurnool, Prakasam and Guntur districts. The area of the present study falls under the southern block.

The Southern Block

The Southern block extends from Nandhyala valley near Nandhyala (a Mandal headquarters in Kurnool district) in the south to the Srisailam (a Shivite shrine) plateau in the north. It is bounded by Athmakur (a Mandal headquarters) in the west and Yerragonda Palem (a Mandal headquarters) in the east. This block comprises 40 per cent of the total area of the Nallamalai.

Six groups of hill ranges are seen in this block: 1. Nandhyala - Ahobilam hill range; 2. Byrluti - Nagaluti hill range; 3. Byrluti - Peddamanthanala hill range; 4. Rollapenta - Peccheruvu-Srisailam hill range; 5. Srisailam

- Dornal hill range; and 6. Chinthala - Yerragondapalem hill range, which is divided into two sub hill ranges: (a) Nekkanti hill range, (b) Nadathadikala - Kayya hill range. Of these Nandhyala-Ahobilam range, Byrluti-Peddamanthanala range and Chinthala Yerragonda-palem range are the widest. These ranges possess a few high peaks like *Ahobilam, Rollapenta (Manthralakanuma)* and *Darabailu,* and harbour patches of evergreen forest, with rich floral species of great importance to the Chenchus. All these hill ranges are more or less contiguous interspersed by deep gorges and valleys.

The southern block comprises five plateaux viz, Peccheruvu plateau, Sivapuram plateau, Gundla Brahmeshwaram plateau, Srisailam plateau and Palutla plateau.

Six prominent valleys are seen in the southern block. They are: (1) Nandhyala valley; (2) Rollapenta valley; (3) Chama valley; (4) Sakirevu kona valley; (5) Peddarevu valley; and (6) Palanka valley. Nandhyala, Rollapenta and Chama valleys are wide and open valleys. Trekking is not very difficult in these valleys. The Chenchus of nearby settlements visit these valleys for various purposes. Peddarevu, Sakirevu kona and Palanka valleys are steep and narrow. Trekking in these valleys is very difficult. However, the Chenchus of nearby settlements exploit honey and the game in these valleys in summer or in the days of scarcity of food resources. The valleys are known for rich floral resources. Many places in these valleys support the Chenchus in the periods of food scarcity. Rollapenta (Manthralakanuma) and Palanka are the most verdurant zones of the Nallamalai forest. Several important medicinal and food plants and superior variety of trees are reported from these two zones.

Topography of the Sample Settlements

The eight settlements selected for the present study fall under two broad topographical locations viz., Palutla plateau and Chama valley. Alatam, Guttalachenu, Nekkanti, Palutla, Panthanala and Ponnalabailu settlements are located on the Palutla Plateau. Chinthala and Marripalem settlements are located in the Chama valley. Srisailam-Dornala hill ranges separate the Palutla plateau from Chama valley.

Palutla Plateau

The Palutla plateau is located 10 kms eastwards from Srisailam shrine. It is the extension of eastern hill range i.e., Chinthala-Yerragondapalem range of the Nallamalai. This plateau is bounded by river Krishna in north and Chinthala-Yerragondapalem hill range in the south. In the west it is bounded by Sakirevu kona valley and in the east by Nadathadikala kondalu - a sub hill range of Chinthala-Yerragondapalem range. Palutla plateau is the largest plateau in southern block of the Nallamalai. It stretches roughly about 30 kms from west to east. The width from north to south on an average is 16 kms. It covers an area of roughly 480 sq. kms. The elevation of this plateau is 700 mtrs MSL.

The Palutla plateau comprises gently undulated terrain traversed by several streams, valleys, hills and level grounds are commonly seen.

The prominent streams in this plateau are *Kamakshamma Vagu* (stream), *Mulamaddi vagu, Ankaleti vagu, Nekkanti vagu, Pedda vagu, Vippalamada vagu* and *Jenkudabonda vagu.* Except *Mulamaddi vagu* the rest are perennial streams.

Three valleys namely, *Peddarevu* valley, *Palanka* valley and *Kamakshi* valley are seen in Palutla Plateau. These are known for rich floral resources. The steep gorges seen in this plateau are; *Palanka, serri* (cliff/gorge), *Boyalakota serri, Gadasala serri, Sami serri, Pedda serri,* etc.

The hills in Palutla plateau belong to two sub-hill ranges i.e., *Nekkanti* hill range and *Nadathadikala-Kayya* hill range. Both hill ranges run from south to north. These ranges are the parts of the Chinthala-Yerragonda palem hill range. The prominent hills in Nekkanti range are *Vajrala konda* (hill), *Tekulapenta konda, Degapilla konda, Hanumanthuni kurava* etc. The prominent hills in *Nadathadikala-Kayya* range are *Bakkachintha penta konda, Palanka konda, Burugundala konda,* etc.

Chama Valley

Chama valley originates at the north-eastern edge of Paccheruvu plateau. It runs from north-west to south-east and finally comes down to plain area near Dornala. It stretches for about forty kilometers. It runs between two hill ranges: *Srisailam-Dornala* hill range on the right bank and *Chinthala-Yerragondapalem* hill range on the left bank.

This valley comprises the patches of thick evergreen forests. Bamboo is the prominent vegetation in this valley. *Chinthala vagu* a perennial stream, flows in this valley. On the sides of the banks some plain alluvial soil is formed with small boulders. Three Chenchu settlements namely Chama, Chinthala and Marripalem are located in this valley.

Soils

Several types of soils are found in the southern block of the Nallamalai. Black cotton soils occur in a limited extent and confined to the terrain portion in the forest and near the river banks or tank basin. Alluvial soils are also confined to the banks of the river Krishna and its rivulets. The red-brown loamy soils are present fairly extensively in valleys, plateaux, foot-hills and hill-slopes. Apart from agriculture these soils support fairly luxuriant growth of trees and grass.

Climate

The climate in the Nallamalai is generally pleasant despite the marked seasonal variation. During March through May the temperature fluctuates around 40°C. Temperature starts decreasing from June and reaches minimum level of 20°C in November and starts increasing from February. During November to February the nights are cool and the area is covered with extensive fog till 8 o'clock in the morning.

Rainfall

The region receives southwest monsoon during June-September with an average rainfall of about 85 cms. Northeast monsoon is active in October and November. Rains also occur during the pre-monsoon periods and in the early summer. Besides throughout the year the rains occur intermittently here and there in the region.

Forest Types

The forest in the Nallamalai is categorized as tropical dry deciduous type (Champion and Seth,1968) located in a semi-arid region in Andhra Pradesh. The Nallamalai is chiefly characterized by uneven distribution of forest growth. Some localities harbour rich verdurant growth and in some localities the tree growth is thin or bushy. Many plants drop leaves in February and March and develop buds in April and May. The forest is mostly mixed type wherein ecotonal formation is highly restricted. The forest largely comprises mixed species. The individual members of the species are highly dispersed. This being a general pattern, certain vegetational types can be identified largely subjected to edaphic, altitudinal conditions: (1) Superior dry mixed deciduous forests; (2) Inferior dry mixed deciduous forest; (3) Hardwickia binata type; (4) Bambusa abundinacia or bamboo forests; and (5) Thorny scrub type (Rajgopal, 1974).

Superior Dry Mixed Deciduous Type

This type of forest is mainly confined to the high hills and plateau areas with an elevation of 450 and 760 meters. This type of forest is seen on *Gundlabrahmeswaram, Sivapuram, Srisailam, Peccheruvu* and *Palutla* plateaux. The major species present in this forest are *thada* (Greswia liliae folia), *gumpani* (Odina wodier), *thabisi* (sderculia urens), etc.

Inferior Dry Mixed Deciduous Type

This type of forest is most predominant over other types of forests in the Nallamalai. It occurs most commonly on low lying grounds, parts of lower plateaux and along foothills. The major species seen in this type of forest are *thella thumma* (Acacia leucopholea), *thuniki* (Dispyros melano xylon), *illinta* (Diospyros cloro xylon), *somi* (Soymida febrifuga), etc.

Hardwickia Binata Type

Hardwickia Binata type locally known as *yepi* or *narepa* forest type is seen in high rainfall zone like Krishna valley and plateaux of *Palutla, Sivapuram, Srisailam, Peccheruvu* and *Gundlabrahmeshwaram.* Hardwickia binata exhibits a gregarious habit and is found growing in isolated belts or patches in the forest. The undergrowth invariably consists of grass of good fodder. Apart from this type, teak type, terminalia type, Anogeissus type, Bosewellia type, Acacia type, Colombus rotang type also occur wherein the respective type species dominate. However such occurrence is only limited and scant.

Bambusa Abundinancia or Bamboo Forest

Bamboo forest occurs over fairly extensive areas of the Nallamalai. It is plentiful in *Peccheruvu, Rollapenta,* and *Nandhyala* valley in Kurnool district, *Palutla, Darabailu, Thummalabailu,* and *Chama* valley areas in Prakasam district. In this type of forest the under growth is very sparse.

Thorny Scrub Type

This type of forest is largely confined to the clear felled areas and fringe areas of the Nallamalai. Sparsely distributed trees and thorny bushes are seen in this type of forest.

Apart form the type of vegetation listed above, patches of evergreen type are also seen along the high altitude hill zones like *Dharabailu, Palanka* valley, *Thambella madugu* etc., in Palutla Plateau and *Maddi gundam, Mondonirevu* etc., in Chama valley.

The forest supplies raw material to various industries including the paper mills. One reason for occurring the dense forest is its favourable location to receive good rainfall both from south-west monsoon and north-east monsoon. The region also possesses several natural springs and patches of fertile soil. Several plants in the Nallamalai exhibit gigantism: the shrubby climber, Marshadenia tenacissima and Hetecteres Isora.

The Chenchus have their own views, ideas, perceptions about the forest in which they live. Different terms are used to denote specific features of forest and forest types. The Chenchus construct a 'category' of forest, which is linked to the socio-cultural fabric in a complex fashion. While the Chenchu construction of the forest comprises several aspects (discussed is Chapter 5), this section is devoted to delineate physical and floristic and faunal composition of the forests as understood and explained by the Chenchus.

The Chenchus view the forest under two broad categories: *konda adavi* (hill forest) and *chadunu adavi* (plain forest). Incidentally the Forest Department has also classified the Nallamalai forest into hill forest and plain forests. Simply defined *konda adavi* is hill forest and *chadunu adavi* is forest on level lands. The native terms for forest are *adavi* or *polamu*. Hill forests include forest in hill tops, hill slopes, ravines, valleys and high gradient undulated terrain. Plain forest is confined to low altitude level grounds and basins. Vegetation is usually superior at hill-slopes, valleys and basins, and thin on hill-tops. Patches of thick vegetation is also seen on the level grounds or high altitude plateaux. As the gradient of plain forest gradually merges with the low levels at the fringe areas of the Nallamalai, the vegetation becomes very thin and thorny bushes dominate with virtual absence of tree coverage.

Based on the density of the floral species/vegetation cover, the Chenchus recognizes three types of forest: (1) *peddadavi;* (2) *chinnadavi;* and (3) *mundladavi*. Thick, dense vegetation with superior floral species with closed crown is referred to as *peddadavi*. The trees are tall, growing to a height of 30-40 feet. These forests are confined to ravines, valleys, high altitude zones and the river sides. In Palutla plateau, this forest is seen in the places like *Darabailu, Thambella madugu, Sankella gundam, Palanka serri,* etc.

Inferior vegetation, slender tree growth with open crown characterizes *chinnadavi*. The density of vegetation is moderate. This type of forest occurs most commonly in the Nallamalai along the hill-top, plain zones, hill-slopes, etc.

Mundladavi is characterized by the presence of bushy vegetation, shrubby growth and very thinly sprinkled tree coverage. This is like open forest in the sense, the whole area is visible. Some localities in the Nallamalai have very poor forest growth owing to the presence of rocky beds, inferior soil types, etc.

Sub-Categorization of Forest

According to the Chenchus, the forest is not a continuous zone of tree coverage. They recognizes finer differences within the forest. The forest is categorized into tangible named bodies, units or zones. These are usually traversed, visited, gleaned, camped, referred to in their day-to-day chores, discourses, inquiries or references. These zones themselves can be divided under two groups. The first group is concerned with division of the forest based on floristic conditions and the second is based on topographical features:

1. *Matta or Mada:* A large patch of thick forest growth is referred to as *Matta or mada.* The canopy of the forest is usually closed. These patches however occur sporadically at high altitude slopes, steep valleys. Some of these patches have specific names like *Vippala mada, Gunnala jedi penta matta, Cheruvu matta, Vagu matta.*
2. *Madhugu* : Patch of thick forest growth.
3. *Sarava :* The term *sarava* is applied to any plain level ground devoid of tree growth. These are usually bigger patches compared to *baraka.* Sometimes grass lands are also termed as *sarava.*
4. *Baraka* : The term *baraka* is applied to any open place in the forest devoid of tree growth. These patches might have formed naturally or by clear-felling. This term is used when the Chenchus kill an animal in the forest and bring out into the cleared area for butchery.
5. *Bayalu:* Patches of moderately open undulated forest with sparse tree coverage with scanty grass is called *bayalu.* The *term bayalu* is used to those forests, which are devoid of crown formation.

6. *Gadda: Gadda* means a plateau. This term is also used to any high gradient zones or flat localities on the hill-top.
7. *Sikaram/Nadikoppu:* The terms *sikaram/nadikoppu* are used to refer to the hill-peaks.
8. *Konda valu :* Hill-slopes and inclines are referred to *kondavalu*. These are the places of rich vegetation.
9. *Sela:* Narrow valley washed by streams is termed as *sela*.
10. *Serri:* Precipice or cliffs are called *serri*. These are mostly rocky places with steep cuttings falling into valleys or ravines. The edge of a hill with a steep cutting is also called *serri*. The localities called as *serris* contain small plants originating from the rocky beds or walls of the hills. Honey deposits are usually seen on these *serris*. In sample settlements *serris* have names like *Thadibandala serri, Garbagundala serri, Kothula serri*, etc. *Serries* are usually associated with a deity or folklore.
11. *Gundam:* A naturally formed moderate sized water reservoir usually with a rocky bed is termed as *gundam*. It is usually located on the hilly areas and in valleys. The stream running from hill peaks or high gradients drain into the *gundams*. The area around *gundams* harbours luxuriant growth of forest. Huge trees are located nearby these *gundams*. Some of these are treated as sacred.
12. *Palugu:* Any gentle to moderate slope land is called *palugu* irrespective of the presence or absence of vegetational cover. These localities are seen on plain grounds or on plateaux.
13. *Jede: Jede* refers to very small open patches of salt-lick amidst thick forest cover. Salt content is high in the soil and hence very poor vegetation may be seen.

14. *Bodu/Katava:* Grounds with rocky beds or boulders are known as *bodu/katava.*
15. *Vagu:* A stream that flows for not less than six months. Some are perennial streams. Some examples are *Vippalamada vagu, Pedda vagu* in the territory of Guttala chenu settlement. The thick patch of forest on the banks of *vagu* is known as *vagu matta.*
16. *Kunta:* A small earthen pond is known as *kunta.*

Catchment Area of the Sample Settlements

Each Chenchu settlement traditionally owns a territory. The extent of the catchment area of each settlement varies from the other settlements. The territory is divided into named localities, where various activities (either single or multiple activities) like grazing the cattle, collection of food, firewood, hunting etc., or combination of these activities are carried out. For instance, the territory of Palutla settlement comprises major localities like *Sulluti, Kuntalabodu Kantrevumadalu, Thota, Korasamani banda, Malla gundam, Tekula penta, Seetha banda,* etc. These localities are exploited exclusively by Palutla people. Each locality may exhibit a combination of different topographical features and locations like *sarava, sela, serri, palugu* etc. Table 3.1 gives the details of certain localities in Palutla territory and the major economic resources of these zones.

Apart from the localities, which are frequently exploited, there are some other localities, which are generally not exploited in normal conditions. These are said to be reserved/restricted zones. They are exploited only in severe famine conditions. For instance, in Palutla catchment *Hanumanthuni kurava sela, Barla madugu, Malla gundam, Katthu madugu* and in Guttla chenu territory *Boyalakota, Birruti* etc., are such examples.

Table 3.1 Named Localities, Their Topography and Major Economic Resources in the Palutla Catchment Territory

Sl. No.	*Name of Locality*	*Topographical Location*	*Dominant resource available*
1	Sulluti	Palugu, Baraka/ bailu, Sarava, Katava, Vagu, Matta, Gundam, Serri	Food, fodder, fibre, instrumental and CNTFP like soap-nuts, *sugandapala* roots, honey etc. and game.
2.	Ankammakunta	Kunta, Jede, Sarava	Food, fodder, fuel and game.
3.	Kantrevu madalu	Palugu, Vagu, Matta, Baraka, Sarava, Katava	Food, fodder, structural material, fibre etc. Grazing.
4.	Thota	Gadda, Sela, Palugu, Matta, Vagu	Food, fodder medicine, fibre, structural material, CNTFP like *sugandapala* roots, soap-nuts, gum etc., game.
5.	Kuntalabodu	Sikaram, Kondavalu, Gundam, Serri, Sela, Matta	CNTFP like soap-nuts, gum, *sugandapala* roots, honey and game
6.	Korasamani banda	Kondavalu, Sela, Jede, Gundam Matta	Game, food and structural items, and CNTFP like gum, soap-nuts and *sugandapala* roots and honey.
7.	Mallagundam	Gundam, Serri, Sela, Matta, Kondavalu, Sikaram	Game, CNTFP, honey, food, structural material.
8.	Tekulapenta	Kondavalu, Sikaram, Katava	CNTFP like *sugandapala* roots, gum and honey.
9.	Seethabanda	Serri, Kondavalu, Sikaram, Sela	Honey, CNTFP, food and game.
10.	Urjala	Matta, Baraka, Palugu, Katava, Vagu, Sarava, Kondavalu	Food, fodder, fuel, structural material etc. and game.

Note: In the above table only few dominant resources are mentioned against the localities. The grazing, collection of firewood, food items, etc., are generally executed in nearby areas of the settlements.

FLORAL RESOURCES

Distribution of Floral Species

Plant distribution is a very important indicator in understanding the nature and type of forest. Some species tend to grow in clusters, whereas other species tend to be dispersed. A simple measurement helps us to know the nature of plant distribution. This measurement involves selection of a sample quadrants of 10 mtrs x 10 mtrs areas and counting of all species with respective densities in each quadrant (Oosting, 1958). This ecological survey has facilitated an understanding of various features of the floral species in the Nallamalai. Totally 88 plots were surveyed, at least 11 plots in catchment territory of each sample settlements, representing from various zones like hill-top, hill-slopes, valley, plateau forest, salt-licks, etc.

The results show that the plants in the Nallamalai are highly dispersed. Each quadrant has several species each with very few individual plants. The maximum number of species recorded is 22 and minimum number of species recorded is 1. The maximum and minimum number of all plants of all species for all plots recorded is 137 and 15 respectively. There are several species represented by single plants. Single variety of grass species dominate interspersed by other grasses, plants and climbers. Creepers also exhibit minimum diversity though domination by single species of climber/creeper is rare. Though the diversity and density of species is high compared to the plantation sites, the diversity may be less compared to tropical forests in Amazon or in South-east Asian regions like Sarawak, East Kalimantan, Malaysia, etc.

An additional feature of the Nallamalai is homogeneity in terms of species composition. Adjacent tracts of forest do not differ greatly in species composition. In other words more or less same species are distributed throughout the Nallamalai. However, there are exceptions wherein certain species are either absent in certain locality or occur in large numbers restricted to certain patches. The net result of this distribution is that the total number of tree species recorded in inventory is not related to the size of the sample area. More or less same species are found even as the area is increased. This is one principal ecological constraint to the Chenchus who have to gradually expand the area of collection as the resources in one area are exhausted. Coupled with this feature is the differential distribution of vegetational type viz., inferior or superior depending upon soil, rainfall, altitude conditions. This is also an ecological constraint that the Chenchus have to negotiate.

Inventory

It is estimated that the Nallamalai forest harbors 743 taxa spread over 109 families (Ellis, 1982). In the area under the present study the Chenchus could point out and show only 333 species. They could name and identify only 284 species. They could not give names of the rest of the species. Of these 284 species the Chenchus use only 256 species for various purposes and the rest were branded as unused.

The enumerated species fall into eight types of floral classes: trees, shrubs, herbs, climbers, creepers, grass, fungi and aquatic plants. The following Table 3.2 shows the frequency distribution of plants under different floral classes.

Table 3.2 Distribution of Plants According to Floral Class

Sl. No.	*Floral Class*	*Physically enumerated*	*Identified by local nomenclature*	*Not identified*	*Plants used*	*Plants not used*
1.	Tree	87	87	-	84	3
2.	Shrub	47	47	-	45	2
3.	Herb	89	69	20	57	12
4.	Climber	34	28	6	27	1
5.	Creeper	36	26	10	20	6
6.	Grass	16	16	-	15	1
7.	Fungi	5	5	-	5	-
8.	Aquatic	19	6	13	3	3
	Total	333	284	49	256	28

Source : The present study.

It can be seen that, almost half of the existing flora in the Nallamalai are alien to the Chenchus when we take the total taxa (743) into consideration. Many plants are either not known to them or not taken into account. Though some species are endemic to certain localities, the floral species identified by the Chenchu are widely distributed in the Nallamalai indicating a high diversity rather than species concentration. Thus, a majority of floral species are common throughout the Nallamalai and known to the Chenchus. Chenchus are unaware of very few species, which their own people in other settlement are familiar with. For example, *chedu gadda* (edible tuber) which is more familiar to the Chenchus of Mahboobnagar district is not known to the Chenchus of present study area.

End-Uses of the Resources

The floral resources which are collected from the forest are utilized for thirteen types of end-uses/purposes by the Chenchus: food, fodder, fuel, fibre, medicine, structural, liquor preparation, fish fuddling, commercial non-timber forest produce (CNTFP), ornamental, magico-religious, instrumental, and miscellaneous purposes. Table 3.3 shows the frequency distribution of 256 species under various end-uses.

Table - 3.3 Number of Species Used for Various End-uses

(N=256)

Sl. No.	*End-uses*	*No. of species*
1	Food	121
2.	Fodder	86
3.	Fuel	46
4.	Fibre	7
5.	Medicine	97
6.	Structural (hut construction)	13
7.	Liquor preparation	3
8.	Fishing	7
9.	CNTFP	18
10.	Ornamental	4
11.	Magico-religious	17
12.	Instrumental and equipment	
	- household	8
	- agriculture	14
	- hunting	3
	- music	8
13.	Miscellaneous	17

Note :
1. Some species have multiple uses. Hence column total does not tally with N (256).
2. Honey and wax are not mentioned in CNTFP.
3. Fuel: Frequently used species only.
4. CNTFP: Only those floral species which have commercial value at the time of data collection. The number may change as the species specific demand fluctuates.
5. Miscellaneous: Include the purposes like *killi* (pan), detergent, bathing, hair growth, *beedi*, leaf plates, etc. (Details are shown in Table 3.9).

Food: Though the number of species used for food is more (121) only a few species are regularly exploited in the respective seasons of availability. The remaining are occasionally or rarely exploited. The following Table 3.4 shows the frequency of species exploited for food.

Table - 3.4 Number of Species Used for Food

(N=121)

Sl. No.	*Types of species*	*No. of total species*	*Frequently collected*	*Occasionally collected*
1.	Tree	41	25	16
2.	Shrub	27	18	9
3.	Herb	18	10	8
4.	Climber	16	9	7
5.	Creeper	10	3	7
6.	Grass		-	3
7.	Fungi	4	4	-
8.	Aquatic plants	2	-	2
	Total	121	69	52

Out of the 69 species regularly collected for food purpose, some are most preferable, while other are not preferable. A list of few most preferred food species is given in Table 3.5.

Table - 3.5 List of Most Preferred Species used for Food

Sl. No.	*Parts eaten as food*	*Preferred species*
1.	Fruits/Pod	*Nemmi*, tamarind, *velaga, jana, nekkara, dadiri, nalla neredu, kaleva, morli, chitimiti, kondeetha, beera, chilukaduddera, alii, ulindha etc.*
2.	Nuts	*Thadi, dela, morli, poliki*
3.	Leaf	*Boddukura, mallakura, chenchalaku, sirrukura, doggalaku, pavalikura, nemalikura, chamakura, chukkakura, mundla kura, dadirikura etc.*
4.	Tubers	*Chenchu gadda, baljawa, kondamucchu thoka, bodagadda, eravalagadda, thokapulchera, gundu mukkarai, baccharavva, kondapulchera, nulu gadda.*
5.	Flowers	*Nemali, vippa.*

Note: The vernacular names are used. Unfortunately for many species scientific names are not available.

Children are not particular about the preferred species. In their daily visits to the forest all the available food items are exploited. Fruits like *ragi* (peepal), *marri* (banian) and nuts like *gotti* and *thadi* are mostly collected by the children. Adults do not pay much importance to these food species. Hence these food species are known as *chinna pillala pandlu* (children's food).

Phenological pattern of food species in the Nallamalai is remarkably seasonal. There is virtually no species providing food throughout the year. Food species are distributed more or less evenly throughout the Nallamalai. As such there is not much difference in the inventory of food species from one locality to the other. However, a few species are found to be endemic to certain localities. The famous *chenchu gadda* (edible tuber) is not reported from several localities in the northern parts of the Nallamalai. *Chedugadda* (edible tuber) is not found in the southern block of the Nallamalai. The Chenchus usually collect multiple tubers, leaves or fruits in any season. It may be due to the nature of dispersed distribution of plant.

Fodder: The Nallamalai is a rich source for fodder. The fodder comprises leaves, grass, fruits/pods and nuts. A few Chenchus owning cattle collect grass like *erra gaddi, karu gaddi, edumulla gaddi* (vernacular names of species of grass), small head-loads of twigs of *yepi, nemali, ulcha* (vernacular names of species of trees, shurb) etc., for the goats and calves. Otherwise the cattle and goats are grazed in the forest. The grass gets dried up during the summer and may be wiped out due to the fire in the forest. Grazing generally restricted to the plain lands and foothills.

Firewood: Regarding the firewood the Chenchus exhibit selection but there is a wide choice. Out of the 46 species used for firewood, the Chenchus prefer to collect the shrub species like *dadiri, korivi, manga, nekkara, veduru* and trees like *nalla maddi, sandra, thella billudu, poliki* and *yepi* as they give much heat and burn slowly for long time with less smoke. The Chenchus generally do not use the species like *rella, thangedu,* etc., as they do not burn smoothly and easily. The trees like *vepa* (neem) *jammi* and *ari* are not used as fuel due to their spiritual values.

As most of the Chenchu settlements are nestled amidst the forest zones, availability of firewood is not a problem. Inspite of the fact, vast stretches of areas are clear-felled for timber and plantation, and several restrictions imposed by the Forest Department, the Chenchus are not under the pressure in fire-wood collection.

Fibre: The Chenchus use fibre for preparation of ropes to get down into *serries,* for agriculture purpose and to tether cattle. Fibre is also used in the construction of huts and corrals. The species and parts used for fibre extraction is shown in the following Table 3.6.

Table - 3.6 Species and Parts Used for Fibre

Sl. No.	*Name of the species*	*Parts used*	*Actual purpose*
1.	Marri	Aerial roots	Prepare rope.
2.	Yepi	Bark	Tether cattle, used in hut constructions, prepare ropes for agriculture purpose and to get down into *serries.*
3.	Jana	Bark	Tying faggots and other head loads.
4.	Shyagalu	Whole	Make ropes for agricultural purpose.
5.	Peddavempalli	Bark	Tying faggots and other head loads.
6.	Dusara theega	Whole	Tying faggots and other head loads.
7.	Theendra theega	Whole	Tying faggots and other head loads.

Out of the seven species used for fibre the *yepi* and *shyagalu* are predominantly used and the rest are occasionally used.

Medicine: The Chenchus use 97 species of plants for healing various diseases. Herbal medicine is a popular mode of therapy. Each disease may be cured by medicine obtained from a single species or alternate species available in specific season. If a certain plant is not available, alternate plants are chosen. Nowadays the availability of medicinal plants has become somewhat difficult as a result of large scale deforestation. (The species and parts used for healing various ailments are given in Appendix I).

Liquor Distillation : Mahuwa flowers, bark of *thella tumma* or *somi* are used for distillation of liquor. Mahuwa flowers are collected in March and April in large quantities and are distilled. These flowers are also stored. *Thella tumma* bark is available throughout the year. Bark of *somi* is used as an alternative to *thella thumma.* They prepare liquor for domestic consumption or for local sale.

Structural Purpose: Structural purposes include construction of hut, corrals, camp shelter, goats' fencing, pandals and *mancha* (a raised platform in the agriculture fields). The Chenchus use 13 species. The important plants are, *yepi, thella, billudi, sandra, sirumanu, nalla maddi, ulcha, butta, veduru, katterra gaddi,* etc., used for various purposes like poles, rafters, fibre, doors, thatching etc. (The names of the species used for structural purposes is given in the appendix I).

Fish Fuddles: Seven species are used to fuddle the fish. They are (1) *manga* (shrub), (2) *somi* (tree), (3) *pulchera* (tree), (4) *naga jenku* (shrub), (5) *gara* (tree), (6) *kaninga* (tree) and (7) *konda butta* (shrub). The bark and pods of these species are pounded and mixed with soil and sprinkled in the pond in order to intoxicate and stupefy the fish.

Ornamental Purpose: Four species are used by women for ornamental purpose. The flowers of *thangedu*, leaves of *sunnapu katte* and *goggerapatthi* are kept in their hair. *Dusara theega* is used as armlet.

Commercial Non-timber Forest Produce (CNTFP): The Chenchus collect the products of eighteen species for commercial purpose and sold them to Girijan Cooperative Corporation (GCC) store or to the private merchants. The forest produce used for commercial purpose are known as Commercial Non-timber Forest Produce (CNTFP). Out of the eighteen species twelve species are prominently collected in the sample settlements. The items used as CNTFP are not constant. They get changed depending on the demand for the items. The following Table 3.7 shows the details of species used for CNTFP.

Table - 3.7 Prominent Species and Parts Used as CNTFP in the Sample Settlements

Sl. No.	*Parts Used*	*Species*
1.	Roots	*Sugandapala*
2.	Gum/exudate	*Thabisi, sirumanu, kondagogu*
3.	Seeds	*Chilla, musti, nekkara, kanuga, morli*
4.	Leaves	*Tuniki*
5.	Fruit/pod	*Chintha*, soap-nut

Note : Honey and wax are also used as CNTFP but not mentioned in the table.

Magico-Religious Purpose: The Chenchus use 17 species as magico-religious devices. These species are used to scare away the evil spirit and healing the diseases caused due to the evil spirit. The species and parts used for the magico-religious purposes are shown in the Table 3.8.

Table - 3.8 Species and Parts Used for Magico-Religious Purposes

Sl. No.	*Names of Species*	*Part used*	*Purposes*
1	Anduga chettu (tree)	Exudate	The smoke of exudate gives good health to the children.
2	Pogapodi (herb)	Whole plant	The smoke of exudate gives good health to the children.
3	Banda bajanika (herb)	*Bajanika*	Kept in amulets to ward off evil spirits.
4	Gara chettu (tree)	*Bajanika*	Kept in amulet to scare away evils and ghosts.
5	Nalla Jilledu (herb)	Root	Used in amulets to scare away evil spirits.
6	Thella Jilleda (herb)	Root	Used in amulets to scare away evil spirits.
7	Pulchara (tree)	*Bajanika*	Kept in amulets to prevent ghosts.
8	Yalthuri (shrub)	Fibre and *Bajanika*	Used in amulets
9.	Buthankam (herb)	Whole plant	Kept in home to scare away devils and ghosts.
10.	Naga jenku (shrub)	*Bajanika*	Kept in home to desert evil spirits
11.	Erra chithramala (herb)	Leaves	Pounded, mixed with milk, and sprinkled on the cattle herd to scare away evil spirits.
12.	Thella chithramala (herb)	Leaves	Pounded, mixed with milk, and sprinkled on the cattle herd to scare away evil spirits.
13.	Naga musti (tree)	*Bajanika*	Pounded, mixed with milk and sprinkled on the cattle herd in order to prevent the evil disease.
14.	Pamutheega (creeper)	Whole plant	Pounded, mixed with milk and sprinkled on the cattle herd in order to prevent the evil disease.
15.	Musti chettu (tree)	*Bajanika*	Pounded, mixed with milk and sprinkled on the cattle herd in order to prevent the evil disease.

16.	Ari chettu (tree)	Fibre and *Bajanika*	Fibre tied around the neck of child to scare evil spirit.
17.	Poliki (tree)	Nuts	Preparation of sacred food.

The trees like banian, *chedepa* or *vepa* (neem) and *ari* trees are associated with sacredness. Some times the trees under which the local deity is worshipped are also treated as sacred. For instance, the banian trees under which goddess *Porlamma* is worshipped in Palutla and Guttalachenu are treated as sacred trees.

Instruments/Equipment: Twenty-eight species are used for preparation of implements used for the agriculture, household equipment, hunting and gathering and musical instruments. Household instruments comprise brooms, pestle, baskets etc. Agriculture implements comprise *gorru, guntaka* (small ploughs) plough, cart etc. Arrows, bow, and fishing baskets *{kodima)* are the instruments used for hunting. (The details of the usage of various species for various implements are shown in the Appendix I).

Miscellaneous: Seventeen species are used for various miscellaneous activities. These activities can be classified as personal, agricultural, food and drinking, leaf plates and fire-making etc. The following Table 3.9 gives the details of usage of various species by the Chenchus for various purposes.

Table - 3.9 The Species Used for Miscellaneous Purposes

Sl. No.	*Local name*	*Parts used*	*Actual purpose*
Leaf Plates			
1.	Pedda chitimiti (tree)	Leaf	Leaf plates
2.	Polimera chettu (shrub)	Leaf	Leaf plates
3.	Thada chettu (tree)	Leaf	Leaf plates
Personal			
1.	Cheekireni (tree)	Leaf	Head bath (used as shampoo)
2.	Manga (shurb)	Pod	Washing cloths, bathing

Sl. No.	*Local name*	*Parts used*	*Actual purpose*
3.	Revagani gadda (tuber)	Tuber	Applied for hair growth*[1]
4.	Sunnapa katte (herb)	Leaf	Chewing as betel leaves*[2]
5.	Thella maddi (tree)	Leaf	Bathing (used as soap)
6.	Yade theega (climber)	Leaf	Prepare *beedi*
Food purpose			
1.	Nalla maddi (tree)	Stem/ branch	Prepare ash and mix with tamarind*[3]
Fire making			
1.	Lukki (herb)	Stem	Fire making by friction
2.	Panchodi (herb)	Stem	Fire making by friction
Others			
1.	Chilla (tree)	Nut	Purifying the water
2.	Jeedi (tree)	Nut	Closing the hole for musical Instrument*[4]
3.	Udumusulli (herb)	Tuber	Fed for dogs to make active*[5]
Agricultural			
1.	Picchhi chettu (tree)	Stem	Fencing agriculture fields
2.	Regu (tree)	Stem/ branch	Fencing agriculture fields.

Note: * 1. The powder of this tuber is mixed with goat's milk and applied to hair for growth.
* 2. The leaves are chewed as substitute to betel leaves.
* 3. The ash of *Nalla maddi* logs is mixed with the tamarind balls. So that the acidity is decreased.
* 4. To close a small hole in the *thappeta* (a musical instrument) by pasting the powder of seeds of *jeedi* and heated.
* 5. The tubers are made into powder, mixed with milk and given to the dogs in order to make them active in hunting.

Types of Flora and End-Use

It is interesting to know about various types of flora exploited by the Chenchus to obtain various end-uses like food, fodder, fuel, medicine, structural, and other requirements. Specifically we would like to know on what floral types (trees, herbs, shurbs, climbers, creepers etc.) the Chenchus depend most. Table 3.10 gives the details of the distribution of plants according to the type of flora and their end-uses.

Table - 3.10 Floral Species Used for Various End Uses

(N=256)

Type of species	*Total*	*Food*	*Fodder*	*Fuel*	*Fibre*	*Medicine*	*Structural*	*Liquor*	*Fishing*	*CNTFP*	*Ornamental*	*Ritual*	*Instrumental*	*Miscellaneous*
Tree	84	41	29	30	2	32	5	3	4	14	-	7	22	9
Shrub	45	27	18	16	2	22	5	-	3	2	1	2	4	2
Herb	57	18	11	-	1	24	-	-	-	-	2	7	-	4
Climber	27	16	10	-	-	7	1	-	-	1	_	-	1	2
Creeper	20	10	7	-	2	8	-	-	-	-	1	1	-	-
Grass	15	3	10	-	.	2	2	-	-	1	-	-	1	-
Fungi	5	4	-	-	-	2	-	-	-	.	-	-	.	-
Aquatic	3	2	1	-	-	-	-	.	.	-	-	-	-	-
Total	256	121	86	46	7	97	13	3	7	18	4	17	28	17

Note: Some species are used for multiple purposes. Hence, total does not tally with the total of respective rows.

It is observed that each end-use is met from multiple species belonging to multiple floral classes. It can be seen that 'tree' is the single largest floral type from which most of the end-uses are availed of. However, for food, fodder, medicine, fibre, the Chenchus depend on other floral types. For these end-uses the contribution from tree works out to be around one-third where as, the contribution from other floral types put together works out to be two-thirds. This pattern of exploitation of floral types indicates that for the Chenchus other floral types are as much important as that of the trees. This clearly indicates the importance of 'lesser' floral types in the life of the forest dwellers. (The uses of various individual resource species are shown in the Appendix I).

The range of end-uses is high for the trees. herbs and shrubs respectively. The other floral types have limited number of end-uses. Food, fodder and medicinal requirements are secured from a wide range of floral types. Herbs, shurbs, climbers and creepers have both food and medicinal significance. Structural and instrumental requirements are mostly met from trees. Commercial products are largely derived from trees.

Number of End-Uses

Out of the 256 floral species reported to be exploited to derive various end-uses, some species provide only a single end-use, where as others provide multiple end-uses. A single species is exploited to meet multiple end-uses like food, fodder, fuel, CNTFP etc. The Table 3.11 shows the number of species used for various end-uses.

Almost half of the available species yield multiple uses. The number of species decreases with the increase in the number of uses.

Table-3.11 Distribution of Species Used for Number of End-Uses

(N =256)

Number of usages	*Total Species*	*Food*	*Fodder*	*Fuel*	*Fibre*	*Medicine*	*Structural*	*Liquor*	*Fishing*	*CNTFP*	*Ornamental*	*Ritual*	*Instrumental*	*Miscellaneous*
One	127	51	26	-	1	37	3	-	1	1	1	1	2	3
Two	78	36	30	15	3	30	3	1	-	4	3	8	13	10
Three	29	19	15	13	2	16	2	-	1	6	-	4	6	3
Four	16	10	10	13	-	11	3	1	5	2	-	4	4	1
Five	6	5	5	5	1	3	2	1	-	5	-	-	3	-
Total	256	121	86	46	7	97	13	3	7	18	4	17	28	17

Number of Parts Used

The Chenchus use several parts of the species for various end-uses. They use 15 parts of the plants like root, tuber, stem, bark etc. These parts are used independently or in combination with other parts, Generally a single part is used for single purpose. Some times single part is used for many purposes like food, medicine etc. The Table 3.12 elicits the frequency of species and number of parts used.

Table-3.12 Distribution of Species According to Number of Parts Used and Actual Parts Used

Number of parts used	*Total species*	*Root*	*Tuber*	*Stem*	*Bark*	*Exudate*	*Branches*	*Twigs*	*Leaves*	*Flowers*	*Fruit/pod*	*Seeds*	*Nuts*	*Spikes*	*Aerial roots*	*Bajanika*
One	114	7	17	6	4	5	3	1	48	1	18	3	-	-	-	1
Two	67	7	-	16	5	3	5	12	41	1	31	5	1	4	1	2
Three	29	3	-	6	8	4	7	10	15	1	22	2	4	-	-	5
Four	11	3	-	5	3	1	6	5	9	1	7	1	1	-	-	2
Five	4	-	-	2	3	1	2	3	4	1	2	-	2	-	-	-
Whole plant	31	-	-	-	-	-	-	-	-	-	-	-	-	-	-	-
Total	256	20	17	35	23	14	23	31	117	5	80	11	8	4	1	10

Note: 1. Total number of parts used does not tally with N = 256, as many parts are used from single species.

2. The number of parts (one, two etc) used, is applicable to the number of species and not to the actual parts like root, tuber etc.

To know which parts of the plant are frequently used and to know the relative importance of several parts of the plants, the floral species are distributed according to the number of parts exploited in the above table the total 256 horizontally across different parts. It is seen that single part is exploited from a little less than half of the total species. More than one part (many parts) are exploited from 53 per cent of the total species. Leaves and fruits are most frequently collected parts and the aerial root is the least collected part.

The maximum number of parts collected from the species is five. These five parts are collected from two spieces namely *morli* and *pulchara* trees for various purposes like food, fodder, fuel, medicine, fibre, fish fuddle, CNTFP and magico-religious purposes (The parts collected and the purposes are shown in the Appendix I). There are fifteen species like *thella nelajammi, erra nelajammi, nelemi, banda nelemi, dusara theega, pamu theega, katterra gaddi, duda gaddi* etc., which are used as a whole for the purposes like medicine, fibre, food, fodder, ritual and structural.

It can be inferred from the table that a wide variety of parts are used though the maximum number of actual parts collected from any species does not exceed five. There seems to be no relationship between the number of species and total number of parts exploited. In fact, lesser the number of parts exploited, wider the range of actual parts used. In other words, as the total number of parts exploited increases the range of actual parts used decreases. Thus, when five parts are exploited the actual parts like root, bark etc., goes up to 8. When only two parts are exploited, the actual parts go up to 15. The implications of such dependence on the floral species by the Chenchus are very obvious. The Chenchus exploit a variety of parts from 3/4th of the total species. Given the large number of plant species in the Nallamalai the Chenchus exploit a minor portion by widening the range of parts actually used.The parts of a few prominent species used for various purposes are shown in the table 3.13.

Table-3.13 Parts of Few Important Species Used for Various Purposes

Sl. No.	*Parts*	*Name of species*	*Purpose*
1.	Root	*Sugandapala, Nelemi, Thella Usiri*	CNTFP Medicine
2.	Tuber	*Chenchu gadda, Baljavva, Boda gadda, Nulu gadda, Gundu mukkarai, Thokapulchera*	Food
3.	Stem/Branch	*Yepi, Bukhara, Billudu, Sandra, Sirumanu etc.*	Structural Instrumental Fuel
4.	Exudate/gum	*Sirumanu, Thabisi, Kondagogu*	CNTFP Food (time of scarcity of food)
5.	Bark	*Yepi, Jana, Gumpani*	Fibre Medicine
6.	Twigs	*Jana, Manga, Dadiri,*	Fuel

Sl. No.	Parts	Name of species	Purpose
		Nekkara, Korivi	
7.	Leaves	*Doggalaku, Sirrukura, Boddukura, Mallakura Nemalikura, Chenchalaku*	Food, Fodder
8.	Flowers	*Mahwa*	Food, liquor
9.	Fruits/pod	*Nemmi, Velaga, Jana, Kaleva, Nallaneredu, Morli*	Food
10.	Seeds	*Nekkara, Musti*	CNTFP
11.	Nuts	*Poliki, Dela, Morli, Thadi*	Food
12.	Spikes/grains	*Adavi korra, Chigirintha*	Food
13.	Aerial roots	*Marri (banian)*	Fibre
14.	*Bajanika*	*Nagajenku, Yalthuri, Ari*	Magico-religious
15.	Whole plant	*Fungi, Nelemi*	Food, Medicine

Note :

1. Several floral types are important apart from trees.
2. Multiple uses from single plants.
3. More than half of the plants are used for multiple purposes.
4. More than half plant species, multiple parts are used.

The parts exploited from various species by the Chenchus for various purposes are mentioned in the Appendix I.

An attempt is also made to understand the number of parts used from various floral types like tree, shrub, herb etc. The following table 3.14 gives the details.

Table-3.14 Number of Parts Used from Various Types of Species

No. of parts used	*Total species*	*Types of Species*							
		Tree	*Shurb*	*Herb*	*Climber*	*Creeper*	*Grass*	*Fungi*	*Aquatic plants*
One	113	26	13	40	21	11	-	-	2
Two	67	29	15	13	6	4	-	-	-
Three	28	17	11	-	-	-	-	-	-
Four	10	7	3	-	-	-	-	-	-
Five	5	5	-	-	-	-	-	-	-
Whole Plant	33	-	3	4	-	5	15	5	1
Total	256	84	45	57	27	20	15	5	3

Source: Present study.

It is obvious that maximum number of parts are collected from tree and herbs followed by shrubs and climbers. Only one part is used from two aquatic plants. Grass and fungi are used as a whole.

RESOURCE AVAILABILITY: SEASONAL AND SPATIAL VARIATION

This section of the chapter discusses the spatial and seasonal variations in the availability of the floral resources. The Nallamalai belongs to tropical dry deciduous forest type, consisting of mixed forest interspersed by small patches of dense stands of single species like tamarind, *thabisi, pulchera* (trees) *nekkara* (shrub) and bomboo forests.

As already pointed out more or less similar types of resources are fairly dispersed throughout the Nallamalai. However, differences in altitude, types of soils, precipitation and topographical conditions produce differences in quality of vegetation (superior or inferior), in quantity (thick or thin vegetation) of the floral resources and floral types.

To understand the variation in the distribution of floral species, the forest is classified into two major zones viz., plain forests and hilly forests. Plain forest encompasses the level grounds, gentle slopes and plateaux. Hill forest encompasses the hills, hill-slopes, hill-peaks, ravines, cliffs, gorges, etc. A survey is conducted to understand the differences of plant growth on hills and plains. Table 3.15 gives the details of spatial distribution of the species.

Table-3.15 Spatial Distribution of Various Types of Floral Species

Sl. No.	*Types of Species*	*Plain Forest*	*Hill Forest*	*Both Forests*	*Total*
1.	Tree	36	21	30	87
2.	Shrub	26	7	14	47

3.	Herb	50	9	10	69
4.	Climber	11	4	13	28
5.	Creeper	12	5	9	26
6.	Grass	4	3	9	16
7.	Fungi	-	-	5	5
8.	Aquatic	-	-	6	6
9.	Total	139	49	96	284

It can be seen from the table that, a majority of the floral species is available in the plain forests. Except fungi and aquatic plants, remaining all types of flora grow in both forests. However, the number of species grows in plain and hill forest varies considerably. Hill forests have less number of species compared to plain forests. In other words, a large number of plants do not grow in the hill forests. Thus, hills tend to be less heterogeneous compared to plain forest. But it does not mean that forest coverage is thin in hilly areas. (The names of the plants growing in hill forests and plain forests are shown in the Appendix I).

Most of the Chenchus' forazing activities are confined to the plain forests. Their day to day needs are fulfilled in the plain forests. Table 3.16 shows the distribution of floral species according to their end-uses in the two categories of forest zones.

Table-3.16 Spatial Distribution of Floral Species According to their Major End-Uses

(N=256)

Sl. No.	*End-uses*	*Plain Forest*	*Hill Forest*	*Common to Both Forests*	*Total*
1.	Food	62	18	41	121
2.	Fodder	42	15	29	86
3.	Fuel	20	10	16	46
4.	Fibre	5	-	2	7
5.	Medicine	48	14	35	97
6.	Structural	7	1	5	13
7.	Liquor making	2	-	1	3
8.	Fish Fuddle	4	-	3	7
9.	CNTFP	8	6	4	18

Sl. No.	*End-uses*	*Plain Forest*	*Hill Forest*	*Common to Both Forests*	*Total*
10.	Ornamental	4	-	-	4
11.	Magico-religious	13	2	2	17
12.	Instrumental	11	8	9	28
13.	Miscellaneous	11	3	3	17
14.	Total	237	77	150	464

Note : Multiple entries take place. Single species is used for more than one purpose. Hence the total does not tally with N.

A variety of end-uses are availed of from plain forest zones. The food resources particularly the leafy foods like *doggalaku, sirruhura, mundlakura* etc., are available only in the plain forests. Grazing of cattle is mostly confined to the plain areas. However, during the peak summer seasons the cattle are taken to the hills. The fire-wood is collected from the plain forests surrounding the settlements. Out of seven species from which the fibre is extracted four species like *marri, yepi, pedda vempali* and *jana* are available exclusively in plain forests. And three species *dusara theega, theendra theega* and *shyagalu* are available in both the forest zones. (The names of species available in different forest zones are mentioned in the Appendix I). The names of few most important species according to their major end-use in different forest zones are shown in the Table 3.17.

Table-3.17 Prominent Floral Species Available in Different Zones and their End-use

Sl. No.	*End-use*	*Plain Forest Zone*	*Hill Forest Zone*	*Both zones*
1.	Food	*Nalla balusa,*	*Morli*	*Velaga, Vippa,*
	(a) Fruit/pod	*Dadiri Nekkara*		*Nemmi, Pacchabotica*
	(b) Leaves	*Dadiri, Nemali, Chenchalaku*		*Dela, Gaddanelli, Pulichintha*
	(c) Nuts	*Thadi*	*Chilla, Morli, Thabisi*	-
	(d) Flowers	*Vippa, Nemali*	-	-

Sl. No.	End-use	Plain Forest Zone	Hill Forest Zone	Both zones
	(e) Exuadate	*Konda gogu*	*Sinruanu*	*Thabisi*
2.	Fodder			
	(a) Leaves	*Thadi, Korivi,*	-	
	(b) Grass	*Erra gaddi, Chigirintha, Edumulla gaddi*	-	*Velaga, Anduga, Chilla, Kattakanthributta, Duda gaddi*
3.	Fuel	*Neredu, Nekkara, Manga, Dadiri*	*Gumpani, Pacehara*	*Dela, Somi*
4.	Fibre	*Yepi, Jana*	-	*Shyagalu, Theendra theega*
5.	Medicine	*Gara, Neredu Thella kommi*	*Gumpani, Pacehara*	*Musti, Surugudu-Pala chettu*
6.	Structural	*Yepi, Sandra, Bandharu*	-	*Jirra maddi, Katterra gaddi*
7.	Liquor	*Thumma*	-	*Vippa, Somi*
8.	Fishing	*Gara, Manga, Pulchera*	-	*Somi*
9.	CNTFP	*Seeds of Nekkara, kanuga, gum of konda gogu*	*Thuniki leaves, chilla* seeds, gum of *sirumanu* and *thabisi*	*Suganda roots*, soap-nuts
10.	Ornamental	*Thangedu, Goggerapatti, Sunnapa katti*	*Dusara theega*	-
11.	Magico-religious	*Gara, Chithramala, Naga jenku, Yalthuri*	*Andhuga*	*Naga musti*
12.	Instrumental	*Nerlinga, Yepi, Chintha, Sandra*	*Jittegi, Nalla maddi*	*Maddi*
13.	Miscellaneous	*Manga, Polimera chettu*	-	*Thada, Nalla maddi, Cheekireni*

Note: Honey is available in hill forest. But not mentioned in the table as it is not a floral resource.

Seasonal Variation in Resource Availability

Peters (1996) observed that the tropical trees exhibit tremendous variability in the flowering and fruiting phenology. He quotes a few studies to prove that different species produce flowers supra-annually (only once in every couple of years), annually, or even several times in a year. Inspite of the diversity of different phenologies exhibited by individual species, community wide flowering and fruiting patterns have been found to be remarkably seasonal in many tropical forests (Peters, *Ibid*).

In the Nallamalai, availability of various food resources is seasonal. Seasonality usually refers to availability of new leaves, flowers and fruits in specific seasons. Certain plants as a whole also exhibit seasonality. The herbs like *doggalakura, chetlakindakura, bacchalakura,* and the tubers like *baljavva, gundummukkarai,* etc., and the grass of all types are generally seen only in rainy and winter seasons. The whole plant dries out in summer and their existence is not traceable. The grass becomes dry and frequently subjected to fire in the forest. Almost all trees and shrubs shed their leaves during the summer.

Traditionally the Chenchus conceptualize seasons in accordance with the availability of various floral resources. They identify a particular period of the year with one or several fruits, tubers, flowers, green leaves etc., available in that period. Thus the year is conceptualized in terms of a series of floral resources occurring in a cycle. In the same way the annual calendar is identified basing on prominent climatic features. Traditionally no specific names were used to designate each season. Gradually, the Chenchus learnt to use Telugu annual calendar by borrowing certain months, seasons that are significant to them. Presently the Chenchus' calendar is a blend of their own names as well as the names borrowed from the Telugu calendar of months/seasons and festivals.

Broadly speaking, based on the climatic conditions, the Chenchus have divided the year into three seasons: (1) *Vana kalam* (rainy) (2) *Chali kalam* (winter) and (3) *Enda kalam* (summer).

Vana kalam (rainy season) lasts from July to October. The Nallamalai receives rainfall by southwest monsoon in June. But the good rains start only in July and last till the end of October. Hence, the Chenchus identify this period as rainy season. *Chali kalam* (winter) begins in November and lasts till the end of February. After the rainy period, the Nallamalai is invaded by fog during the nights and experience severe cold during November to December. Hence, the Chenchu identify this season as *chali kalam* (a cold season). *Enda kalam* (summer) starts in March and continues till the end of June. The temperature goes upto 40°C in May and June. Based on weather changes in this season it is sub-divided into; (1) *gadpulu* (hot winds) and (2) *tholakari* (light showers). Hot winds blow in March and April. In May and June light showers are received. These showers are called *tholakari* (the first showers in the year).

Based on the availability of floral resources the Chenchus have sub-divided the seasons into six sub-seasons like; (1) *Nemmi pandla kalam* (2) *Dadiri pandla kalam* or *Chenchu gadda kalam* (3) *Thuniki pandla kalam* (4) *Banka kalam* (5) *Vippa putha kalam or Morli pandla kalam* and (6) *Jana pandla kalam or Thenelu theese kalam*. *Kalam* is a local term used to denote the season.

Nemmi Pandla Kalam

Nemmi pandla kalam lasts during the months of July and August. During this season the fruits of *nemmi* species ripen and available bountiful. These fruits are tastier than any other fruit in this season and they are collected in large quantity. Hence, this season is named as *nemmi pandla kalamu.* The other fruits ripen in this season are *nekkara, beera, alli, chiluka duddera, chitimiti, kaleva,* etc.

Dadiri Pandla Kalam or Chenchu Gadda Kalam

Dadiri pandla kalam or Chenchu gadda kalam follows the *nemmi pandla kalam.* It lasts from September to October. During this season the collection of the edible tuber *chenchu gadda* is important activity of the Chenchus. The fruits of *dadiri species* available bountiful. Hence, this season is known as *chenchu gadda kalam or dadiri pandla kalam.* The other tubers available in this season are *guddavva, pandi boda gadda, alavara gadda, nulu gadda.* Fruits *kattakanthri butta, nalikira butta, udinda* etc., are also available.

Thuniki Pandla Kalam

Thuniki pandla kalam follows *Chenchu gadda kalam.* It lasts from November to December. During this season the fruits of *thuniki* species are available in plenty. Besides these fruits *regu, pariga, nalla balusa* fruits and edible tubers like *baljavva, boda gadda, kondamucchu thoka* and the nuts like *poliki* are available.

Banka Kalam

Banka kalam follows *Thuniki pandla kalam.* It lasts from January to February. The collection of gum from species like *thabisi, sirumanu, konda gogu* is the major economic activity. Though gum collection takes place in other seasons also, it is the most important activity in this season, hence it is named as *banka kalam.*

Morli pandla Kalam or *Vippa putha Kalam*

Morli pandla kalami or *Vippa putha kalam* follows *Banka kalam.* It lasts from March to April. During this season the fruits *of morli* species are available in plenty. Fruits like *kondeetha,* tamarind also available. Besides the fruits; the flowers of *vippa* (mahua) and *nemali* species are also available. The Chenchus are fond of collecting the mahua flowers. They eat the flowers as food. The most important usage of mahuva flowers is brewing liquor for domestic consumption. Hence, this season is called as *morli pandla kalam* or *vippa putha kalam.*

Jana Pandla Kalam or *Thenelu Theese Kalam*

Jana pandla kalam follows *Morli pandla kalam.* It lasts during May and June. During this period the Nallamalai receives pre-monsoon showers known as *tholakari vanalu.* In this season the fruits of *jana* species are available in plenty and the Chenchus are fond of collecting these fruits. Besides these, other food resource leaves of *boddukura, mallakura, bankakura,* etc., are available in this season. The other most important activity is honey collection. In this season, the quantity and quality of honey available in the *serries* is very high and this season is more suitable for honey collection. Hence, this season is called as *jana pandla kalam* or *thenulu theese kalam* (season of honey collection).

Availability of major floral resources and their collection in the respective seasons are shown in the Chart 3.1.

Seasonal Variation of Floral Food Resources

The Chenchus use various parts like leaf, root, tuber, fruit etc., as food. Each part is available for a limited duration in specific seasons. Only three edible tubers of plants like *kaluva, thamara* (aquatic tubers) and *theendra* provide food through out the year. The seasonal variation in the availability of various parts of the species is shown in the following Table 3.18.

Chart 3.1 : Indigenous Annual Calendar of the Chenchus : Availability Floral Resources

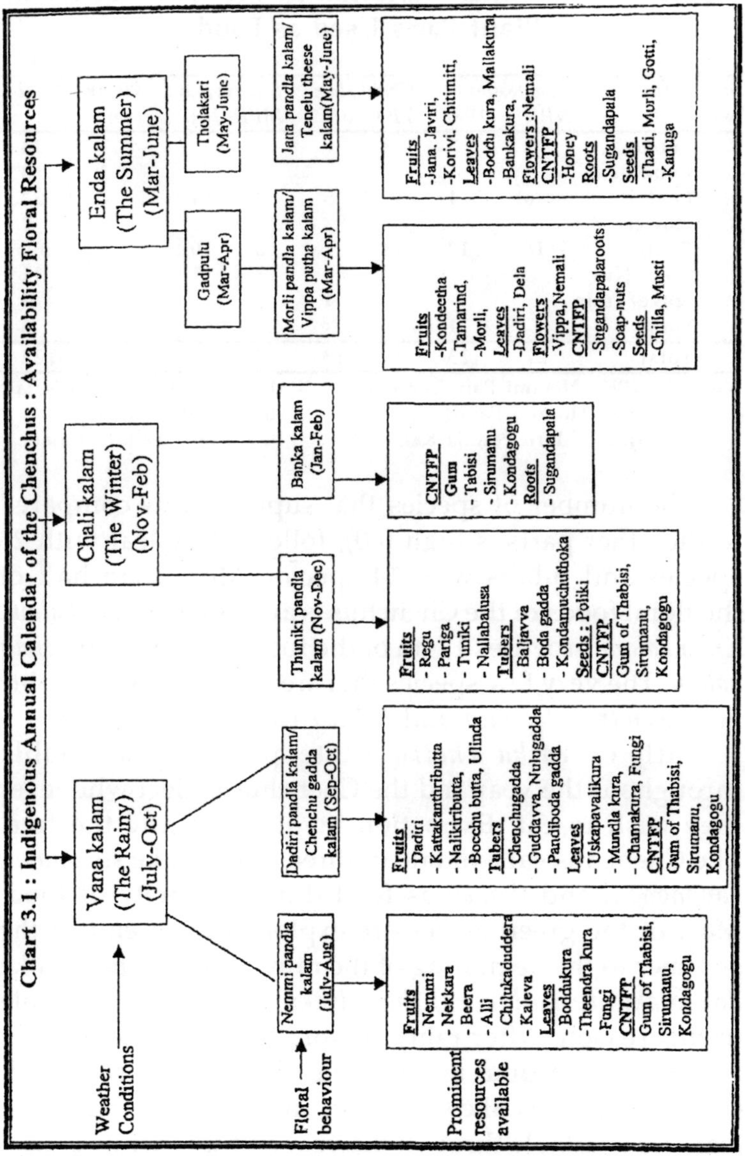

Table-3.18 Seasonal Variation in the Availability of Plant Parts Used as Food

(N=121)

Sl. No.	*Parts used*	*VanalKalam*		*Chalikalam*		*Endakalam*		*Whole year*	*Total*
		NPK	*DPK*	*TPK*	*BK*	*MPK*	*JPK*		
1.	Tubers	3	3	5				3	14
2.	Exudate							3	3
3.	Leaf	6	4		5	2	4	2	23
4.	Flower					3	1		2
5.	Fruits	18	12	14		6	10		60
6.	Seed/Nut				4	3	4		11
7.	Spike/grain				4				4
8.	Fungi		4						4
	Total	27	23	19	13	12	19	8	121

Note: NPK.: Nemmi Pandla Kalam; DPK : Dadiri Pandla Kalam; TPK: Thuniki Pandla Kalam; BK : Banka Kalam; MPK : Morli Pandla Kalam; JPK : Jana Pandla Kalam

The number of species that supply fruits compared to the other parts is high (60), followed by leaf with 23 species and tubers with 14 species. More than half of the floral foods of the Chenchus is available in *vana kalam*. *Enda kalam* provides 1/4th of the foods, followed by *chali kalam*. The very few species that are perennially available are *theendra, thamara* and *kaluva* (tubers).

Pith of *eatha chettu* (date palm) is available throughout the year and the Chenchus collect whenever they wish to eat. Extraction involves cutting the tree. The Chenchus eat exudate of three species like *sirumami, kondagogu,* and *thabisi* as food during scarcity of food. Most of the green leaves are exploited from end of the summer to the beginning of the rainy. Various herbs like *doggalakura, mallakura, theendrakura* etc., are available in this season. After rainy season, leaves of the most of the species become unpalatable and are not collected. Only two species like *karivepaku* and *chinthaku* (tamarind leaf) are available through the year and Chenchus collect them for preparation of chutney.

Flowers of two species *nemali* and *vippa* (mahua) are used as food and available in *enda kalamu*. The nuts of *thabisi, gotti, morli* and *thadi* are available in *tholakari kalamu; poliki pappu* is available in *chali kalam*. *Chilla ginja* (seeds) are available in *enda kalam*. *Poliki* seeds are roasted and chutney is made. Some are eaten raw on the spot in the forest. The grains from the spikes of four species like *doggalaku, buraga* (herbs), *adavi korra* and *chigurintha* (grass) are available in *chali kalam*. These grains are cooked by mixing with rice, *korra* or *ragi* (food grains). Generally these are eaten when the latter food grains are in scarcity.

Four species of fungi are used as food. (1) *bumi puttakokku*, (2) *nemitadugu puttakokku*, (3) *puttakokku* and (4) *puttaputha*. All these are used to prepare either soup or curry. These are available in *vana kalam*.

FAUNAL RESOURCES

The Chenchus recognise 115 faunal species. The enumerated species can be classified into six types viz: mammals, reptiles, birds, amphibians, aquatic species, and insects. Out of the identified 115 species the Chenchus use 89 species for various purposes and the rest are not used. The Table 3.19 shows the frequency of usage of various types of faunal resources.

Table-3.19 Types of Faunal Resources

Sl. No.	*Type of Fauna*	*Identified*	*Used*	*Not used*
1.	Mammals	33	32	1
2.	Reptiles	17	5	12
3.	Birds	43	38	5
4.	Amphibians	4	1	3
5.	Aquatic	8	7	1
6.	Insects	10	6	4
	Total	115	89	26

Birds and mammals constitute a class of animals used more than any other faunal class by the Chenchus.

End-Uses of Faunal Resources

The faunal species are exploited by the Chenchus to avail of various end-uses like food, medicine, magico-religious services, instruments and equipment, commercial purpose and miscellaneous purposes. The following Table 3.20 shows the utilization of faunal resources for various end-uses.

Table - 3.20 Utilization of Faunal Species for Various End-Uses

Sl. No.	*Types of fauna*	*Total*	*Food*	*Medicine*	*Magico-Religious/ Symbolic*	*Scavenging*	*Instrumental*	*CNTFP*	*Miscellaneous*
1.	Mammals	32	27	8	9	4	4	2	1
2.	Reptiles	5	1	-	3	-	1	-	-
3.	Birds	38	35	12	5	-	1	.	1
4.	Amphibians	1	1	-	-	-	-	-	
5.	Aquatic	7	7	2	-	-	-	-	-
6.	Insects	6	2	-	3	3	-	1	1
	Total	89	73	22	20	7	6	3	3

Note: Some animals and birds are used for multiple purposes.

Food and medicine are two important end-uses availed of from the faunal species. The meat of some animals has medicinal value. The parts of some animals are used to treat some ailments. For instance, the skin of wild squirrel or fox is made into a cap and worn it in order to cure headache. Some animals and birds are deified and are ritually or symbolically associated with deities. For instance, tiger is treated as Goddes *Peddamma,* cheetah is treated as Lord *Bayanna* and bear is revered as Lord *Pothuraju.* The behaviour of some animals is also associated with some symbolic meanings. (These are discussed in Chapter-5). Four mammals, one reptile and one bird are used for making instruments, etc. The skin of *manubothu (nilgai)* and *kanithi* (Indian elk) is used for rope making. The skin of *duppi* (spotted deer), *kondagorre* (wild goat) is used as a membrane of *dappu* (a musical instrument). The skin of *udumu* (wild lizard) is used as rings inserted into the bow stave. Finally the feathers *of juttu gadda* (eagle) are fixed to the free end of the arrow.

The horns of sambar and spotted deer have commercial value. The Chenchus however hunt animals for food purpose. For miscellaneous purpose one mammal, one reptile and two birds are used. (The details of the utilization and process of usage are shown in appendix II).

Water Resources

Various types of water bodies are seen in the study area. They are (1) *cheruvu* (tank), (2) *kunta* (pond), (3) *madugu* (a naturally formed deep pond), (4) *gundam* (a naturally formed deep pond in hill areas), (5) *koneru* (small pit), (6) *dona* (puddle), (7) *chalama* (water spring), (8) *vagu* (rivulet) and (9) *kaluva* (stream). The first two water bodies are man made, whereas, the rest are naturally formed. These water bodies can be grouped into two types : perennial and seasonal. Different types of water sources which are seen in Marripalem settlement are given in Table 3.21.

Table - 3.21 Availability of Water Bodies in Catchment Area of Marripalem

Sl. No.	*Name of Water Body*	*Location*	*Purpose*
1.	*Cheruvu*	Plain land	Drinking water, hunting, fishing, grazing and food collection
2.	*Kunta*	Plain land	Drinking water, fishing, hunting and food collection
3.	*Madugu*	Valleys	Drinking water, fishing and hunting

4.	*Gundam*	Valley	Drinking water, fishing and hunting
5.	*Koneru*	Plain land	Sacred/ritual purpose and drinking water
6.	*Dona*	Slops/hills	Drinking water, fishing and hunting
7.	*Chalama*	Stream bed	Drinking water, fishing and hunting
8.	*Vagu*	Plain/hill	Drinking water, irrigation and fishing
9.	*Kalava*	Plain/hill	Drinking water and fishing

Generally *madugu, gundam, koneru,* are perennial bodies, where as *dona, chalama, kaluva, cheruvu* and *kunta* are seasonal bodies. Some *vagus* are perennial as in case of *Pedda vagu* in Palutla and Guttalachenu territory. Many of these water bodies are known by specific names. A few of them in Palutla catchment are: (1) *Palutla cheruvu* (2) *Ankamma kunta, Rellamani kunta* (3) *Katthu madugu, Barla madugu* (4) *Malla gundam* (5) *Thota koneru* (6) *Pilligundala dona, Pandi dona,* (7) *Senjala chalama, Banda chalama* (8) *Peddavagu, Kantrevu madalu vagu* (9) *Erra kaluva, Jauku kalava.*

Some water bodies are considered as sacred. Menstruating women are prohibited from drawing water from sacred water bodies. Each Chenchu settlement customarily owns one or more sacred water bodies. A few more details are given in Chapter 5 on the sacred water bodies. The number of water bodies present in the catchment of one settlement varies from that of the other settlement. Generally, Chenchu settlements are established a bit far away from the water sources, in order to avert the man-animal encounter. If this possibility does not exist a clear division of the water body is demarcated, so that humans and animals use different points of the water body and do not come in contact with each other. Table 3.22 gives details of water bodies in each sample settlements.

Table - 3.22 Number of Water Bodies Present in Each Sample Settlement

Sl. No.	Water Bodies	Alatam	Chinthala	Guttalachenu	Marripalem	Nekkanti	Palutla	Panthanala	Ponnalabailu
1.	*Cheruvu*	-	-	-	1	-	1	-	-
2.	*Kunta*	-	-	1	-	-	1	-	-
3.	*Madugu*	2	4	2	3	3	5	2	3
4.	*Gundam*	3	4	4	3	2	4	3	2
5.	*Koneru*	-	-	-	-	-	1	-	-
6.	*Dona*	2	3	2	4	4	3	2	4
7.	*Chalama*	-	6	3	2	-	3	-	-
8.	*Vagu*	1	1	2	2	1	3	2	3
9.	*Kalava*	-	1	1	-	-	1	-	-

To sum up, the ecological conditions in the Nallamalai have some significant features having implications for the Chenchus to organize themselves in order to cope up with the physical constraints. Marked seasonality and phenology are the most conspicuous markers. The terrain is more or less continuous in a broad sense. The distribution of floral species is more or less even with patches of ecotonal occurrence. Generally speaking there is no significant difference in the distribution of floral species between the catchment territories of the sample settlements. The species diversity is moderate and domination of a single species is relatively in frequent. In a patch of land, one or two species may exhibit greater density (individual members of a species) but do not out number other species.

Marked difference is seen in the distribution of type of vegetation. Depending upon altitude, edaphic features some zones are endowed with rich verdurance vegetation as against bleak desolated sparse patches of inferior vegetation.

The forest is perceived in terms of various features - topographical and vegetational. The forest is divided into named zones which define the nature and availability of resources. The forest is visualized from a macro-perspective to micro-perspective.

All types of flora (tree, shrubs, herbs, climbers, creepers, etc.) are all very important to the Chenchus. Forest resources serve the Chenchus in a wholesome fashion catering to almost all needs of survival. One significant aspect is multiple uses of floral species which in itself increases their value.

4

The Consumption of Non - Timber Forest Produce (NTFP) at Household Level

In this chapter an attempt is made to discuss the dependence of the Chenchus on various forest resources for fulfilling various needs. The main aim is to quantify various Non-Timber Forest Produce (NTFP) utilized by the Chenchus for various end-uses at the household level in order to know the degree of dependence on the forest produce.

The tribal people particularly those inhabiting the forests depend on forest produce to fulfil various needs like food, fodder, fuel, medicine etc. They treat the forest as a storehouse not only for economic purpose but also for socio-cultural purposes. Their dependence on the forest is total. Deeney and Fernandes (1992) write that "the tribes and forests are interdependent and each one's survival is metaphorically attributed to the other".

Even though the dependence of the tribals on forest produce is well known, we know very little about how much produce is actually utilized by them. There could be seasonal differences in the quantities of NTFP used by the tribals. There might have been temporal changes in the utilization in terms of both type and quantity of the forest produce. Certain produce would have either depleted or become extinct. Changing conditions would have necessitated dependence on new produce. Further, these changes would have also brought in certain behavioural and attitudinal changes towards forest produce, the method of exploitation, utilitarian values, etc.

The Chenchus depend directly on the forest resources in order to satisfy their basic needs. About four to five generations ago, the ancestors of the Chenchus in the present study area are reported to have led a pure hunting and gathering life. They exclusively depended on forest resources not only for food but also for meeting various other needs like medicine, fuel, fibre, structural, instruments, etc. In the last five decades the sample settlements have been increasingly opened to the outside contact. The Forest Department and the merchants were the chief agents of contact. Gradually the Tribal Welfare Department also entered the Nallamalai with men, money and material to ameliorate the Chenchus. New occupations like wage-labour, agriculture, commercial sale of forest produce were introduced by these agencies mainly to break the bond between the Chenchus and the forest.

However, the elder informants have reported that their dependence on the forest is gradually intensified and increasing. Their ancestors' requirements on forest produce were minimal. The informants reported that their ancestors had no permanent big huts, corrals, enclosing fence etc. As the Chenchus learnt to build strong permanent huts, practice wage-labour, agriculture, animal husbandry their requirement for various NTFP and dependence on the forest also increased. Collection of commercially valued NTFP has increased the dependence of the Chenchus on the forest. Sedentarization, time bound wage labour, cultivation etc., have induced new habits which in turn increased the dependence on forest produce. While demand for a few items of produce is increased, it declined in case of some other produce.

The non-timber forest produce (NTFP) collected by the Chenchus can be classified into two categories viz., regularly collected items and occasionally collected items. The regularly collected items are those used for food, fuel, commercial purpose etc. These items are collected several days in a week if not the whole week. The occasionally collected NTFP items are those for such end-uses like structural, instrumental / equipment, medicinal, fishing, magico-religious and ornamental purposes. These items are collected as and when the need arises.

Methodology in Quantifying the NTFP

Quantifying the NTFP used by the Chenchu households is an extremely difficult task. It is difficult to collect such data from a considerable number of sample households by a single researcher. Accurate information can be gathered from each household by maintaining daily records. However, such a record is to be maintained for one full annual calendar, in view of the seasonal availability of various NTFP, which is a difficult job. It is also uncertain that all the selected sample households would recall quantities collected long back say about 2 or 3 months ago. Besides it is also uncertain that all the informants would stay within the village throughout the year. Had the researcher decided to stick on to one single village, it would have entailed reduction in the sample size and elimination of differences between sample settlements. In order to overcome these difficulties a strategy is worked out. Accordingly the sample size for this particular study aspect is reduced to five settlements from eight, so that reasonable representation is achieved in terms of topographical features. In each settlement a sample of five households is selected. Each settlement is visited many times in one year, each trip roughly synchronizing, with each season. Thus each season is covered. During each visit the sample households were interviewed so as to recall how much quantity of various NTFP was actually collected during that particular season. During these trips as well as in other visits, the loads of NTFP collected by the Chenchus were also actually weighed whenever such opportunities surfaced. Further the help of key-informants was also taken in order to assess the quantity of NTFP as accurately as possible. A spring balance was used to weigh the sample head-loads of various NTFP. These measurements have helped in arriving at standardized estimates of weights of NTFP used for various end uses. Recall method, sample weighments, key-informants' assessments have increased the accuracy of quantification of NTFP. A brief note on the methods of data collection for each end-use is presented in the next few lines.

Apart from the sample households, one typical Chenchu household, which in all probabilities represents the Chenchu society, was selected. This household had a family size of 5 (one couple and 3 children) and practiced minimum agriculture, depended mostly on sale of Commercial Non-timber Forest Produce (CNTFP) and on forest food. This household was selected from Ponnalabailu settlement. It provided actual quantity of various NTFP used by it for various end-uses. These quantities have been taken as standardized measures of the NTFP used by the Chenchus in general, though in reality each and every household differs in the quantity actually consumed. This typical household, it is hoped, will give us an idea about the quantity of NTFP utilized by an average Chenchu household.

The collected data is presented in the form of average for 25 households (5 sample households x 5 sample settlements) and range, that is the minimum and maximum quantity of NTFP utilized for each end-use.

The food items, which were collected and brought home, were weighed and based on several such observations, an estimate is made per household. Fruits, tubers and leaves are the important food items for the Chenchus. The daily collection of these items varies in quantity from one household to the other household. The food items eaten in the forest was also approximately estimated.

Cattle are usually taken to the forest for grazing. Stall-feeding is done only during the period when the oxen are used for agricultural operations. Cows and goats are not stall-fed. Households, which kept oxen, collect fodder and stack it. A few households also stack agricultural hay though a majority does not cut the stalks. But the quantity of agricultural hay does not last more than a fortnight. Since it is difficult to estimate the amount of grass grazed by an animal in the forest, an indirect estimation suggested by Singh (1989) was adopted, according to which, 2% of body weight of the animal is taken as the weight of fodder consumed, per day by one animal. The average weight of bull, cow, calf and buffalo were estimated most conservatively as 225, 220, 100, 275 kg respectively (Govt. of India, 1987 quoted in Malhotra, et al, n.d.). The average weight of an adult goat and sheep of the Chenchus area were determined from the local market to be 12 kg and 13 kg respectively. The estimation of grass grazed by one cow per one year is 220 x 0.02 x 365 and per one goat is 12 x 0.02 x 365. The Chenchus do not keep buffaloes. Oxen are very few and are not kept for long.

Many faggots collected were weighed on the spot with the spring balance. An average weight of faggot is arrived at. The number of days an average faggot lasts was estimated. From this, the annual requirement of firewood per household is estimated after making appropriate adjustments for the seasonal variation.

The major purposes for which fibre is used were identified. Purposes for which a negligible amount of fibre is used were not considered. For each major purpose, the quantity of fibre needed is estimated. The Chenchus keep bundles of fibre in their huts for any sudden necessity. Sample bundles were weighed and an average weight is arrived at. Number of bundles required for major end-uses are elicited from the informants. From this total fibre requirement per annum per household is estimated.

The end-use of structural purpose refers to NTFP used for hut construction, household and agricultural fence, corrals, watch-posts etc. During the fieldwork, six huts of all types were under construction. The material used for various parts of the hut was actually weighed. For each huts a sample number of bundles of thatch are weighed and a total weight of thatch was arrived at by multiplying the average weight of one bundle with the number of bundles actually used. The quantity of material required for each type of hut varies. Certain Non-timber forest produce is sold either to local merchants who make periodic visits to the Chenchu settlements, or to the Girijan Cooperative Corporation (GCC) stores. The records maintained by the GCC and merchants provide details on the quantity of produce and the names of the individuals. This information is collected. A small amount of CNTFP is also sold to the ryots by a few individuals in some settlements, who are identified and the quantity sold is also recorded. Several NTFP items are seasonally available. Produce like gum, *sugandapala* roots (cusscuss), are collected for most part of the year.

The items used for magico-religious purposes, medicinal, ornamental and miscellaneous purpose are not quantified because these are collected in very small quantities and procured occasionally. The household articles like pestle, cots, leaf mats, brooms, baskets and the implements used for agricultural purposes like bullock cart, plough, *gorru* etc., were roughly calculated.

The NTFP collected is used for both domestic consumption and sale in the market in order to earn some income. The actual utilization of NTFP varies from one household to the other household, and settlement to settlement. Various factors intervene at the household level influencing the quantum requirement of NTFP at each household. For a few households the total quantum requirement of NTFP may be very less compared to other households. In the same way for a few households the requirement of a specific NTFP is more than their counterparts. One important aspect in the utilization of NTFP is that a great proportion of what is collected and utilized remains within the Nallamalai. Only a small proportion of biomass collected goes out of the Nallamalai into the wider market. These items have commercial value and form a chief source of income generation.

In the following pages, each end-use is discussed in detail giving information on: (1) significance of each end-use in the life of the Chenchu, (2) number and important species used for each end-use, (3) seasonality, (4) number of households depending on NTFP for specific end-uses, (5) pattern of availability and exploitation, (6) quantitative estimates for each end-use, (7) variability of consumption between households and between villages, (8) determinants of the use of NTFP (9) finally the ecological impact on the collection of NTFP.

Consumption of Forest Food

Food resources available in the forest have been a chief source of subsistence to the Chenchus from times immemorial. About half a century back, it is said that they were almost exclusively depending on the forest for food. Agriculture was almost absent in the Chenchu society during those days. The traditional forest food comprised a variety of fruits, tubers, leaves, flowers etc. Honey and tubers constituted the staple diet. The forest produce was easily available throughout the year.

Even today, the Chenchus depend on the forest food resources for the major part of the year. Several species of forest food are consumed: 121 species of flora and 73 species of fauna are used as food. Out of the floral species categorized as food only 69 are regularly collected. The prominent species are fruits like *nemmi*, tamarind, *jana, kaleva, chitimiti, nekkara, beera, alli,* etc., the seeds and nuts of *poliki, thada, dela, morli,* the tubers like *chenchu gadda, baljavva, kondamucchuthoka, baccharavva, boda gadda, alavara gadda, gundumukkarai,* the green leaves like *boddukura, chenchalaku, doggalaku, sirrukura, nemalikura, nellikura, chamakura,* and the flowers of *vippa* and *nemali* etc. The food resources are seasonally available.

The consumption of forest food resource is high in *vanakalam* (rainy) and least in *chalikalam* (winter). In rainy season fruits of many species get ripen. More number of tubers and green leaves is also available in this season. After the rainy season the tubers become unpalatable and gradually decay. The new leaves in early *vanakalam* (rainy season) are palatable and later on they become unpalatable and most of the herbs die in late *chalikalam* (winter). The Chenchus collect the resources initially in the nearby areas of their settlements and gradually expand the area to far away places. On an average Chenchu women and men walk for a distance of 5 km in pursuit of food collection. If distance increases, temporary camps are established. In both cases, the 5-km distance is the standard and food collection takes about 4 to 5 hours. Approximately the Chenchu men and women go to forest for 250 days in a year for collection of various food resource. In the peak seasons, they visit the forest as many as four to five times in a week. The food is consumed on the same day, or the next days. The collected food in each time lasts for one or two day. Food is generally collected by women in groups. They also carry out other pursuits like firewood collection, grazing goats etc. The quantity of food collected by a typical Chenchu household during each season is shown in the Table 4.1.

Table-4.1 Flow of Biomass, used as Food at a Typical Chenchu Household Level and the Seasonal Variation (Weight in kgs)

Sl. No.	*Important food components*	*Vanakalam*		*Chalikalam*		*Endakalam*		*Whole year*	*Total*
		NPK (Kg)	*DPK (Kg)*	*TPK (Kg)*	*BK (Kg)*	*MPK (Kg)*	*JPK (Kg)*	*(Kg)*	*(Kg)*
1.	Fruits	50	34	12		34	50		180
2.	Leaves	10	8	-	3	3	6	-	30
3.	Tubers	20	30	18	10	-	-	2	80
4.	Flowers	-	-	-	-	10	-	-	10
5.	Seed/nuts	-	-	-	3	6	1		10
6.	Fungi	1	1	-	-	-	-	-	2
7.	Honey						I		1
8.	Insects						2		2
9.	Meat							20	20
	Total	81	73	30	16	53	60	22	335

NPK :Nemmi Pandla Kalam DPK: Dadiri Pandla Kalam
TPK : Thuniki Pandla Kalam BK: Banka Kalam
MPK: Morli Pandla Kalam JPK: Jana Pandla Kalam

Note: 1. Rarely eaten foods (pith of date palm, grains of *Chigirintha, buruga, adavi korra* and gum of *thabisi, sirumanu* and *kondagogu)* are not listed in the table.

It is observed that the fruits are eaten in large quantities. Different varieties of fruits are available almost throughout the year. Tubers are also consumed. Green leaves are used along with rice, jowar, bajra or millet and *korra*. The typical Chenchu household collects 312 kg of plant food, 20 kg of animal food, 2 kg of insects and one kg of honey per year. The average quantity of forest food consumed by the 25 sample households is 300 kgs. The range of difference between the minimum and maximum utilization is 100-400 kgs.

Dependence on forest food continues to be quite substantial even though several new occupations are practiced by the Chenchus. Firstly, forest food is preferred most compared to the food that is cultivated or purchased. The elderly Chenchus report problem of digestions, fatigue and weakness as resulting from eating the newly introduced food items. Agricultural food as well as purchased food lack variety. Besides, the Chenchus cannot depend upon the purchased food althrough the year. Cultivation is practiced only by 40 per cent of the total households in the sample settlements. The following table 4.2 gives the details of income and expenditure of the typical household.

Table - 4.2 The Annual Income and Expenditure of the Typical Chenchu Household

Sl. No.	*Source of Income*	*Amount (Rs.)*	*Sl. No.*	*Expenditure*	*Amount (Rs.)*
1.	Agriculture (sale of chillis)	400	1.	Food (only purchased)	2250
2.	Sale of CNTFP	5400	2.	Cosmetics/ Ornaments	350
3.	Wage-labour	600	3.	Liquor and tobacco	1500
4.	Live-stock	500	4.	Amusement and visiting towns	900
			5.	Cloths	1000

Sl. No.	*Source of Income*	*Amount (Rs.)*	*Sl. No.*	*Expenditure*	*Amount (Rs.)*
			6.	Household equipment	300
			7.	Miscellaneous	600
	Total	6900	Total		6900

It is observed that the typical Chenchu household spends a small amount on the food. It buys both food grains and the other items (salt, edible oil, pulses etc.) used for food. The Chenchus rarely use the pulses, edible oil for food purpose. The general food contains rice of *korra* or rice and chutney made of dried chillies, tamarind and salt. On an average the household spends Rs. 2/- on other than food grains per day. Hence out of Rs. 2250/- only Rs.1520 (2250-730) is used to buy food grains, which fetches 304 kg of rice (Rs. 5 per one kilogramme). The typical household cultivated 150 kg of *korra* (food grains). The household needs 2 kg of food grains per day. Hence the food grains 454 kg (304 kg purchased grains and 150 kgs of cultivated grains) support the household for 7 months and 15 days. The wild foods supported the remaining four and a half months in the year.

Besides, agricultural produce as well as purchased food contains mostly cereals to which some curry or vegetable dishes are needed. The green leaves, and some wild seeds and nuts of *thadi, poliki, dela, chilla* and *gotti* from the forest are eaten along with the cereals purchased or produced. All the households collect food resources from the forest either regularly or occasionally irrespective of their dependence on cultivation and sale of CNTFP.

Generally the Chenchus collect the food items either by plucking or digging or picking the fruits/seeds/ flowers fallen on the ground. They do not lop the branches of fruit bearing trees. Honey is exploited by driving away the bees by means of smoke torches. By employing these methods they neither over exploit the resources nor disturb the ecology. The implements used in the food collection are very simple. The *Karra para* (digging stick) and *doti* (a long slender pole with a hook fixed to one end). The other implements like, *goddali* (axe) and *chenchu katthi* (knife) are rarely used in the food collection.

The meat is collected in two ways: directly killing the animals and scavenging. Hunting was not a major pursuit though meat is a prized food. Hunting is not a successful occupation each time. The average meat consumption is minimal. The Chenchu food is dominantly vegetarian than non-vegetarian.

Consumption of Fodder

Animal husbandry is adopted by the Chenchus from the people of the plains, who used to entrust their cows with Chenchu individuals for grazing. In lieu of this service, the Chenchus were paid either in cash or kind. They used to get one or two calves. Now, a considerable number of Chenchu households are involved in cattle rearing, either their own or those of the peasants of the plain area. Forest is the chief source of fodder to the live-stock. The fodder is freely and easily available from the forest. Cattle are usually taken to the forest for grazing. Oxen are stall-fed during agricultural operations. Remaining live-stock is not stall-fed. The few households keeping oxen collect the fodder and stack it. The Chenchus do not stack dry grass. They depend mostly upon green grass. It is reported that 86 species are grazed by the cattle in the forest. *Javiri, kattakanthri butta, ulcha, thella papidi, nulla papadi, kaleva* are some of the important species. Most of the species grazed are shrubs, herbs and climbers. The small twigs and branches of *yepi, arti* are lopped off for grazing the cattle. The major species which the Chenchus collect from forest for bulls, calves and lambs are *erra gaddi, karu gaddi, edumulla gaddi* (grass), and the twigs of *yepi, nemali* (tree) and *ulcha* (shrub) respectively.

In the case of fodder out of 86 species, some are available seasonally and some are perennially available. Species like *karu gaddi, oopa chattha, golla savaram, adavi korra* etc. belong to the grass family. The parts like flowers, nuts, seeds are available only in specific seasons. The flowers like *vippa, nemali, billudu,* the fruits like *nemmi, morli, nekkara* and nuts like *gotti, thadi* are seasonally available. The perennially available fodder items are mainly the leaves of species like *yepi, ragi, pulchara, jana, thumma, billudu,* etc.

In the studied area, 50 per cent of the Chenchu families possess livestock. The typical Chenchu household possesses one bovine (cow) and five ovine (goats) animals. The range of live stock is 2 to 20. But on an average the Chenchu household possesses one bovine and two ovine animals. In the Chenchu region cows and goats population is predominant. Sheep and buffalo population is negligible. The reason behind this is cows and goats are more suitable in the hilly areas.

In rural Andhra Pradesh, fodder requirement is expressed in terms of *mopulu* (grass bundles) of dried paddy stalks or green grass. The Chenchus do not use this term. However, the quantity of fodder consumed by live-stock of the Chenchu can be expressed in terms of bundles by approximately arriving at the weight of each bundle. The researcher weighed sample green grass bundles in his own village and the average weight of a bundle is estimated as 20 kgs. Dividing the quantity of total fodder consumed for household with this weight of bundle of green grass, the number of bundles required can be arrived.

Given the average number of live-stock (one bovine and two ovine) per household, an amount of 1780 kgs

(89 bundles) of fodder per annum is required. The typical Chenchu household requires 2044 kg (102 head-loads) of green fodder per annum. The details of fodder requirement to typical Chenchu household is shown in the Table 4.3.

Table - 4.3 Fodder Requirement to the Typical Chenchus Household per Annum

Number of cattle		*Weight of Animal*	*Fodder Consumed per annum (Kg)*	*Total (Kgs)*
Bovine (cow)	1	220 (Kg)	1x220x0.02x365 = 1606	2044
Ovine (goat)	5	12 (kg)	5x12x0.02x365=438	

Generally the bovine and ovine animals are taken together into the forest for grazing either by women or children. They take the cattle to the forest by around 9.30 a.m and return to the settlement by 5 p.m. In the rainy and winter, the grazing is confined to nearby surroundings whereas in summer the cattle are taken to distant places like, hill-tops and valleys for grazing. The cattle of a single settlement are grazed in several groups in different localities in the forest.

The variation in the requirement of fodder between households is influenced by the number of cattle. However, the variation is not maximum because most of the households keep only minimum number of live stock.

The consumption of fodder by a typical Chenchu household is less than that of an agricultural household in the rural areas of Andhra Pradesh. In the *Akepadu** rural region of Cuddpah district of Andhra Pradesh, from which the researcher hails, a household keeps on

* Akepadu comprises 14 villages with agriculture as a main stay. This region is a representation of Rayalaseema a major region comprising 4 districts of Andhra Pradesh.

an average five bovine animals (oxen, cows and buffaloes) and two ovine animals. The former are kept for agriculture purpose, the latter are kept for milk. The ovine animals are kept for meat. The average weight of a bovine animal is estimated as 255 kg (2 x 225 + 3 x 275 x 5),. In this region the quantity of fodder requirement for household per year is 9482 kg (5 x 220 x 02 x 365 + 2 x 12 x 02x 365).

The impact of grazing on the vegetation in the Nallamalai is only marginal. Cows usually feed on the grass. But goats eat away small plants, leaves, pods, fruits and flowers. Usually the plantations are fenced and hence there is no threat to them from cattle. The Chenchus are very much afraid of the Forest Department which penalize them if their cattle is found grazing in plantations or in prohibited areas. Forest fires are common in summer. It is alleged that the Chenchus themselves resort to burning away dried up grass in order to get fresh shoots in rainy season. The Chenchus say that burning of forest is done by the Forest Department itself and ryots of plain areas. Accidents-natural or otherwise are common. Comparatively speaking, forest fires are more commonly confined to peripheral areas in the Nallamalai than in the interior areas. Soon after rains the peasants from the plains drive their flock to the Nallamalai. They also cut green grass to be taken back in head-loads or cart-loads to their villages. In spite of these, bovine and ovine animals are also good agents in spreading the seeds to different places.

Fire-Wood

Fire-wood is the sole source of fuel for the Chenchus. Naturally they collect fire-wood from the forest which is their immediate environment. Wide varieties of species are available in the forest. Other means of fuel like kerosene stoves, solar cookers and cow dung cakes etc., are not available in the area under present study.

It is reported that two to three generation's ago, usage of fire-wood by the Chenchus was very minimal compared to the present days. They used to depend much on raw wild foods. The animal meat used to be roasted. They used to boil only a few varieties of tubers and hence cooking time was also less. The consumption of fuel has radically increased only after the introduction of agriculture in the Chenchu society. Due to acculturation they started cooking two times per day and taking bath with hot water. This has increased the cooking time and in turn increased the quantity of consumption of fire-wood. Earlier they used to take bath once or twice in a week in the streams. Even today some Chenchus retain this habit of bathing in the streams, Now-a-days, taking hot water for bathing is also picked up. Further, use of fire-wood has increased because of watching crops during nights. In order to make the presence of humans known to the wild animals, firewood is burnt throughout the night (known as *negadu)* at the agriculture fields. Fire is also necessary to protect themselves from the cold and scare away wild animals. Firewood is used to warm the hut during nights in the winter, to make glowing torches while walking in nights, and keep flame during nights in the huts to get some light and make bonfire in nights during communal activities like amusement, playing, dancing etc.

Usually women collect fire-wood twice or thrice in a week or on day-to-day basis. In the rainy season they keep one or two bundles extra in the hut. Firewood is not collected in large quantities and stacked. Generally dried/dead wood and fallen twigs are collected. Cutting green wood and fresh branches are not resorted to.

Forty six species are cited by the Chenchus as useful for fire-wood. However, a few species like *dadiri, kaleva, manga, korivi, nallabalusa, yepi* and *nallamaddi* are prominently used. A typical Chenchu household consumes 1800 kgs (90 head-loads) per annum. The average Chenchu household requires 1700 kgs (85 head-loads) of fire-wood per year for various purposes listed above. The range of consumption for the sample households is 720 to 3600 kg (36 to 180 head-loads) per year. Consumption of fire-wood is high in households which practise agriculture. Crop watching consumes almost three times the quantity of fire-wood used for cooking food per day.

The consumption of fire-wood by a Chenchu household is less than that of the peasant household in the *Akepadu* region. The average consumption at household level per day in *Akepadu* region is estimated as 7 kg per day or 2560 kgs per annum. The more consumption of fire-wood in this region is due to: (1) longer periods of cooking time, cooking for more number of people and cooking twice or thrice per day; (2) people generally take bath with hot water every day. The Chenchus generally bath once or twice in a week. Besides they prefer to take bath in the streams. The agrarian people use other types of fuel namely logs, cow dung, coal, agricultural waste etc.

Sometimes the Chenchus use specific varieties of fuel-wood for specific purposes. The logs of *yepi, jirra maddi, chilla, billudu* and *sirumanu* are used for *negadu*, (night fire at agricultural fields) which gives much heat and last for longer time. The twigs and branches of *manga, korivi, dadiri, nekkara, gotti, kaleva, ulcha, somi, nemmi, poliki,* which burn speedily and softly are used for cooking food and boiling water. *Veduru* (bamboo) and *korivi* are used to make glowing torches. The

Chencus do not put off the fire in hearth completely. They allow the embers to be glowing in the hearth.

Consumption of Fibre

Fibre is used mainly for building huts, corrals and fences, rope-making, collection of honey, and for agriculture. Fibre is an important material to the Chenchus as it is necessary for various minor purposes like tying the faggots, tethering animals like oxen, goats, calves, fastening the bow string etc. Several species available in the forest yield strong fibre from which ropes and threads are twined.

Out of seven important species used for extracting fibre two species namely *yepu* and *shayagalu* are predominantly used. The ropes made of *yepi* fibre are used for agricultural purpose mainly for plough and cart harness. The ropes are used as hangers by which the Chenchus descend into the *serris* for honey collection. The ropes used in agriculture and for tethering animals last for one year. Fresh ropes are made for honey collection each year.

Fibre is extracted by soaking the stems of *shyagalu* for 20-25 days. The fibre is dried in sun light for a few days and made into bundles. The green fibre from *yepi* bark can be used immediately after extraction for making ropes or spin into thread and make bundles. The aerial roots of *marri* (banian) are pounded and ropes are made. The bark of *pedda vempali* and *jana,* and the creepers like *dusara theega* and *theendra theega* are used to tie the faggots and other head-loads in the forest. The consumption of fibre for various purposes used by the Chenchus are shown in the Table 4.4.

Table - 4.4 General Consumption of Fibre for Various Purposes

Sl. No.	*Purpose*	*Quantities (Kg.)*
1.	Hut (traditional hut) construction	10
2.	Corrals (for hut and tethering cattle)	15
3.	Fencing to hut	5
4.	Agriculture*	15
5.	Honey collection*	25
6.	Others	5
	Total	75

Note: * Fibre requirement for one year.

Ropes and threads or strands of fibre used for binding are to be replaced at least every year. Ropes once used in honey collection are not reused. All the fibre that is used for huts, corrals and fences are replaced as and when they worn out or wither away.

The consumption of fibre by the typical Chenchu household per annum is 30 kilograms. The household possesses only one big rope for honey collection and small ropes for tethering the cow and goats in the corral. The average consumption (for the 25 households) of fibre is 25 kg. The consumption varies from household to household ranging from 10 to 45 kgs depending on the possession of live-stock, corrals, agricultural implements and ropes for honey collection, size of the hut and various implements. Generally all the Chenchu households do not possess all implements. They borrow from the neighbours when the need arises.

There is substantial increase in the use of fibre on account of adoption of agriculture, cattle rearing and construction of relatively bigger, permanent huts, corrals, fence etc. The Chenchus usually keep stock of fibre or ropes, threads made of fibre. Extraction of rope do not involve much damage to the trees. *Yepi* twigs yield ample quantity of fibre. All other plants are shrubs and small plants.

Traditionally, the Chenchus did not consider the hut as an important asset as they were leading a nomadic life. The earliest Chenchu hut was a small conical shaped with a small entrance. They had to crawl into the hut. It was made of pliable branches which used to be covered with leaves and grass. The Chenchus learnt the art of building solid, permanent huts through their contact with the neighbouring plain area people. Due to the adoption of agriculture and cattle rearing, the size of the huts is increased. Apart from hut, the Chenchus have learnt to construct various other structures like *mancha* (a raised platform at agriculture field to watch crop from wild animals), fence, corrals etc. All the materials needed for these structures are procured from the forest.

The Chenchus of present study construct three types of huts: (1) *chuttu gudisa* (2) *mula gudisa* and (3) *kottamu* (figures and measurements are shown in Chapter (2). The materials used for huts last for 8 to 10 years, after which the thatch, rafters and wattles have to be replaced. Total hut is abandoned or burnt out and a new hut is erected in the event of frequent incidence of diseases and death. Generally the Chenchus construct a new hut after 10 years. The biomass needed for each type of hut is shown in the Table 4.5.

Table - 4.5 Materials and Quantity Required for Structural Purpose

Sl. No.	*Hut components*	*Standard Weight of single piece (kg.)*	*Types of huts*					
			Chuttu gudisa No.	*Weight (kg.)*	*Mulagudisa No.*	*Weight (kg.)*	*Kottam No.*	*Weight (kg.)*
1.	Pole	20	15	300	10	200	11	220
2.	Central Pole	30	1	30	1	30	2	60
3.	Bamboo walls (bundle)	25	8	200	8	200	12	300
4.	Rafter	3	80	240	100	300	150	450
5.	Thatch (head	20	12	240	14	280	23	460

	load)							
6.	Fibre (bundle)	1	10	10	15	15	20	20
7.	Beam on poles	5	7	35	8	40	12	60
8.	Fencing to hut*	200	-	200		200		200
9.	Miscellaneous		10	10	15	15	20	20
10.	Long beam on central poles	20						20
	Total			**1265**		**1280**		**1810**

Note: * Size of fence do not vary with the type of hut owing to lack of large difference in the extent of area of the enclosure.

The families practicing agriculture erect a *mancha* (a platform) at the agricultural field to watch crops during nights. There may be more than one *mancha* in one field depending on the extent of area of the field. The materials and quantity required for *mancha* are given in the Table 4.6.

Table - 4. 6 Quantity of NTFP Used for Mancha

Sl.No.	*Components*	*Average weight of piece (kgs)*	*No*	*Weight (kgs)*
1	Poles	10	6	60
2.	Platform	15	-	15
3.	Rafters	1	20	20
4.	Long poles	20	2	40
5.	Beam	5	1	5
6.	Thatch	20	2	40
7.	Miscellaneous (fibre etc.)	-		2
	Total NTFP			182

The round hut is the traditional type and is more predominant in all the sample settlements. The selected typical Chenchu household possesses two round huts. One is used for residing and the other is used as corral. Both huts do not have fencing. The quantity of NTFP used for structural purposes by the typical Chenchu household is 2530 kilogrammes. The requirement of NTFP for different households ranges between 1060-3000 kgs. The average consumption of NTFP for (25 households) hut construction is 1360 kgs. The flow of NTFP used for structural purpose varies across the households and settlements, depending upon the size and number of huts, live-stock, fencing to hut and agriculture practice. The wide gap between the two extreme ends of consumption of biomass is due to that some households do not have fences, and corrals, whereas few other households are big and possess *kottam,* fence, corrals and *mancha* etc. Households practicing agriculture have big huts, whereas households practicing animal husbandry have small huts.

The materials required for the structural or house construction are available throughout the year. The branches and stems of the species like *yepi, sandra, bidludu,* bamboo are available perennially. However, for roofing two types of grass species like *chedu boda* and *katterra gaddi/gudisa gaddi* are available only in the winter.

Fernandes, Menon and Viegas (1988) report that the tribals of Orissa use less than 2 cubic metres of wood for house construction. They also report a study conducted (by ORG) in Puri district according to which the average requirement per household for repairs is 22 bamboo poles and 0.11 cubic metre of timber. In comparison, a middle class urban house needs more than 3 cubic metres of timber.

The consumption of biomass for house construction by an agricultural household in the *Akepadu* region is almost double than that of the Chenchu household. The average house size of an agricultural household is 55 m^2 (11 mt x 50 ml). The average biomass used for construction is 2500 kgs. The items used for house construction are shown in the Table 4.7.

Table - 4.7 Biomass Used for House Construction in Agrarian Society

Sl. No.	*Items*	*No.*	*Weight*	*Total Weight (kg)*
1.	Poles	8	30	240
2.	Beams on poles	4	100	400
3.	*Addapattelu* (beams on poles)	10	30	300
4.	Small beams	2	20	40
5.	Rafters	170	3	510
6.	Thatch (head loads)	40	20	800
7.	*Pendi*	-	20	20
8.	Miscellaneous	-	-	50
9.	Fibre	20	1	20
10.	Door and Frame	1+1	50	100
	Total	-	-	2480

The house in agricultural village is very strong and lasts for fifteen to twenty years. The agriculture society needs bigger houses than the Chenchu society. The huts are compartmentalized and the number of poles, rafters etc., is high. The agricultural hut comprises a sleeping room, *pooja* (worship) room, store room and a cooking room. The Chenchus do not have any *pooja* room within the hut. Generally, they do not keep the idols of gods and goddess in the hut.

The Chenchu prefer to use species like *yepi, sandra, thella billudu* and *sirumanu* for hut construction. They collect only two types of grass species like *katterra gaddi* or *chedu boda* for thatching. Traditionally the bamboos were used for wattle walls of the hut. At present because of stringent forest rules the usage of bamboos is declined. The forest officials are punishing the Chenchus, while the latter were found cutting bamboos. Hence, they are using the species like *nalikirabutt* and *bandanru* (shrubs) for the wattle walls. Most of the structural material used for hut construction is collected from moderately grown up trees. Very small trees or very big trees are not chosen as they do not serve the purpose.

The impact of collection of material for structural purposes on forest seems to be minimal because the huts and corrals are repaired or totally replaced once in ten years. The thatching grass is available in plenty in the forest. The species like *nalikiributta, bandaru chettu* (shrubs) are used for wattle walls. These species grow again speedily. The species like *sandra, yepi, billudu* used as poles and beams are slow growing trees.

The Chenchus are facing the problems in collection of material for structural purposes, as a result of various forest rules. The local forest officials punish them while they are found cutting the trees. The Chenchus are not allowed to carry the axe and knife into the forest. They have to collect the material secretly. They have to walk long distance for collection of material as the large tracts of land are reserved for plantation programmes. They express their grief that though they have been residing in the forest since times immemorial, they are afraid of the forest officials and they lost their right to collect the materials.

Commercial Non-Timber Forest Produce (CNTFP)

Commercially valued forest produce has been a medium through which, the Chenchus have been in contact with the plain's people. Traditionally the Chenchus used to exchange the forest produce like honey, tamarind, soap-nuts, *vippa* flowers and nuts of *morli* with the plain people for food grains, chilli, salt, iron or cloths etc. Since long, the Chenchus have been collecting the forest resource for both domestic consumption and for commercial purpose. The sale of CNTFP had been and continues to be an important source of income to the Chenchus. The produce used to be either exchanged or sold in market for cash. Now-a-days, essential commodities including food grains are procured by means of income raised by selling CNTFP in the Girijan Cooperative Corporation (GCC).

The Chenchus collect eighteen items for commercial purpose. But only 12 items are predominantly collected. These are tamarind, soap-nuts, *sugandapala* roots, seeds/nuts, of *nekkara, kanuga, chilla, musti* and *morli*, gum of *thabisi, sirumanu, kondagogu* and *tendu* leaves. Gum and *sugandapala* roots are being collected for the past two decades only. These two kinds of produce fetch the Chenchus considerable amount of income. The quantity and income generated by sale of CNTFP by a typical Chenchu household, average Chenchu household and the range of difference between the maximum and minimum collection per annum is shown in the following Table 4.8.

Table-4.8 The Quantity of CNTFP Collected by Chenchus per Annum (in kgs)

Sl. No.	*Items*	*Typical Household*		*Average for 25 Household*		*Range of difference*	
		Kg.	*Rs.*	*Kg.*	*Rs.*	*Kg.*	*Rs.*
1.	Tamarind	45	252	24.53	137.50	15-50	75-250
2.	Soup-nut	135	820	73.00	500	20-40	100-200
3.	*Sugandapala* roots	213	2556	137.70	1640	60-500	600-5000
4.	Seeds/nuts	43	228	37.40	200	15-70	75-350
5.	Gum	16	984	7.0	427	5-20	300-1200
6.	Honey	8	560	4.87	340.90	5-20	750-8400
	Total	460	5400	284.50	3244.40	120-700	1900-8400

Note: The rates are not constant. They are subjected to change even in the same season. Hence the income by selling the same quantity and quality of the same item of different households may vary depending on the fluctuation in the prices.

It can be seen that *suganda pala* roots account for major quantity out of the total CNTFP collected.

Majority of the households are involved in collection of *sugandapala* roots. The collection of CNTFP varies from season to season in the year. The gum is prominently collected in rainy and winter seasons. *Sugandapala* roots are collected from late winter to the end of summer. Tamarind and soap-nuts are collected in early summer. Honey and seeds/nuts are collected only in summer. Details of seasonal collection are given in Chapter III.

The CNTFP are collected by both wife and husband. Camps are also established for 5 to 15 days at distant places to collect these roots. Tamarind is collected by both the male and female. While the male climbs to shake the branches in order to make the fruits fall down, the female collects and piles. Drying, cleaning, shelling etc., are all done by women.

Collection of gum and honey are exclusively male tasks. The gum collection usually does not involve seasonal camp. Single individual goes in the morning and remove a small portion of the bark on the stem of gum trees and comes back in the evening. After one week the individual goes and collects the gum. Even though gum is available throughout the year, the collection takes place only in rainy and winter seasons because the yield is high during these seasons.

Honey collection is a group activity executed by men. Series of honeycombs are deposited by the bees at the *serris* on the vertical surfaces of cliffs. Seasonal camps are executed for honey collection in summer.

The quantity of NTFP collected for commercial purpose varies from household to household. Very few households which are successful in adopting agriculture and individuals employed in government department do not show much interest in collection of CNTFP.

Presently the gum and *sugandapala* roots have much commercial value and are over exploited. In order to extract as much gum as possible, more deep incisions are made on the stem of single gum tree. Ultimately the stem is gradually thinned and collapses. This happens mostly in the case of *kondagogu* and *thabisi* trees. *Sugandapala* roots are also now extracted indiscriminately without any care to refill the pit or leave a root intact so that the whole plant would not die.

NTFP Used for Medicinal Purpose

The Nallamalai was once said to be a source of large number of medicinal plants. It was called *moolika seema* (region of herbal medicine). The Chenchus of the sample settlements have been using indigenous medicines for healing various diseases. Even though allopathic medicine is known to the Chenchus, they prefer to depend more on herbal medicine. Treatment procedures of using herbal medicine is known to many adult Chenchus.

They use 97 species of plants for healing various diseases. Alternate or multiple herbal formulas exist to treat a specific disease. The quantity collected is very less and it is occasionally collected when the need arises. Even in the changing circumstances, herbal medicine plays an important role. Thus, the young generation is also acquainted with various medicinal plants like *thella usiri, naga musti, nelemi, pulchera, balintha chettu* etc. (details of medicinal plants are given in Appendix I). This is unlike forest food with which the young generation is gradually getting separated. Collection of medicinal plants involves great care. Some of the procedures of collection are discussed in the Chapter 5.

The Chenchus are encountering problems from local forest officials like guards and watchers in collection of medicinal plants. For instance to set the broken parts of limbs of the domestic animals, they use the bark of *gumpani* tree. But the forest rules do not allow them to use axe on the tree to collect bark.

NTFP Used for Fish Fuddling

The Chenchus practise four types of fishing methods viz., rod and hook, *kodima* (a bamboo fishing trap), bow and arrows and fuddling. *Kodima* and bow and arrow are used in flowing water at shallow streams. Hook and fuddling are used in the stagnant waters. There are six plants, which are used for fish fuddling. The parts used for fish fuddling are pods, leaves and bark. The names of the plants are shown in the Chapter 3. The species are used occasionally.

NTFP Used for Magico-Religious Purpose

The Chenchus use eighteen floral species for magico-religious purpose. Mostly these species are used to ward off evil spirits, evil dreams etc. Parts like root, *bajanika,* bark etc., are used. Parts of some species like *ari, thella jilledu* are kept in amulet or tucked in the thatch or tied to rafters. Some are mixed with water and sprinkled on the cattle herd in order to ward off evil spirits. At any point of time only a few people will be exploiting these plants. The important species are *ari, naga musti, yalthuri, buthankam* etc. Further details are given in Chapter 3. Very small quantities are used for this end-use.

NTFP Used for Ornamental Purpose

Traditionally the Chenchus, particularly women, used to wear various kinds of ornaments like anklets, armlets, necklaces made of slender stems of climbers. The flowers and leaves were also used by them as ornaments. At present they use four species for ornamental purpose. The flowers of *thangedu,* leaves of *goggerapathi* and *sunnapakatte* are adorned in hair. *Dusara theega* is used as armlet.

NTFP Used for Implements and Equipment

The implements and equipment used by the Chenchus can be classified into four categories viz, agricultural implements, hunting and fishing implements, household equipment and musical instruments. Agricultural instruments comprise bullock-cart, plough, *gorru* and *guntaka* (types of ploughs). Bow and arrows, *kodima* (fishing trap) are used for hunting and fishing purpose. Household equipment comprise baskets, granaries, brooms, pestles, mats etc. *Dappu* is a musical instrument. The Chenchus use various plants for making these implements. Except the agricultural implements all the other implements are seen in almost all the Chenchu households. Only a few Chenchu households possess the agricultural implements.

The Chenchus use 14 species for agricultural implements. The prominent among them are trees like *adavi dirisena, bonthada, jirra maddi, maddi, muriki nimma, nalla maddi, nemali, nerlingu, sandra* etc. Three species like bamboo, *ulcha* and *polimera chettu* are used for hunting and fishing purpose. Eight species are used for preparation of household utensils. The important species are bamboo, *pusikapullanattu, eatha, palapariga, thabisi, thada, thaluku* etc. Three species are used for musical instruments. They are tamarind, *yade theega* and *yepi*.

The selected typical Chenchu household possesses the agricultural implements like *gorru, arku* and *guntaka* (ploughs), hunting implements of bow and arrows and one fishing trap. It also has one *dappu* (musical instrument) and some household equipment like one basket, one mat, pestle and broom. The quantity of biomass used by the typical household for various equipment is mentioned in the Table 4.9.

Table - 4.9 Consumption of Biomass for Various Equipment by the Typical Chenchu Household

Sl. No.	*Implements*	*NTFP (kg)*
1.	Agriculture	
	(a) Gorru (A type of Plough)	25
	(b) Araka (Plough)	35
	(c) *Guntaka* (A type of Plough)	20
2.	Hunting and fishing	
	(a) bow and arrows	5
	(b) *kodima* (fishing trap)	5
3.	Household equipment	25
4.	Musical instrument	10
	Total	125

The variation in the consumption of biomass for equipment is not much, because, most of the Chenchu households generally possess very few implements. Variation may arise due to possession of additional implements. For instance, a few Chenchu households in the sample village possess bullock-cart where as many households do not have. A household may have two bows and many arrows. Some families, which practice agriculture, possess granary and baskets where as the other households which do not involve in agriculture do not have granaries, baskets and agriculture implements.

The range of difference between households in utilization of NTFP for instruments and equipment is 20 kgs to 460 kgs. The large difference is because, some household have all agriculture implements like bullock-cart (350 kg) and other implements where as the other households possess only bows and arrows and very few household equipment. On an average the Chenchu household consumes 100 kgs of biomass for instrumental and equipment purpose. Fernandes,

Menon and Viegas (1988) report that the tribals of Orissa use 0.65 cft or 0.019 cubic metres of timber for implements and household equipment.

Most of the implements/equipment last for longer periods. For instance, the baskets, musical instrument and bow and arrows and fishing trap may last for three to four years. But the bullock cart and household instruments like pestle, etc., last for many more years. Hence the requirement of NTFP for this end-use is usually minimal. Sometimes a suitable log of wood may be stored for future use.

Collection of material for instrumental or structural purposes may implicate the Chenchus under criminal offences. For instance, in 1997 Seelam Muttahiah of Guttlachenu was arrested by forest guard, while he was carrying an *yepi* log for making plough. He was kept in the forest bungalow in Gutalachenu for a complete night. The next morning he was asked to present before the Forest Range Officer in Yerragonadaplaem. Knowing this all the villagers attacked the forest guards and freed Mutthaiah. The guards were beaten up. Later Mutthaiah and some other villagers left the village for three months due to the fear for forest officers.

Consumption of NTFP at Village Level

Basing on the data collected from 5 households from each Chenchu settlement, total bio-mass requirement for the whole village is estimated by multiplying the average for 5 households with the total number of households in each settlement. Depending on the number of households the quantity of consumption varies from one settlement to the other. Following Table 4.10 shows the details.

Table-4.10 Consumption of NTFP at Village Level (in kgs)

Sl. No.	Items of NTFP	Alatam (kg)	Guttalachenu (kg)	Nekkanti (kg)	Palutla (kg)	Ponnalabailu (kg)
1.	Food	1860 (310)	5600 (280)	3300 (300)	20300 (290)	3200 (320)
2.	Fodder	12000 (2000)	34000 (1700)	20900 (1900)	126000 (1800)	15000 (1500)
3.	Fuel	9000 (1500)	36000 (1800)	19360 (1760)	128800 (1840)	16000 (1600)
4.	Fibre	66 (11)	200 (10)	121 (11)	840 (12)	60 (6)
5.	Structural	8880 (1480)	27000 (1350)	15400 (1400)	102900 (1470)	11000 (1100)
6.	CNTFP	2040 (340)	4800 (240)	2750 (250)	17150 (245)	3500 (350)
7.	Instrumental	360 (60)	2800 (140)	1100 (100)	9100 (130)	700 (70)
	Total	34206	110400	62931	405090	49460

Note: Averages are shown in the brackets for each village. Averages are for 5 households in each settlement.

The average consumption of biomass for various end-uses varies across the settlements. But the gap is not much wide. Agriculture and cattle population are the two major variables, which influence the consumption of biomass at village as well as household level. The consumption of food and collection of CNTFP are highest in Ponnalabailu settlement followed by Alatam, and minimum consumption is reported from Guttalachenu. It is observed that in Ponnalabailu and Alatam agriculture is almost absent except for a few households. Hence, there is a greater dependence on the wild foods and the consumption of NTFP as food is high. Some food grains are purchased by selling the CNTFP. In the remaining settlements agriculture is practiced. Particularly in Guttalachenu and Palutla settlements both food crops and cash crops are cultivated, however the yield is low. Hence the dependence on wild foods and collection of CNTFP is comparatively less.

The consumption of biomass for fodder and structural purposes also varies. The highest and lowest consumption is reported from Alatam and Ponnalabailu settlements respectively. In Alatam, Palulla and Nekkanti the cattle population is high and the consumption of fodder is also high. Many households possess cattle sheds. They use more biomass for structural purpose. In Ponnalabilu very few households possess live-stock and the consumption of biomass for fodder and structural material is least. Fire-wood consumption is highest in Palutla followed by Guttalachenu and least in Alatam. Palutla and Guttalachenu people produce food grains, and cook more times than Alatam and Ponnalabailu people, who cook once per day or couple of days when food grains are not immediately available. As agriculture is practised in Guttalachenu, Palutla and Nekkanti they use fire wood as glowing torches and *negadu* (fire in the fields) during nights. Apart from this Palutla and Guttalachenu Chenchus are influenced by the non-Chenchu tribals (*Sugali* tribes). Usually the practice of bathing with hot water is adopted. Whereas, the Alatam and Ponnalabailu people take bath once in a week, in the streams or with cold water.

NTFP used for instruments and household equipment is high in Guttalachenu and Palutla and least in Alatam. Guttalachenu people possess more agriculture implements like bullock-cart, plough, *gorru* and household equipments like baskets of various types, cots, etc., apart from the implement used for hunting and gathering. The consumption of fibre is more or less equal in four settlements but, in Ponnalabailu it is a half that of the other settlements. In Ponnalabailu the agriculture and cattle population is almost nil, hence, the consumption of fibre is very less.

Money Value of Various NTFP Items Used by the Chenchus

In the preceding pages it is shown adequately the importance of the forest produce, and its utilization for each end-uses. In this section an attempt is made to estimate the economic value of various forest produce in terms of money. It is tempting to know how much income a Chenchu household generates by way of selling the forest produce. In the same way, it is also interesting to know how much income the Chenchus would have invested on various forest produce used for domestic consumption, if at all these produce were to be purchased from the market. Such an exercise provides crucial insights into the development interventions involving the rehabilitation programmes. Such data are essential in order to know how much dependence on what produce the forest dwelling people depend to meet different survival needs.

The value of NTFP was determined based on the criteria : (a) the price of the item in the local market and (b) price of an equivalent item or produce, sold in market in case the NTFP in question is not sold in the market. Regarding food, many varieties fruits, leaves and nuts are eaten by the Chenchus which are not available in the market. For instance, *chenchu gadda, baccharavva* etc., (the edible tubers) which are prominently eaten by the Chenchus are not available in the market. The equivalent tuber *ganisa gadda* cultivated by farmers and sold in the market is taken as an equivalent item in arriving at the rates for the above tubers. The market rates of fodder, fuel, fibre, structural and equipments which are sold in the near by plain areas are taken for calculating the value of NTFP used for various purposes. NTFP items used for food, CNTFP, fodder, firewood, fibre and structural material are thus evaluated. An opportunity cost exists for various produce and services such as hospital treatment, which can be compared with the values derived indirectly for various NTFP. Wherever possible a comparison is made between NTFP procured by the Chenchus from the forest and an alternate that could have been purchased or availed of from the market. Several NTFP used for end-uses like medicine, small food items like berries, plums eaten in the forest or collected in very small quantities for which, arriving at an equivalent money value is rather difficult.

Estimating money value for NTFP used for ornamental and religious purposes is also difficult as virtually there is no market equivalent. The magico-religious objects and material (such as coconut, camphor, incense sticks, flowers, turmeric etc.) available in the market cannot be compared with the NTFP used for magico-religious and ornamental purpose.

The estimated values for different NTFP are only relative and subject to fluctuations. The values refer to the local prices existing during the months of June-September 1998. The estimated money values of various NTFP are given in Table 4.11.

Table-4.11 Estimated Money Value of Various NTFP Items used by the Typical Chenchu Household

Sl. No.	*NTFP end-uses*	*Estimated price per unit (Rs.)*	*Number of units*	*Money Value (Rs)*	*Total value (Rs)*
	Food				3740
	(a) Fruits	5 (per kg)	180 (kg)	900	
	(b) Leaves	5 (per kg)	30 (kg)	150	
	(c) Tubers	5 (per kg)	80 (kg)	400	
	(d) Flowers	20 (per kg)	10 (kg)	200	
	(e) Nuts/seeds	50 (per kg)	10 (kg)	500	
	(f) Fungi	40 (per kg)	2 (kg)	80	
	(g) Honey	70 (per kg)	1 (kg)	70	
	(h) Insects	20 (per kg)	2 (kg)	40	
	(i) Meat	70 (per kg)	20 (kg)	1400	

Sl. No.	*NTFP end-uses*	*Estimated price per unit Rs.*	*Number of units*	*Money Value (Rs)*	*Total value (Rs)*
2.	**Fodder**	20 (head load)	102 (head load)	2040	2040
3.	**Fuel**	20 (head load)	90 (head load)	1800	1800
4.	**Fibre** (other than structural)	15 (one bundle)	30 (one bundle)	450	450
5.	**Structural***[1]				2400
	(a) Poles	25 (one pole)	30	750	
	(b) Central pole	50 (one pole)	2	100	
	(c) Bamboos for wattle	25 (head load)	16	400	
	(d) Beam	10 (one)	2	20	
	(e) Fibre	15 (bundle)	30	450	
	(f) Rafters	40(bundle)	4	160	
	(g) Thatch	20 (head load)	24	480	
	(h) Miscellaneous	20	2	40	
6.	**CNTFP**				5400
	(a) Tamarind	5.60 (kg)	45	252	
	(b) Soap nuts	6 (kg)	135	810	
	(c) Sugandapala roots	12 (kg)	213	2560	
	(d) Seeds/nuts*2	6 (kg)	43	258	
	(e) Gum*3	60 (kg)	16	960	
	(f) Honey/wax	70 (kg)	8	560	
7.	**Instruments and equipments**				1100
	(a) Agriculture				
	(1) *Gorru* (a plough)	200(one)	One	200	
	(2) *Araka* (a plough)	200 (one)	One	200	
	(3) *Guntaka* (a plough)	150 (one)	One	150	
	(b)Hunting and fishing	50 (one)	One	50	
	(1) Bow and arrows	100 (one)	One	100	
	(2) *Kodima* (fish trap)	150 (one)	One	150	

Sl. No.	*NTFP end-uses*	*Estimated price per unit Rs.*	*Number of units*	*Money Value (Rs)*	*Total value (Rs)*
	(c) Household equipment	100		100	
	(d) Musical instrument	150	one	150	
	Total value of NTFP used				16930

Note : 1 The typical household possess two huts; one for residing and the other for cattle. Hence the number of units used for hut are multiplied by two.

2 & 3 The prices of CNTFP like seeds/nuts and gum varies based on quality and species. The average price is taken into consideration for each item.

Relative Contribution of Income from Different Occupations

The Chenchus earn their subsistence through five major means: (1) direct dependence on forest resources, (2) agricultural produce, (3) sale of CNTFP, (4) wage-labour and (5) live-stock. Excepting agriculture, for the rest of the activities, forest resources (floral and launal) form the base. Sale of CNTFP and wage labour fetch them money. The first two activities, on the other hand, do not fetch any money. However, the produce acquired by these two means is quite significant to the Chenchu life. Food, fodder, fibre, firewood as well as a score of other material are all procured from the forest. Even though they are procured at free of cost, these resources have value in terms of money. The forest produce and agriculture produce utilized by the Chenchus for domestic consumption were valued and estimated in monetary terms, in order to assess the relative value of these produce vis-a-vis income generated by sale of forest produce and income earned by wage labour and live-stock.

The quantity of food grains *(korra)* cultivated by the typical household in 1997-98 is 150 kg. The rate of food grains in the nearby market area is kg. 5.00 per one kilogramme. The money earned by household by selling the commercial crop (chillis) is Rs. 450. The income earned by selling the CNTFP is estimated by consulting the GCC stores and by interviewing the household. The value of food collected from the forest is estimated based on the price of equivalent items in the nearby market. The money earned by wage-labour is also estimated. Both wife and husband in the typical household worked for repairing and constructing the tank bund in *Rellamani kunta* in Palutla which was organized by Forest Department. The husband worked for 10 days and earned Rs. 300/- and the wife worked for 15 days and earned Rs. 300/-. The following Table 4.12 shows the contribution of various sectors to the subsistence of the typical Chenchu household.

Table-4.12 The Contribution of Different Sectors to the Subsistence of the Typical Household

Sl. No.	*Item*	*Value of each item (Rs.)*	*Percent contribution to total value*
1.	Agriculture		
	(a) Cultivated food grains	750.00	6.67
	(b) Sale of commercial crops	450.00	4.00
2.	Food collected from forest	3740.00	33.27
3.	Sale of CNTFP	5400.00	48.05
4.	Wage (forest) labour	600.00	5.34
5.	Live stock	300.00	2.67
	Total value (Rs.)	11,240.00	100.00

It is observed that agriculture, wage labour and live-stock together contribute only 19% of the subsistence needs of the typical household. For the remaining 81% of their needs are fulfilled by direct depending on the forest, by collecting the food resource and selling the

CNTFP. Even for keeping the live-stock, the forest is the major source which provides fodder. It is obvious that the forest occupies a central role in the Chenchu economy, and the dependence of the Chenchus on forest is almost total.

Ecological Impact of NTFP Collection

According to Peters (*ibid*) almost any type of resources extraction from the forests will have an ecological impact. It is extremely difficult to gauze and point out exact nature of this impact. Intensive annual harvesting of valuable market produce can gradually eliminate the species from the forest. The felling of large adult trees can produce a similar ecological result in a much shorter time. Harvesting of fruits, nuts, and seeds results in removal of plant embryos from the site, and hence reduces the total number of seedlings that can be potentially recruited into the tree population. Thus, patterns of resource extraction and their use influence the forest ecosystem.

The Chenchus depend upon reproductive propagules (fruits, nuts and seeds), plant exudates (latex, resins, gums) and vegetative structures (containing a diverse assemblage of different plant parts to be used as food, fodder, fuel, fibre, building material, medicine, fish poisons, etc). Destructive harvesting of any of the above produce results in severe ecological consequences. At the outset, the Chenchus adopt a harvesting technology that is simple, elementary and suitable only for small-scale harvesting. They do not simply cut down trees to harvest its fruit or collect honeycomb deposited at intractable locations on tree-tops. Mostly the fallen seeds, flowers and fruits are collected. Plucking is another method of fruit collection. Another popular method is to shake the tree branches in order to make the fruits (eg. *morli,* tamarind) and flowers, (mahua), fall on the ground. A long stick with a hook end is used to pluck out fruits (e.g., *velaga, manchi neredu* and *madapa* seeds). Women also are expert tree climbers. Most of these propagules are collected in quantities that are sufficient to the family and its immediate neighbours.

Many items of reproductive propagules are not collected in commercial quantities. Usually the Chenchus collect any food produce during periods of good yield. When the produce is less its collection is usually refrained. A tree yet to bear fully blossomed flowers or fully mellowed fruits, is usually left untapped. These practices reduce the ecological negative impacts owing to extraction of reproduction propagules. The collection of propagules per se however impair the process of seedling recruitment (germination of new seedlings and their establishment) as the collection reduces the potential seeds that could have otherwise germinated and get recruited into the plant population. The Chenchus are also competitors with forest frugivores and as such, their collection reduces the total food supply to the arboreal and ground-foraging animals.

The Chenchus report that the trees like soap nut, *morli, kanuga* (pongamia) nux vomica, mahua and *chilla* are getting depleted. The reasons for this depletion can be attributed to logging rather than to the practices of collecting the reproductive propagules. Logging impact on the genetic composition of the tree population being exploited is also getting evident. The Chenchu complain that the yield of many CNTFP are inferior— an observation which the Girijan Cooperative Corporation also shares. It is most likely that trees producing superior propagules might have been excessively targeted or felled down in the selective logging because these trees might be the 'aged' ones. The Forest Department itself prefers to cut superior trees as they fetch revenue and if left unlogged, it only amounts to uneconomical. The value of these trees in terms of its yield of commercial produce is not taken into account that warrants its retention timber value as the priority to the Forest Department. That is why the Forest Department regards most of the propagules and other NTFP as minor forest produce and timber and industrial utilities of forest produce (e.g. bamboo to paper mill) are considered as major forest produce.

Tapping of latex, resins and gum can be quite destructive. This activity may results in disturbance of the forest canopy or killing of the exploited tree. If the exudate is removed properly, the exploitation can be sustainable. Destructive harvesting and major concentration on limited number of species may lead to species extinction.

The Chenchus are involved in the collection of gum only for the past two decades. The GCC and Forest Department have given training to the Chenchus and imparted the proper procedure of gum extraction. The Chenchus use the hatchet to remove the bark of the plant. The standard method of tapping, involves chopping a rectangular box of 50 cm length and 20 cm width into the trunk of the gum producing trees. Usually the bark is removed to make the inner wet trunk visible. This wet trunk is lightly shaved to cause injury to the stem tissues upon which the gum slowly starts dripping. The flow gradually stops after two or three days or sometimes more, as the gum starts to build up and harden along the upper surface or bottom of the box. The gum is removed with the hatchet itself. A single box is to be shaved for two to four times to get gum. A fresh box is to be made on the other side of the trunk opposite to the previous one, once the existing box does not yield any gum. Boxes may be carved at different heights. The span of gum dripping depends upon the season and health of the trees. The gum yield is said to be high during rainy and winter seasons.

Adhering to the said procedure is not always ensured. Some Chenchus lament over the simultaneous multiple deep gashes made by their greedy fellow and the poachers from the plains. Such practice is said to have caused destruction of large number of trees. Gashes are so deep that the upper portion of the trees gets collapsed leading to death of the tree itself.

Further there is concentration on only a few species: *thabisi, sirumanu* and *kondagogu*. As the gum fetches more money than any other CNTFP, the Chenchus show great interest in gum collection. No information is available on the replacement levels of these gum trees.

There are several important vegetative structures exploited by the Chenchus: bamboo poles, tubers, platter leaves of *madapa* climber, fibre, bark of *thumma* thatching grass, *sugandapala* roots. Many more vegetative structures are also collected such as tender leaves for food, twigs, pith and meristem of date palm, various parts for medicinal usages. Superficially it may appear that exploitation of vegetative structures do not disturb ecology. Ecological impact, however, depends mostly on large-scale logging, the manner of collection of various vegetative structures and the quantity collected.

As already pointed out, the Chenchu mode of extraction is characterized by the use of simple technology and exploitation of minimum quantities. The Chenchu also take certain precautions, that help regeneration after exploitation. The Chenchus are said to be expert bamboo cutters. The cutting of bamboo does not involve severe tugs that result in breaking of companion poles, their leaves etc. Besides they know the vantage position to cut the pole from its meristem such that the chances of regeneration and regrowth of the stalk left after cutting the bamboo pole are ensured. While collecting the yams or tubers the Chenchus take care not to cut the mother root. Besides the pit is refilled once the tubers are extracted.

Collection of some of the vegetative structures causes injuries to the tree population. For preparation of arrack (local made liquor), the Chenchus use the bark of *thumma* tree. The stem of this tree gets badly affected due to the extraction of the bark along with some portion of the inner layer. Many trees are reported to have died because of this practice. Now-a-days, the Chenchus are using jaggery, sulphate and other chemicals in making of the liquor. This has reduced dependence on the *thumma* bark.

The extraction of *suganda pala* root by the Chenchus is very recent phenomenon. As there is good market demand for these roots, the Chenchus are busily engaged in the collection of these roots. In the beginning the Chenchus used to collect these roots more carefully not to kill the whole plant. Nowadays, the Chenchus are too greedy to collect as much quantity as possible without paying much heed to the survival of the plant.

Honey has been an important food that the Chenchus collect with great skill. It is a dangerous and arduous occupation. However, the Chenchus are expert honey collectors. It is alleged that the tribals lop down big tall trees just to collect honey. When the researcher raised this issue with the Chenchu informants, they doubted about the existence of such practices in their region. They were skeptical because lopping of tree is not always possible unless there is enough gap for tree falling. There is a risk that the tree crown may get lashed to the neighbouring tree canopy or stems as the tree falls rendering the collection a futile effort.

On the other hand, the Chenchus cited two techniques

of collecting honey deposited at some end of a top branch. The first one involves use of a bamboo pole with short spikes. The pole is used as ladder to reach the most vantage point from which honey can be collected. Yet another mode involves arranging a hook to the slender end of a lengthy bamboo pole to be hanged at a vantage point. The collector ascends by means of the pegs on the bamboo pole to reach the comb. The second technique involves using a long but relatively thick vine, which is lashed to an arrow. The arrow is shot to pierce the comb such that honey drips out and trickle down along the vine to be collected in a receptacle.

These practices indicate that the extraction of NTFP has no dangerous impact. However, it must be mentioned that the Chenchus exhibit safe methods with respect to the traditionally utilized produce. Commercially valued produce does not attract this attention.

The forest resources are gradually declining due to introduction of agriculture, afforestation and deforestation programmes. Large patches of forestland around Chenchu settlements have been converted to the agricultural lands. The species providing fruits, tubers, leaves, flowers etc., are all lost in the deforestation. Large patches of forestland are being utilized for plantation. In the afforestation programme only a few trees like eucalyptus, bamboo, teak are grown. The Chenchus are not allowed into the plantation grounds. Due to these reasons the area of resource base is getting decreased. Hence the Chenchus have to go for distant places for collection of forests resources used for various end-uses.

The major aim of this chapter is to critically evaluate the importance of forest produce to the Chenchus. The typical Chenchu household requires 7324 kgs of bio-mass for recurring as well as non-recurring purposes.

In terms of money value, this bio-mass costs about Rs. 16,930/- excluding the bio-mass used for other end-uses like medicine, ornamental, magico-religious etc., and the cost of labour in the collection.

5

Cultural Construction of Forest and Traditional Knowledge

The place of nature and the environment in anthropology, particularly in Indian context is inadequately addressed. Reference to nature is found under the caption of world-view which is more an abstract idea (Redfield, 1962; Mehra,1977; Bose, 1971; Sinha, 1958). The existing notions of natural world are based on the categories of thought unique to each community or groups of communities. These categories are socio-cultural in origin. Thus there are different constructions of the nature manifesting cultural variation. The nature and meaning of the forests are constructed not precisely based on physical characteristics. The people imbue the forest with meanings for different species and spaces. For example, which areas are to be gleaned and which areas are proscribed to human action, may not be decided by means of rationalized understandings. The socio-cultural meanings attributed to the forest are beset with contrast comparisons. For instance, in the dominant discourse, to the modern society and for the multinational corporations, forest is a source of raw material to be harnessed in order to maximize profits. On the other hand, for the forest-dependent small-scale hunter-gatherers or subsistence farmers, the forest provides collective resources and forest is visualized in symbolic/sentimental dimensions.

In Indian ancient literature and epics, mountains and forests are represented absolutely realistically and corresponded to botanical descriptions. But at the same time it is the symbolic meanings that are ultimately represented in a given situation. In *Brahminical* tradition Malamoud (1996) has shown the ever-present dichotomy between the village and forest. Here the forest is conceptualized as a place of violence and wicked practices through asceticism, (Chatterji quoted in Chattopadhyay, 1984).

Most of the literature in anthropology gives cursory statements of tribe-forest relation. Recently there is a growing concern on understanding the cultural construction of the forest and nature.

Gadgil (1985) and Gadgil, et al (1993), have been arguing that the Indian lore were concerned with the special attention and special affiliation the local indigenous communities bestowed on the forests since ages. Though these studies highlight the symbolic and sentimental dimensions of the forest and indigenous community relation, instrumental relations are also underscored to highlight these conservation practices.

This chapter is intended to explicate cultural construction of the external environment particularly focussing on floral and faunal resources. The objective is to understand the beliefs, ideas, notions and explanations the Chenchus have towards their immediate physical environment. Further, the traditional knowledge concerning the ecology, flora and fauna is also presented.

The intention behind this chapter is to assess and show that the forest and its resources are intricately linked with the culture of the Chenchus. A simple comparison reveals a big difference. Planting trees are very common with the Indian politicians and with *adivasis* (tribals). A politician plants a sapling and his job ends there. But when an *adivasi* plants a sapling, a series of actions follows which include continuous nurturing, emotional attachment, symbolic associations involvement and action of proper dedication to the posterity. In the same way the forest to city dwellers is a space of greenery and commercially valued timber, whereas to an indigenous community, forest is related holistically through cultural relations.

Traditional knowledge has been understood from different perceptions. In broad terms, on one hand, it is conceptualized as practical knowledge or specialized expertise and on the other as esoteric and abstract ideas, notions. Notes and Queries on Anthropology (1971) defined traditional knowledge as "practical knowledge based on observation and experience, but myth, magic, and supernatural beliefs are also preserved and may be mingled with *empirical knowledge* (emphasis added).

Traditional knowledge is the cultural capital of traditional society held in the memories of people and transmitted orally. The scope of traditional knowledge is much vaster than what is represented in this chapter. In view of various constraints, only peripheral treatment is given to traditional knowledge.

Traditional knowledge or indigenous knowledge has been viewed as ethnoscientific knowledge. Chambers (1983) views indigenous knowledge as "stock of knowledge" as well as "systems of concepts, beliefs and ways of learning" held by a culture group. Indigenous knowledge is said to be produced by people in direct contact with the physical environment (Howes and Chamber, 1980). In a sense it is common sense knowledge and the views, ideas and perceptions about every day realities of life in a given physical space rather than abstract ideas that can be applied universally

(Kloppenburg, 1991; Clarke, 1994). Browder (1995) maintains that because indigenous knowledge is more locally rooted, they are "spatially and culturally pluralistic, polymorphic and polychronous" (quoted in Bordt, 1997). Some scholars considered the indigenous knowledge as holistic encompassing technical knowledge together with cultural traditions, norms, values and insights that are tied to mystical or religious beliefs (Thrupp, 1989).

Traditional knowledge has been distinguished from scientific knowledge, often termed "western scientific knowledge", which has been systematically produced in research institutes and universities by professionally trained scientists and publicized in written documents since the beginning of standardized application of the scientific method in Europe in the 17th century (Meehan, 1980).

It is difficult to judge and validate indigenous knowledge. Numerous colonial officers expressed great interest in these knowledge systems, particularly knowledge about the biological realm (Dalziel, 1937; Keay, 1989). Historically resources have been used under pre-scientific, traditional systems. Indigenous systems are significant because of their potential survival value. However there is an ongoing scholarly debate among anthropologists and others on the nature and origin of resource management practices that have conservation consequences.

What is important in the case of tribals and traditional communities is the cultural perception of knowledge and its application in the utilization of natural resources in day to day life rather than how scientific their knowledge is. Writing about cultural and scientific images of nature by man, Roy Rappaport (1971) distinguishes cognized model - description of knowledge and beliefs concerning the environment entertained by a people, and operational model - a description of the same ecological system including the people in accordance with their survival. Any information useful for their survival is knowledge to them. Even their religion is looked in terms of functionality. Worshipping ancestral spirits, gives stability to the society and the worship of benevolent spirits gives wealth and good harvest to the community. Appeasement of malevolent spirits is also essential because it is negatively functional. Neglecting of these spirits brings doom on the community in the form of epidemics, disease, pests, natural calamities, scarcity of resources etc. Magic is used for various purposes like good monsoon, increasing the fertility of the soil etc. Reddy (1988) writes "The natives of Nicobar Archipelago use magico-religious ceremonies in their gardens to improve the quality of root and tuber crops.

Oral transmission of knowledge plays a major role in these societies. The most important methods of oral transmission of knowledge are : story, folk tales, songs, dance, testimony, report, chatting, participation in decision making and picture etc. These methods of transmission of knowledge in these societies serve two purposes: firstly, they reinforce the already existing knowledge and secondly they impart new knowledge. Some of the folk methods like decision making, chatting, dialogue etc., involve the persons in the process of knowledge acquisition.

In several traditional societies the parents encourage the children to become self-reliant and allow them to learn things by experience. Even if a child is attempting to do a dangerous thing, which is likely to cause injury, parents generally do not dissuade them. Their attitude is 'let the child know by experience that a knife will injure if it is mishandled and fire will burn one's body if touched. It is a lifelong learning process in the art of socio-economic living according to the changing environment. The cultural values and beliefs are reinforced through the participation in songs, dances, story telling etc. Reinforcement of belief and value systems are very important in any culture to keep the individuals within the boundaries of their cultural traditions. In fact the reinforcement mechanisms of beliefs and values give stability to tribal cultures.

Cultural Construction of Forest : The Chenchu

The Chenchus visualize a world comprising their own territories and the territories belonging to the peasant communities. They designate the latter as *pallapollu* or *pallapu vallu,* meaning people from the plains or low lands as distinct form highlands known to the Chenchus as *konda* and alternately as *adavi* meaning hill and forest respectively. Though the Chenchus include within the category of *Pallapollu* all the people other than themselves, they do not look upon all of them as entirely a different category. In their day-to-day interaction, the sharp distinction of *konda* and *pallam* becomes lessened. The ethnic groups like *mala/ madiga* - the scheduled castes, the *boya, dasari, chakali, mangali* - the service castes in the villages are known to the Chenchus. The peasant caste-the *kapu* (whose title— is *reddi)* is much respected. In spite of this, the Chenchu maintain a distinct territorial identity namely the forest dwellers as opposed to the people of plain areas. Some Chenchus take pride of their habit of inhabiting hills and elevated places. Implicit in this residence and habitat are several meanings such as safety, greenery, fresh air, assured food supply, cool water and healthy ambience. A tacit expression of superiority vis-a-vis plains peoples is also indicated in such viewpoints.

There is a significant continuity between the human (socio-cultural) world of the Chenchus and the natural and supernatural universe. They consider the forest as their home and proclaim themselves as the people of the forest. The forest is a space, which is their microcosm, and its manifestation is found in their day-to-day life. The forest is an animated space and presided over by ancestral spirits and supernatural deities called *devatha* or *devara*. Some of their ancestors are said to inhabit the space surrounding the catchment territory. The spirits can influence the life of the Chenchus by way of creating problems. Hence in order to ensure their subsistence needs from the forest, the Chenchus regard their ancestral spirits with great respect and propitiate various deities to for their benevolence. At the same time the Chenchus act in accordance with the rhythm of nature in terms of residential shifts, proliferation of kin relations and network, ingenious ways of negotiating with the floral and faunal exploitation etc. Albeit their empirical knowledge about the utility of many plants and animals and awareness about natural rhythm of time and space, they do not think that they can control and regulate them without any benevolence from the ancestral spirits and supernatural deities. The Chenchus are also aware that there is a dire necessity to renew the empirical information and enrich it in the light of the dynamism inherent within the natural world.

The Chenchus have a few myths and tales concerning the origin of earth, water bodies and plants. Some of these myths are also seen in the folk culture of the caste Hindus. The Chenchus believe that all the living beings, land, streams, rivers are created by *Paramathmudu* or *Bagavanthudu* (the supreme God) incarnated as *Varaha* (pig). After killing the *asura* (demon) king *Hiranyaksha*, Lord *Vishnu* brought up the earth from the bottom of ocean. Later he asked goddess

Rampala ganga to cut the earth so that it can become as a mat to spread on the sea water for the humans to inhabit. When the earth was lifted up from deep sea, the earth was in a marshy state. As the earth is lifted all the water started flowing down which resulted in the formation of streams, rivers etc. Some organisms like fish, frogs, leech etc., which also came up along with the earth, wallowed themselves in the semisolid marshy land and due to their action *donas, chelamas* (the springs and water holes on the earth) and other water bodies had come into existence.

The Chenchus say that goddess *Parvathi* had sprinkled the seeds of all floral species in the newly formed earth. Lord *Shiva* showered rains. With these divine actions, various plants have come into existence. Due to the flowing action of water most of the seeds sprinkled in the main lands were washed off into the valley, riverbanks etc. Hence these valley and bank locations are rich and dense with plants in large numbers compared to upper gradient areas.

The Chenchus believe that earth also exhibits growth and decay just as living beings. The action of termites and other worms is likened to the growth of earth wherein the termites deposit mud on earth itself or on various plants in the form of ant-hills. The termites also eat away wood and in turn generate mud. Due to action of rain, light and wind, the mud generated by termites and other worms, get dissolved to be mixed up with earth. This action is likened to the process of decay. The physical bodies of animals and plants grow and later die to be transformed into mud and become earth. Thus the Chenchus say that the earth exhibits the process of growth and decay.

Forest forms a central category around which the Chenchus weave their own culture and day to day life. Their rituals, normative practices derive as well as reflect the meaning attributed to various beings and sites in the forest. Forest is regarded, as a space inhabited by animals and plants. Forest is also a place inhabited by malevolent and benevolent spirits or being. Forest is also a place for regulated exploits: a certain discipline, code of conduct among their own people as well as towards other species and spirits are to be observed. Property rights and the moral imperative of sharing information, environmental updating constitute the chief ingredients in the interaction between themselves in the context of their association with forest. The forest is a familiar place but has to be negotiated by means of various rules and restrictions in view of the above conceptualization. On one hand the Chenchus are pragmatic in their daily trips to the forest in search of survival needs and to negotiate with the dynamic changes occurring in it. On the other hand they are also afraid of the supernatural entities and seek protection from hurdles. Knowledge about the forest is essential and is a subject of their every day life, as also deduced by Siva (1988).

There is a clear separation of human beings from that of plants and animals. The lairs of animals are recognized. These are excluded or forbidden for a thoroughfare, occupation (temporary stay) or frequent visits. In a sense, it can be stated that hunting of animals usually takes place at sites other than their lairs or nests or breeding sites. There are exceptions especially for small animals like iguanas, rabbit and some birds. Certain places like *sela* (ravine), *vagu* (stream), *matta* (patch of thick forest) are avoided for resting by the Chenchus. Certain areas are said to be unsuitable to human entry due to the presence of some plants that cause confusion or loss of sanity and produce mysterious sounds; for instance, *Pacchipalanka* in Guttalachenu territory is proscribed place wherein Chenchus believe some dangerous trees grow and kill the trespassers. The

Chenchus say that they live in the forest but maintain their own habitational place distinct from the rest. A commonly repeated answer to the query about the uses of hut and *gudem,* is that these will aid in keeping the wild animals away (there are other uses like a meeting place, to share the 'spoils' between each other in the manner of social obligation of sharing). Further, the animals live in close intimacy with plants/ground/hills but the resting-places of the Chenchus are different. A hut is a perfect place that assures shelter, safety and rest. Their traditional hut - a tiny conical one with a low narrow entrance is a nest to the Chenchu. The Chenchus view that the hut separates them from animals, plants, insects and spirit beings.

The non-human entity is negotiated with various beliefs, myths and practices. The Chenchus keep alive the interface between the humans and non-humans by a notion of *jiv*. It is through *jiv* that meaning is derived in myths.

The term *jiv* is a hazy notion. It is applied to indicate both 'soul' and 'life-spirit' or 'consciousness'. Every life-form is believed to possess consciousness. This consciousness is something that is said to be common to both the humans and non-human life forms. Animal comportments are cited to illustrate the viewpoint. When a wild dog dies, the pack assembles around it three times, each time yelping. The last yelp is louder and shrilly signifying a final farewell to and detachment from the deceased dog. When a Chenchu dies, the *thappeta* (a musical instrument) is beaten thrice the last one is the final and prolonged one. The grief in both is deemed as similar: it is the same *jiv* in the dogs and the Chenchus that express the anguish and sorrow.

The barking deers sleep in groups with their heads to the exterior and their backs and tails huddled closely to each other in a circular form. This mode of lying is said to facilitate easy sniffing of predators. The Chenchus exclaim that these animals are as careful as the human beings and hence must have a same consciousness in both. Construction of the nests and voice modulation of birds are said to be of great dexterity that is matched to that of human beings. Such abilities are possible because the *jiv* is present in birds too. Thus, animals and humans are closely related and share commonality.

To the Chenchu the essence of forest is an ever elusive entity and a space for varied enigmatic encounters. The elusiveness exists in spite of their thorough familiarity with the forest. This appears to be paradoxical. Simultaneous existence of elusiveness as well as familiarity arises due to the nature the physical environment itself. Particular reference may be made to such features like (1) fugitive nature of certain resources ; (2) seasonality of various forest produce; (3) greater diversity of floral species in a given unit area giving raise to the pattern of dispersed resource distribution; and (4) relative scarcity and abundance of floral resources distributed uneven. These features are the constraints, which the Chenchus overcome by means of an ever-renewed information about the environment. The foremost principle a Chenchu learns and makes it an internalized guiding force is "keen observation with eyes and ears kept open in a state of high receptivity". An ever renewed familiarity with the environment is thus an adaptive strategy to cope up with the phenology in a tropical, deciduous forest ecosystem and fugitive nature of animal resources. One noteworthy point here is that not all events and entities are feasible for familiarization. For instance, it is not possible to get familiarized once for all with the exact sites of certain food giving lianas. Availability of food, hunting success, animal attacks are all difficult to forecast and ascertain. Further the Chenchus explicitly recognize that the seemingly stationary external physical environment is actually very dynamic. They are conscious about seasonal changes and phenology, periodicity of synchronous flowering and fruiting, localized mast-fruiting, the boom (abundance) and bust (scarcity) rhythm and prediction, senescence, fugitiveness of animals etc. This information is very much essential to their survival strategies. However, this continuous process of familiarization is not merely a matter related to art of subsistence. There are ample incidences and events, animal comportments and plant powers not amenable to their cognition. These are elusive for them. The implication of their elusiveness of their ecology is not without any significance. In ecological parlance, this elusiveness reminds the Chenchus of their own place amidst other beings, the dynamic relations with the other organisms and the fragile nature of the environment vis-a-vis their own needs.

During their usual trips to the forest, the Chenchus indulge in keen observation, which may not be intended for any immediate action. Mostly such observations are of pure inquisitive in nature in order to know the ethology, new changes in the floristic distribution and physical ambience which would form a basis for deriving meanings, symbolic experiments and expressions, and relations and devising subsistence strategies etc. This observation helps them to perceive the environment as other animals do. To borrow Ingold (1993) this observation is like a salient conversation between the Chenchus and the surrounding landscapes of biotic and abiotic regimes. This ecological relationship however does not stop at a mere 'walk' but comprise observing with evident pleasure and interest the movements of animals, the progress of fruit maturation or simply the growth of vegetation. One's body takes the smell of the forest and ceases to be extraneous to the forest world.

The Chenchus conceive forest in the manner of myth and by the means of metaphor over and above what is understood as objective reality. The Chenchus do not attribute sentience simply to other biotic organisms. Basically the sentience is conceptualized in terms of their own feelings and their own beings. At a very broad level they distinguish the 'others' as benevolent and malevolent but there are varied other manifestations. By implication, the Chenchus tend to develop a discourse about the unseen reality hidden in the partially intelligible things, beings and events. By means of myth and metaphor the meaning of the hidden reality is manipulated to derive an opportunity to learn ecological principles and develop a certain attitudinal configuration in harmony with the nature. Ideas pertained to a totality of the "nature" seem to be rather dormant or dwarf if not totally absent. What are explicit are episodic narratives reflecting an interface between the Chenchu and the specific plants or animals and certain locations or sites. An ordered interaction is carved to deal with the elusive forest.

Rainfall

The Chenchus view that the rain is given by *Vaana devatha* (rain goddess). They equate rain as mother and earth as its child. By giving rain, the mother rears her child, the earth. The forest is also the child of rain mother. Its survival is dependent on rain mother who in turn loves her child by showering rain.

The Chenchus say that certain localities and sites receive heavy rains compared to other areas. Hills, ravines and dense forest receive first rains. Plain areas receive rains afterwards. The Chenchus say that the hilly areas like *Gangaram, Kuntalabodu, Tekulapenta,* in Palutla territory and *Darabailu, Revagani banda* in Nekkanti territory receive heavy showers.

The Chenchus also view that rainfall is associated with the sanctity of certain sites owing to the fact that the deities have chosen these places as their abodes. Further the Chenchus also draw causal link between *dharma* and rainfall. Where people practice *dharma* the rainfall is regular and adequate. *Dharma* is conceptualized by the Chenchus specifically by means of (1) observance of reciprocal sharing (2) respecting elders and practicing moral values ; (3) restricted entry to the sacred places or abodes of deities and restraint in polluting; and (4) conserving and exhibition of reverence towards plants like *ari, baniyan, jammi* etc., and snakes like *dasaripamu* or *namalapamu* and *vanakokila*. The habitat of these snakes is considered sacred and very rich with floral species. Several deities are reported to be associated with the sites/zones/localities in the forests, which are treated as sacred. The following Table 5.1 gives the details.

Table - 5.1 The Sacred Places Receive Heavy Rainfall in the Sample Settlements

Sl. No.	*Settlement*	*Name of the Zones*		*Name of the deity*
1.	Alatam	Gundampenta	-	Pothuraju
2.	Chinthala	Maddi gundam	-	Bayyanna
3.	Guttalachenu	Palanka	-	Veeraiah
		Sankella gundam	-	Divine cows and
		Gadasala seri		Dasari pamu
			-	Pothuraju
4.	Marripalem	Jangala kona	-	Pothuraju
5.	Nekkanti	Darabailu	-	Bayyanna
		Thambella madugu	-	Namalapamu,
				Peddamma
6.	Palutla	Thota	-	Lord Siva
		Kuntalabodu		Peddamma
7.	Panthanala	Kamakshamma Vagu	-	Lingamaiah
8.	Ponnalabailu	Challapidathala revu	-	Pothuraju

Further inadequate monsoon rains are said to be the result of disappearance of trees especially big tall trees. The Chenchus say that good many trees were felled. Consequently, they say, the temperature is increasing and rainfall is decreasing. Regular heavy monsoon rains now exist only in people's memories as images. Droughts were also said to be rare in the past. Because of delayed rains there is change in the phenology of plants. In the absence of first rains *(tholakari)* immediately after *navami* (late April), blossoming of flowers are delayed which in turn affected the honey deposition by bees. The first rains now occur in late June. Hence honey is not available and there is perceptible reduction in the yield of honey. Due to the same reason, changes are occurring in agriculture cycle and sowing of *korra* and *sadda* (bajra) during June are dispensed with. Adequate rainfall, they say, occur in September and October, during this period only *jonna* (jowar) is sown. Three to four decades ago their country was isolated. No outsiders (contractors, labourers from outside) used to visit their area. Forest cover was relatively thick and tall big trees were numerously seen. Due to timber extraction and expansion of agriculture, this forest had diminished gradually. Vanishing of trees is said to have irritated goddess *Parvathi* and Lord *Siva* who had originally enjoined that trees and humans should live in harmony, protect each other and fend for each other. The Chenchus say, that *manigulu* (humans) now have flouted the divine order and are insolent towards such restrained behaviour. The gods are angry over such behaviour and caused reduction in rainfall.

Other reasons attributed to less rainfall are that *"manigulu soyam pattinaru"* (human beings are not respecting gods and elders), and failure to lead righteous life. Hence the gods are also angry and not bothered about giving rains in right times and in adequate quantities.

The Chenchus view that plants either die or do not grow well if rains are not adequate and if there is shortfall in the number of days of rainfall. The drastic reduction of trees on the hill tops and rocky places is attributed to decline in rainfall. The Chenchus say that these areas are very hot during summer and moisture is absent. Under such condition if a drizzle occurs, it results in sudden shoot-up in the temperature of the rocky bed, causing death to the plants and trees in the area. Several instances of death of plants were cited to substantiate their view permit.

The Chenchus perform a ritual to Goddess *Porlamma* (village common deity) in order to receive adequate rains. They believe that if she is propitiated she asks *Vaanadevatha* (rain goddess) to give good rains. As she is the village deity almost all Chenchu settlements place a stone slab under a baniyan or neem tree as a symbol of goddess and practice community worship in drought conditions. The ritual is a direct address to the goddess as follows:

"Emi	*thalli*	*maa*	*bathuku*	*baruvae;*	*maameda*	*inka*
(what)	(mother)	(our)	(life)	(difficult)	(onus)	(now)
dayaleda;	maa	*thappulunte*	*manninchi*	*Mammilla*	*kaapadu;*	*eea*
(no pity)	(our)	(faults)	(pardon)	(us)	(protect)	(this)
penta meeda		*Neeku*	*kolavu*	*kavalante*	*vaana kuripinchu"*	
(on the settlement)		(to you)	(worship)	(if you want)	(let be showered)	

The ritual involves decoration of the idol *Porlamma*, animal sacrifice and offering of *naivedyam* (sacred food). During the field-work, the informants reported that such rituals were conducted regularly in the past and specifically referred to the one that took place in Guttalachenu during the year 1970 when there was severe famine condition. Palutla people performed this ritual in May 1998 at the shrine of goddess *Porlamma* who stands under a banian tree in the north eastern side of the settlement.

The Chenchus have their own perceptions about changes in landscape, weather and *dharma* (ethic)/*neethi* (moral)/*nyaya* (justice). They derive causal linkages between these. The understanding of change as conveyed to the researcher by the informants is fundamentally related to ecological domain in its inter-connectedness. The growing gulf between the Chenchus and the forest is expressed in their contempt towards the government officials, contractors and other merchants. The alienation from the forest is most dramatically displayed by the Chenchus themselves who tend to withdraw from outsiders and the external environment. Deforestation is also apparent. Deforestation and forced alienation from the forest are attributed to both external factors as well as internal changes especially perceptible alterations in social relationships. Foremost is the role of contractors who cut forest indiscriminately. Their unabated illegal felling is very much resented. This behaviour of the contractors is deemed as a result of wanton increase in pursuit of selfish or familial interests. Deforestation is also a result of expanding agricultural land.

Deforestation, forest policy, adoption of agriculture, sale of CNTFP and wage-labour have resulted in dietary changes. The people believe that food grown by usage of chemical fertilizer not only spoils physical health but mental health. The latter is conceptualized in terms of selfish attitudes, testy temperaments, crime etc. Diet containing chemical fertilizer cause rudeness and lowers immunity to diseases.

Chenchu Concept of Animal World

Chenchus conceive that all living and non-living organisms including man are created by supreme god called *Paramathmudu/Bagavanthudu.* No discrimination is exercised between human life and animal life and man is not considered superior to the animals. They hold the view that the forest produce is to be shared by the human beings and animals. The Chenchus believe that all the organism live in and share the same environment. It seems the Chenchus in their day to day life observe the animal behaviour and learn some techniques from the animals.

The Chenchus say that their ancestors used to live under the shade of large rocks and trees, when they did not know the art of hut construction. They used to roam in the forest for foraging. Philosophically the people muse that their ancestors also had led a life like animals.

It seems that the art of hut construction might have been learnt by the Chenchus by observing the wild pig, which builds a small hut at the time of breeding, with the thatching grass on a thorny shrub. It stays in the hut for twenty to thirty days till the piglings are able to eat and run as fast as their mother. In early days Chenchus used to construct the hut with the support of pliable branches of tree and thatched them with grass or leaves. It had a small low lying entrance through which, they had to crawl in and out. The most elementary type of hut erected by the Chenchus bears similarities with that of the 'hut' constructed by the wild pig. Just as the pig or any other animal is safe and secure in its own lair, the hut of the Chenchus is also a safe place. Once in side, the Chenchu feel not only secure and entrenched but also insulated from supernatural force.

The foraging trips of the Chenchus are scheduled during times that usually fall outside the browsing times of most ungulates and other animals. The browsing times of the animals fall during twilight hours in the morning and evening. Some animals like spotted deer, sambur and nilgai continue to browse into late hours in the night. The daily rhythm of birds almost match with that of the Chenchus, that is, leaving the nests in the morning and returning in the evening. Regarding family system there is close relationship between the Chenchus and birds according to the people. The birds like *gokiragadu, garibichuka, erraburaka, nalla keechugadu, gadapitta* etc., though gregarious, each pair has its own nest with its eggs and young ones. Both the birds feed the young. If one of the adult birds goes out in search of food, the other bird stays back to look after the young one. In the same way, the Chenchus live in groups in *gudems* but each couple and their young children stay in separate huts.

The animals are said to possess emotions like love, pity, and anger just as humans. The birds cited above live in pairs, with their young ones. If any one in the pair dies, the 'bereaved' takes in a new mate and leads a family life. In the same manner if one of the spouses of the Chenchu dies, a new partner will join, the bereaved, and he/she feeds the children as his/her own children. Just as Chenchus feed the orphan children, the gregarious birds feed the young birds if their mother and father birds die. For instance the birds like *kandiledipitta* and *pikkalavva* etc., feed the small orphan birds.

Some animals, fight with other animal till any one of them dies. For instance, while the pig, bear, tiger etc., were with young ones they fight with their enemies till death to guard the kids. The birds like *chiluka, gorinka* etc., will fight tooth and nail to kill large snakes in order to protect the young ones. The snakes like *chatterika pamu, thrachu pamu* are said to revenge on the enemy. If a wild dog is injured by a tiger, the pack attacks and kill the tiger. In the same way, the Chenchus also kill their enemy in order to fulfil their revenge and leave the area. The more arrogant and testing persons are described as *thrachu pamu* (snake).

Seasonal nomadism of some animals like *kondrigadu, edupandi, manupothu, kondagorre* and the birds like *chiluka, garibichuka,* is likened with the nomadic habit of the Chenchus. The Chenchus draw a similarity between themselves and a snake called *ralla gotham* with respect to the hunting technique of ambush. This snake is said to lie hidden to pounce upon an approaching prey, just as the Chenchu hunter sneaks on *mancha* (a raised platform) or into a bush waiting to release an arrow at the animal visiting the salt-lick or water body. Many animals' hunting manners like tracking, trapping, surrounding the prey—are also likened with their own hunting strategies.

If a fellow Chenchu exhibits peculiar comportment, parallels are drawn from animal or birds' characteristics. For instance, if a boy or girl has a big mouth, she/he is nick named as *kapparagadu* (bird) which has a large mouth. A slothy person is called *mattipinjara* or *rallagothamu* (snake) which is said to move very lazy ; the one with big eyes is called *kundeligadu* (rabbit). If a person is unnecessarily cautious, he/she as called *thikkatheethi* (bird) which is said very much active. More eloquent people are called as *jillamayapitta* (bird).

Some unmarried Chenchu boys are irresponsible and do not bother about their duties toward family. They roam in the *gudem*. Sometimes they go to other *gudems* and return after ten or fifteen days. This type of roaming of the boys is described by the Chenchus as *bedaguvva thirugudu* (the aimless roaming of a bird called *bedaguvva).* This bird does not stay at one place for some time. It builds nest only at the time of laying eggs. The rest of the time it does not have the residing place and roams in the forest.

The Chenchus add a suffix *gadu* to the names of Chenchu males. For instance a person whose name is

Bayanna is referred to as *Baigadu.* In the same manner certain animals and birds are referred to suffixing *gadu* to their names. Thus there are animals like *kondri gadu, dondlankadu, gottisiddadu,* etc, and the birds like *pasalapoli gadu, tick tick gadu, kappara gadu, kaviri gadu, theethavva, thondalathochu gadu.* The term *gadu* indicates informality and closeness. Some animals and birds are given names, which reflect specific feature or attribute. For instance, *ragi guvva* is the name given to a bird as it always stays on the tree called *ragi* (pipal tree). Like wise *kundeti salava* which, always predates on *kundelu* (rabbit), *guddiburaka* a bird which always closes one eye and looks like *guddi* (blind). *Chakali pitta* - when this bird flies the feathers on the neck looks like a *muta* (a sack of cloths) carried by a *chakali* (washerman). *Pasalapoligadu* is a bird that always move along with the domestic animals called, *pasulu.* Hence it is called *pasalapoligadu* (herdsman). *Resulu* (wild dogs) are known as *polamu rajiulu* (kings of forest) because they can kill any animal in the *polamu* (forest), *Revula elugu* it always move in the *revu* (brook).

Some animals are said to represent the deities. Tiger is treated as goddess *Peddamma* ; cheetah as *Bayanna* ; bear as *Pothuraju* ; and wild dogs as divine dogs. Chenchus have some beliefs regarding the animals and birds. If an animal or man is killed by a tiger or cheetah the act is considered as sacred because the prey is believed to have fulfilled god's hunger. *Dasaripamu* is treated as a god's snake and the forest will be prosperous where it is present. If it moves from one place to other, rain will come soon. Some birds are also believed to posses divine characters. *Sompitta* (bird) is treated as priest, because it is a fore-teller of the Chenchu fate. It crosses the Chenchus several times making unusual sounds as indication of danger. The testicles of *gadda pilli* (a type of wild cat) are tucked in the thatch as a sign to scare away ghost and evil spirits. The spines of *edupandi* (Porcupine) are worm around the neck in order to relieve the evil spirits haunting on individual. The bones of *peddapakshi* and *jigi pitta* are suspended in the neck of an individual suffering with disease owing to the action of evil spirits.

Traditional Knowledge

This section of the chapter is devoted to traditional knowledge. As already pointed out, traditional knowledge encompasses various aspects (as given in Notes and Queries, *ibid*) including reckoning of time, measurements, cosmological descriptions etc. In this section, the scope of traditional knowledge has been restricted to the immediate physical environment and resources. The limitations do not, however, negate the existence of 'relations of association' between resources, environment and other aspects. Seasonality and other related issues concerning land are discussed in Chapter 3. This section mainly concentrates on floral resources as they are used by means of practically learnt and transmitted empirical knowledge that facilitates day-to-day existence.

Plants are classified under four categories *chettu manu/maku* (trees), *gadda* (tuber), *theega* (climbers or creepers), and *gaddi* (grass). All these are blanket terms in which different species are included. Herbs and shrubs are also called as *chettu* a term more akin to a tree. *Mokka* is another term is used for all small plants even though some of them grow into trees later. *Mulla poda* is the term used to designate an aggregate of bushes.

The Chenchus are well versed with various uses of plants and animals. They can identify the flora which are suitable for fodder, fibre, construction of huts or manufacturing various implements. They choose selectively those plants which serve their purpose efficiently. Thus there are preferred flora to each end-use, among a wide choice. For instance, the cattle are not given certain types of grass like *chedu boda, kattera gaddi. Karu gaddi/duda gaddi* is the most preferred grass and cattle are grazed in places where this grass is grown. This grass is also collected and stacked for feeding animals and young calves. The latter are also fed with leaves of *yepi, ulinda, nemali.* The leaves of *nalla balusa* tree are said to cause some aberration to the young calves. In order to enhance milk production in the mother goats and cows powder of sun-dried tuber called *pala gadda* is orally administered.

Even though there are large variety of species for use as firewood, selection is exercised for specific purposes. For cooking food, selection is not exercised usually. However, certain species like *rella, sandra* are avoided as they do not burn smoothly. *Dadiri, korivi, manga, nalla balusa, yepi* are said to burn well, produce smoke-less flame and give more heat. *Manga* and *korivi* twigs burn well even in high humidity conditions. For making bonfire, *yepi* and *jana* logs are used as they hold consistent flame. While walking during dark, flame torches are made out of bamboo, *pachha botika, korivi, manga. Maddi, yepi, yegi* are used for *negadu* (fire lit in night for warmth and light) as these burn very slowly like embers and can emit flame if air is blown. Plants such as *vepa* (neem), *marri* (banyan), *ari, jammi,* are treated as sacred and not used as firewood. To make fire by friction, *pachha botika* and *konda ragi* twigs are used.

Strong and unbrittle wood is used for hut construction. Further, the wood must be pest/termite resistant, do not snap and endowed with long life. *Sandara* and *yepi* poles are much resorted for hut construction. The beams are made out of bamboo or *thella billudu* as they are weightless but very strong and unbrittled. Bamboo is used for rafters for similar reason. The fibre extracted from *yepi* is said to be not only strong but also highly durable. *Thutthera* twigs, grass like *katterra gaddi/gudisa gaddi, chedu boda* are used as thatch. The wall are made of splinters of bamboo (wattle) or twigs of *ulcha* and *nalikiri butta*.

Agricultural implements are made from mellowed wood of *sandra, thella billudu, yegi, yepi*. Usually well developed weighty logs are chosen. But the Chenchus use these trees occasionally mainly because they lack appropriate instruments/tools of carpentry.

The stave and string of the bow are made up of bamboo which do not snap easily. On the other hand bamboo provides ample tension which facilitates forceful release of arrow. The arrow is made of *ulcha* twigs which are very light but hard and is amenable for straightening any curves. Bamboo is used for making fish traps *(kodima)*, handles of implements like axe, hatchet, digging stick etc. Bamboo is one of the key-stone species that provides various utilities : food, medicine, instrumental, structural besides a score of other small uses.

Musical instrument *(dappu)* is made of a wooden frame and the skin membrane of deer/sambur, wild sheep or domestic goat. The dappu comprises a hallow wooden rim/ring to which the membrane is tightly attached. The wooden ring is made of *chintha* (tamarind) or *yade theega* (climber) wood, sliced into flat elongated plate which is bent gradually into a ring. This wood is preferred because it does not snap and when kept in a curved position, it retains the curvature and does not return to its original shape.

The iron point of the arrow is hafted into the shaft by applying an adhesive of resin from a plant called *andhuga*. The rear end of the arrow shaft is equipped with feathers of *juttu gadda* (an eagle). Three feathers are cut in the shape of parallelogram and affixed vertically to the shaft by means fine sinew or a thread. The feather attachment prevents the released arrow from getting floated. The art of making arrow is specific to an individual or a territorial group. There are three types of arrows like (1) *botteguddu* (an arrow with blunted edge); (2) *gachika* (a small arrow with sharp edge) ; and (3) *Chevulambu* (a big arrow with long sharp edge) and individuals use of small, medium or big arrows depends progressively on ones own dexterity and size of the game. Usually birds and small animals like rabbit, iguana, wild cat are killed by *botteguddu* and *gorika* respectively. *Chevulambu* is used to kill big animals like sambur, nilgai, deer etc. The Chenchus maintain a particular mode of arrow-making and are adept at recognizing each others arrow.

The food regime of the Chenchus is considerably wide : 14 tubers ; 60 fruits; 23 green leaves; 11 seeds and nuts; 3 exudate ; 2 flowers; 4 spike/grain ; 4 fungi; 36 animals are used as food. The Chenchus recognize several features or properties of the various food species. Some items can be eaten raw as in case of most of the fruits. Some items like tubers and green leaves are needed repeated washing or prolonged boiling in order to remove some pungent smell or taste or harmful ingredients. Certain food resources can be stored for a couple of days (Examples are fruits of *nemmi, morli jana, velaga* seeds of *thadi, dela, poliki* and tubers) whereas many are eaten almost the same day or immediately after collection. Certain fruits *nekkara, chitimiti, jana* etc., are to be consumed in limited quantity. Taste of the food also varies : sweet, sour, stale, salty, bitter, pungent. The forest food is categorized as to their physiological effect on the human body (of the Chenchus). There are several such properties : diuretic, purgatory, appetizing, energy boosting, prophylactic, heat/cold effect, acidic, satiating, causing heaviness in stomach, burning sensation, drowsiness, indigestion, blood purifying, increasing virility, libido reduction, etc.

Many floral and faunal species used by the Chenchus are utilized both as food and medicine. When an individual does not get sleep for many days, he eats the chutney prepared by using the *thadipappu* (nuts) which causes drowsiness. Eating *chilla ginja* (nuts) and the meat of birds like *Chiluka odcereeka, odureeka, kandiledipitta* and animals like *revula elugu* produce heat in the body. These food are eaten by the Chenchus for easy digestion and to cure the tumors in the stomach etc. To cure cough the Chenchus eat the meat of a bird called *garibichuka,* fish called *jalla,* and the intestines of the rabbit. To cure fevers like typhoid, malaria etc., the soup made of crabs or a bird called *thella jemudu kaki* or *erra jemudu kaki* is taken. *Thella ustha* or *nalla ustha kayalu* (Pods of shrub) are cooked and eaten for few days to cure the scabies. The Chenchus believe that sexual potentiality of man is decreased due to the decreasing heat in blood. The treatment is to eat the meat or the blood of bear and the birds like *thella jalla maya pitta* and *erra jallamaya pitta.*

The Chenchus believe that the immunity of human body increases on account of eating food that taste bitter such as *ustha, musti, pulchara* etc., the meat of mangoose, *dega* (eagle) and fruits of neem, *thella usta* etc. The plant species like *reppadi chettu, korivi chettu* (trees) possess more brightness. If the fruits are eaten vision is protected and clear sight is effected. The Chenchus say the twigs of these species gives more light and burn easily for long period.

As a people residing in the forest, the Chenchus have developed their own medical system in order to cope up with the disease, ailments, injuries and ill-health and health management. Treatment of disease comprise either administering herbal medicine or recourse to magical formulas and ritualistic observances. The notions of disease causation are not clearly discernible because this knowledge is secretly guarded. Evidently there is the concept of hot-cold states of human body. Many ailments and indispositions are attributed to the fluctuations in the hot-cold states.

Another important cause for disease is consumption of something unsuitable to the body of an individual. Such substance may cause several ailments such as vomits, swellings, indigestion, becoming thin etc. Another reason for ill-health is 'spoiling of blood'. This is a degenerative symptom ensuing owing to prolonged bad habits like excess drinking, illegal sexual contacts, irregular food habits, cruel comportment etc.

The principle behind the treatment is to administer a medicine that has an oppositional property vis-a-vis the nature of the disease or disease causation. For instance to cure excess heat of the body, medicine that induces cold is given. However in certain cases, the medicine administered has the same property as that of the agent causing ailment or ill-health. Treatment for snake-bite involves administering a medicine *(musti, pulchera, jilledu, gotti, vepa)* which is actually poisonous.

The Chenchus attribute certain diseases (body pains, colds, stomach pain, loose motions, indigestion, fatigue, fever, hot-cold condition of the body etc., to the influence of weather conditions in each season. These ailments are managed by switching over to food items which act as antidote to seasonal ailments. In summer, the Chenchu drink the water mixed with the bark of *pacchara* and *neeru mamidi* or water mixed with the leaves of *dusara theega, ari* or fruit of *manchi neredu,* species to protect themselves from the seasonal ailments. In winter season, the Chenchus switch over to a different class of food for keeping their bodies warm. The plant food like *chenchu gadda* (tuber), and the meat of rabbit, nilgai etc., are preferred.

There are several medicinal herbs (see Appendix I) used for treatment of various diseases. The Chenchus treat such diseases like dysentery, cough, indigestion, jaundice, body pains, childlessness, impotency etc. They do not know herbal medicines to treat such diseases like malaria, typhoid, tuberculosis, migraine, leprosy and other degenerative and chronic diseases. Generally they suffer from body pains, injuries, snake-bites.

Children below 5 years of age are most vulnerable to infectious diseases and a substantial number of them die. Maternal mortality is also high. The Chenchus say that if an individual survives till the age of 15 years, he/she will easily survive through most of adulthood.

The Chenchus are acquainted with medicinal properties of various plant and animal species. *Vaidugudu* is the name by which a medicine man is referred to. Medicine man may also be an expert devinator *(gadda cheppe vadu)*. Medicine man is approached whenever the individual's attempts at treatment fails when the ill-health is somewhat unfamiliar. Many usual ailments are treated by the individuals themselves.

Collection of medicinal plants involves a definite procedure or method. The required part of the medicinal plant is usually collected from the eastern side during early sun rise. It is the belief of the people that early sun rays falling on the plant enhance its potentiality. Collection invariably precedes recitation of prayer.

The Chenchus are expert honey collectors. It is no grotesque to pronounce that no other occupation that the Chenchus pursue stipulate so much preparation, interest, strain and danger. Honey collection involves property rights, ritual observances and are replete with folklore and episodes of excitement, treachery and valour. The Chenchu identify five varieties of honey based on the type of bee, location of the deposit and taste of honey. Table 5.2 shows various types of honey combs identified by the Chenchus.

Table - 5.2 Types of Honey bees and Location of Honey Comb

Sl. No.	*Name of honey*	*Location of honey comb*	*Size of bees*	*Grading honey*	*Approxi-mate yield*
1.	Pedda pera	Serri and giant trees	2 cms	Sweet	5kgs
2.	Junnu	Trees and shurbs	1 cm	Sweet	1kg
3.	Musara	Inside the hallow trunks and ant hills	0.50 cm	Sour	1/2 kg
4.	Thondhi	Inside hallow trunk	0.50	Sour	2 kg
5.	Kannugulla	Inside the hallow trunk	0.50	Sweet	1/4 kg

The honeycombs are traced by (1) *puvvam* and (2) movement of bees. *Puvvam* is the excreta of bees deposited in the vicinity of the site of honey deposit. Bees are said to be active and move only during morning and evening, when nectar is collected from flowers. Bees are said to visit water bodies to drink water. The Chenchus observe the movements of bees from the water bodies. *Kannugulla* bees drink only sweet and fresh water from perennial sources. Other types of bees drink water from all resources, especially from marshy lands. The sweetness and good taste of *kannugulla* honey is attributed to the pure water. The bees are said to be ferocious during *tholakari* when *jana* and *nemmi* flowers blossom. During this season, nectar is available only from these two flowers and hence there is relative scarcity of nectar. The bees are very busy in searching and drinking nectar and do not like to be disturbed.

The honey bees are said to have the habit of returning to the same deposit or site every year. However the site should not be disturbed. The Chenchu are careful in not damaging the site chosen by the bees for deposition of honey hive. Further they only drive away bees by mean of emitting smoke and do not indulge in burning the bees. They also exhibit restraint in cutting branches of tress if honey hive are located at top branches of trees. In the recent times, this restrained behaviour is questioned by a few Chenchus because the contractors are any way destroying the forest and honey will also vanish away. Hence it is prudent to collect honey instead of not collecting simply because it involves cutting of a branch or a tree. Honey collector should also observe purity rites like abstinence from sex, and smoking, liquor consumption, taking bath before honey collection. Honey collection precedes a small ritual celebration in the name of *Malalamma* (the goddess of honey).

Conservation of natural resources has been said to exist in the culture of traditional societies. Cultural construction of nature would reflect conservation tradition. In the culture of the Chenchus the nature and its resources—flora, fauna, water, earth, air, sun, wind are treated as having supernatural qualities. In comparison, plants and animals are treated as beings equal to themselves. No status formulas mediate between the Chenchus and flora and fauna. Favourable dispositions emanate from such relationships.

There is no strong evidence to show that the Chenchus have indeed possessed management systems and conservation tradition. However there are a few practices which reflect management and conservation tradition.

One important management tradition is simultaneous importance given to all types of resources. Fruits, tubers, gum, fibre and timber species are all managed simultaneously. Management of only the commercial species is not reported. However when a patch of forestland is clear-felled for agricultural purpose, mango, soap-nut, mahuwa, tamarind and any big trees are retained. Retention of big trees is more due to the difficulty in clearing the slash and the risk of effecting lashing than conservation consideration. The other trees are retained obviously for the value of the produce. However, the Chenchus resent to bring down a huge tree which has seen ages and must have rendered the service of satisfying many needs of their ancestors. Adoption of agriculture has taken away many giant trees.

A second feature is absence of any drastic canopy opening. Traditionally tree-felling is usually of a low-intensity selective nature. The Chenchus do not adopt any growth-enhancing practices to increase the yields of commercially valued species. In case of bamboo, it is reported that the Chenchus cut the poles in such a fashion so that strong tugs and trails are avoided. Besides, they exercise enough caution not to cut the heart or apical meristem so that the bamboo can resprout.

This chapter may present itself as incoherent with the rest of the chapters. Cultural construction of the forest and its resources and traditional knowledge, however occupy a significant position in a study dealing with availability and utilization of natural resources. This chapter is guided by the philosophy that proper attention and emphasis is to be given to the ways in which the people concerned see themselves, their world and themselves in their world. The Chenchus when talking to the researcher about the availability and utilization of resources could not help themselves but to present their own perceptions, which in certain ways are esoteric. This way of perceiving resources (in terms of beliefs, values, ways of procuring, manners of consumption) is somewhat inseparable from the resources as physical objects.

To sum up this chapter, it can be seen that the Chenchus are involved with the resources most intimately. Their construction of the physical world and resources is marked by instrumental, symbolic and sentimental linkages. Their intimate association with the resources is evinced from their knowledge regarding various properties of resources which facilitate resource utilization. Further they also enter into a sort of communication with plants and animals which seem to enter into the culture of the Chenchus as symbols. In their day-to-day interaction, discussion on or reference to animals and plants occur not merely from an instrumental point of view but as if an inseparable entity.

6

Institutional Dimensions in Resource Utilization

This chapter deals with various institutional aspects pertained to utilization, management and conservation of forest resources, as seen among the Chenchus in the area of the present study. Specifically, this chapter aims at addressing the notions of property, rules pertained to defining and maintenance of resource boundaries, social organization of the village community, authority structure and conflict resolution mechanisms in respect of utilization and conservation of forest resources.

Generally speaking an institution is an established way of behaving. North (1990), Nobel Prize Laureate 1993, defines institutions as "the rules of the game in a society or, more formally, are the humanly devised constraints that shape human interaction". Institutions regulate social activity. They tend to achieve certain measures of regularity of action, goals, and interpersonal relations. It is important to understand the nature of the institutions of a society that shapes the use of environmental resources. Indigenous communities have devised various institutions, which facilitate exploitation of resources in a certain acceptable ways to its members. These institutions largely comprise various rules and norms, which act like guidelines.

The anthropologists (Winick, 1964; Madan, 1989) define the institution as a fairly permanent cluster of social usages. It is a reasonably enduring, complex, integrated pattern of behaviour by which social control is exerted and through which basic social desires or needs can be met. To Malinowski (1994) institution is an "isolate of organized behaviour". He proposes a universal structure of the institution comprising charter, personnel, norms, material operators, activity and function. Institutions are essential to fulfil the basic needs of human beings in an organized manner.

The resources may have different characteristic features. Some resources are fixed in a location and some are fugitive. Some are renewable and some are non-renewable. Some resources like animals tend to 'learn' the subsistence strategies or predator's mode of attack and adapt accordingly. Resources also have different 'values'. For instance, animal food (meat) is valued higher than vegetable food. Some are divisible whereas others are indivisible. Resources may be scarce or abundant, concentrated or dispersed. Resources also exhibit some special features, say overlapping. The inclusion and exclusion of 'insiders' and 'outsiders' in respect of determining access to the resources also vary depending sometimes upon type of resource, its scarcity or abundance and fragility, resilience, sometimes upon the special circumstances or sometimes upon the person in question.

Natural resources are considered 'free gifts of nature'. In reality, however, natural resources are almost never altogether free. Many natural resources are difficult to be replenished without incurring some cost. If some resources are over exploited exceeding the capacity of the resource to replenish itself, depletion will result. In the same way exploitation of one resource may impose costs on other resources. For example, if a patch of forested land is clear-felled for fire-wood or for charcoal preparation, many smaller plants yielding food to tribals die causing an externality. In the same way honeycombs may not get deposited if more and more trees and flowering plants are depleted. A resource may be treated (and exploited) as a free good but ensuring sustainability involves some cost, which may be manifested in several forms like restraint, minimal exploitation, the ethic of sharing etc., or some form of organized exploitation, which is conceptualized here as institutional.

Given the nature of resources, certain constraints are to be negotiated in order to harness them. For instance, seasonality is a constraint in the sense, availability of certain resources are season-specific. The fact that certain resources not only seasonal, limited but also need collective effort in its exploitation impose constraints that can be negotiated by collective action which in turn stipulates some institutions. Norms constitute important components of institutions. Norms are expectations about one's action and/or that of others which express what action is right or what action is wrong (Coleman, 1987: 135). The concept suggests a standard of conduct which people believe they ought to follow lest they should expose themselves to some forms of sanctioning or to some unpleasant experience. Obedience to the norms will occur when the sanctions or discomfort are sufficiently great and sufficiently certain to make disobedience less immediately attractive than obedience (*Ibid.* 141-2).

Territoriality and Resource Boundaries: Sample Settlements

Territory is defined as an area occupied exclusively by a group or community by excluding or repulsing other groups from entering through overt defense or through some means of communication (Dyson-Hudson and Smith, 1978; Wilson, 1975). Most hunting-gathering groups use defined territories. But to what extent these occupied territories are accessible to outsiders and by what mechanism, such territories are shared or defended are not addressed adequately. The question of territoriality among hunting-gathering societies has revolved around two generalizations; (1) One holds that the territorial band was the characteristic form of hunter-gatherer social organization (Service, 1962); (2) the other states that groups were flexible and fluid, their form varying according to ecological factors (Lee and Devore, 1968). Some researchers doubted the existence of territorial ambits among hunters-gatherers (Lee, Pilling and Hiatt, 1968). Andrews (1994) argues that the earlier discussions were strained by a lack of a clear definition of territoriality and the complex variations in socio-territorial organizations cross-culturally. Interrelation between territorial space and associated resources has not been defined. Andrews (*ibid*) defines territory as "a more a less delimited area, within which a population carries on resource harvesting activities over the course of a year in a customary pattern".

It is generally assumed that in *adivasi* (tribal) communities in India, accessibility to resources is always freely available. However, recent literature has shown the existence of territoriality and property rights involving bundles of rights to manage and right to exploitation and disposal (Gokhale, 1977; Das, 2000; Roy Burman, 1994). Among the Chenchus, different rules and rights operate in controlling a defined area, and access to utilization and conservation of resources.

Catchment Territory

As already pointed out, customarily each Chenchu *gudem* (settlement) is in possession of a territory loosely called as *polam*. The Chenchus do have some notions of boundary even though these boundaries are not strictly rigid. Each *gudem* identifies its *haddulu* (limits/ boundary line) usually identifiable by means of some landmarks such as hillocks, streams, trees etc. These boundaries are loosely applied to the area that is supposed to be the property of such and such *gudem*. The *polam* is a place, which is habitually gleaned by the Chenchu of each *gudem* or the village community. The catchment area of each settlement carried with it an explicitly stated exclusion rights. Usually the *polam* is a zone that excludes the Chenchus belonging to other *gudem*. In a majority of the cases, the boundaries ambits are big hills (*Dornala konda, Nadathadikala konda* and *Urjala konda*), large trees *(Thavisi chettu kona)*, streams *(Vippala mada vagu, Erra vagu), serri (Boyala kota serri)*. The following table 6.1 gives the details of boundaries and extent of the catchment area of the sample settlements.

Territorial ownership is vested in the community of settlement. The community comprises individual families and in aggregates belonging to different *kulams* (exogamous surname groups). Though the community is divided into *mirasidars* and *punnapollu*, the prerogative claim or manorial rights on the territory by the *mirasidars* is not evident. All the members of the settlement community are well versed with various places in the territory. In principle, any member is free to forage and collect any resource excepting a few resources like tamarind, soap-nut, and honey. The strong norm of sharing food, pooling resources and redistribution reflect the feeling of oneness within the community of consumers. The harvester himself/herself plays as little role as possible in the distribution of the produce collected. Any member can volunteer in the distribution of resources. The community of the settlement expresses a notion of ownership of resources vis-a-vis other communities of other settlements. Thus,

Table-6.1 The Boundaries and Extent of Catchment Area of the Sample Settlements.

Sl. No.	Name of Settlement	Catchment area sq.km	Boundaries East	West	North	South
1	Alatam	35	Kayya	Boyalakota	River Krishna	Jenkulabonda
2	Chinthala	50	Daddanala Konda	Dornal konda	Kuthapa	Ontimarri baipenta
3	Guttalachenu	85	Vippala Mada vagu	Erra vagu	River Krishna	Darabailu
4	Marripalem	70	Jangam middela	Dornal konda	Onti marri baipenta	Bommalapuram
5	Nekkanti	90	Urjala konda	Peddarevu	River Krishna	Darabailu
6	Pallutl	80	Erravagu	Urjala konda	River Krishna	Sankella gundam
7	Panthanala	120	Peddarevu	Sakirevu	River Krishna	Jangam middela
8	Ponnalabailu	70	Nadathadikala konda	Vippalamada vagu	Burugundala	Thavisi chettu kona

Note: The area is estimated based on the information given by the key-informants.

territorial ownership is valid only in opposition to the territories.

In terms of the definition given by Dyson-Hudson and Smith (*op cit*), territoriality found among the Chenchus is beset with some problems: exclusive occupation by a specific group and overt defense mechanisms are not strictly tenable in the case of the Chenchus. Though the community of the *gudem* exhibits relative permanence, members may not stick on forever to the *gudem*. A part of the total span of the adult life of almost every individual is spent in other territories. Entering into other territories becomes a necessity due to (a) strife/hassle in one's own community, (b) scarcity conditions in one's own territory, (c) lack of any relatives in one's own territory, (d) pull factors like employment opportunities, (e) kin obligation, (f) marital dissolution and concomitant dispersal etc. Further no *kulam* explicitly proclaims territorial ownership, irrespective of its claim as first settlers. Such movements are usually confined to adjacent territories, though, sometimes, may extend to distant territories crossing the River Krishna. Kin connections, cutting across descent, alliance, sex, generation, collaterally, bifurcation, facilitate such movements. In the absence of defined kin relation, *kulam* relations are taken as a point of reference. As a kin group, each community in a settlement has marital connections with many other settlements.

But the territoriality is a matter of community interest. At any point of time there are a certain number of core members who are long established in the *gudem* and the notion of community and its allegiance to its territory is carried along by these members. Though the members belonging to the *kulam* that settled first, may live, its claim to the territorial ownership is always a matter related to the community at large and not the first settled *kulam* members.

Overt defense mechanisms for the territorial safety is conspicuously absent. Trespassing of adjacent territories is not uncommon. No naming conventions, symbolic ceremonies, warfare etc., are reported. But territorial rights are mutually recognized by different *gudems*. It is a matter of convention to respect territorial rights of each other settlement.

Another important feature of territoriality among the Chenchus is the existence of accessibility to neighbouring groups to enter other territories during certain seasons for the annual camps. Thus, members belonging to different territories may meet at specific camp sites and harvest resources together at the same site.

When territoriality is defined loosely and members of different groups harvest in each others territories, even under special circumstances, a question can be raised as to why territoriality (or territorial demarcation) exist among the Chenchus at all ? At the outset, it must be mentioned that exclusion is a matter of resource-specific and not strictly pertained to the space or territory. However, the notional territorial demarcation is unmistakably recognized and specified. The probable reasons could be that there is an explicit feeling among the people of the territory about the idea of "subtractibility" of resources. They say that *manaku dorakadu* (to us not available) meaning that resource that is exploited by an outsider is subtracted and hence it is lost. Such a feeling shows the existence of pressure on resources. Finiteness of resources at least in case of a few CNTFP are clearly recognized by the people. If territorial allegiance is absent, then competition obviously increases and disorder is bound to ensue. Territory obviously manifests and symbolizes social identity of the community. Territoriality simultaneously serves to articulate a sort of tacit corporate ownership structure wherein all the members of the community establish a sense of oneness and belongingness. These are some reasons behind the existence of territoriality. The lack of rigidity of territoriality may be attributed to the pattern of resource distribution, seasonality. Further discussion on this aspect is given in the following pages.

The catchment territory itself is categorized into specific sites or zones with varying rights and restrictions to access.

Sub-Catchment Territory

In case of certain settlements, the catchment is sub-divided into smaller units so that each unit is habitually exploited by the sub-divisions of the village community. The internal boundaries are demarcated. The catchment area of the settlement is divided by formal or informal arrangements. Generally the division of the catchment territory takes place in order to facilitate equal opportunity to each *gumpu* to exploit the resources equally. It also imposes certain barriers on some shrewd individuals to over exploit the resources. The increase of population and number of *gumpus* also forces the village community to sub-divide the catchment territory. For instance, in Palutla settlement it is said there were three *gumpus* of *mirasidars* in the beginning. Each *gumpu* comprised three to five families. These three *gumpus* were headed by Chevula Letha Kannadu, Chevula Nadipothadu and Chevula Errapothadu respectively. Nadipothadu and Errapothadu have more relatives, who, gradually immigrated and settled in Palutla *gudem* on account of which the numerical strength of these two *gumpus* has increased. Chevula letha kannadu thought that his counterparts were exploiting more resources than him due to immigration of their relatives from neighbouring *gudems*. Hence, he demanded for equal allotment of territory among

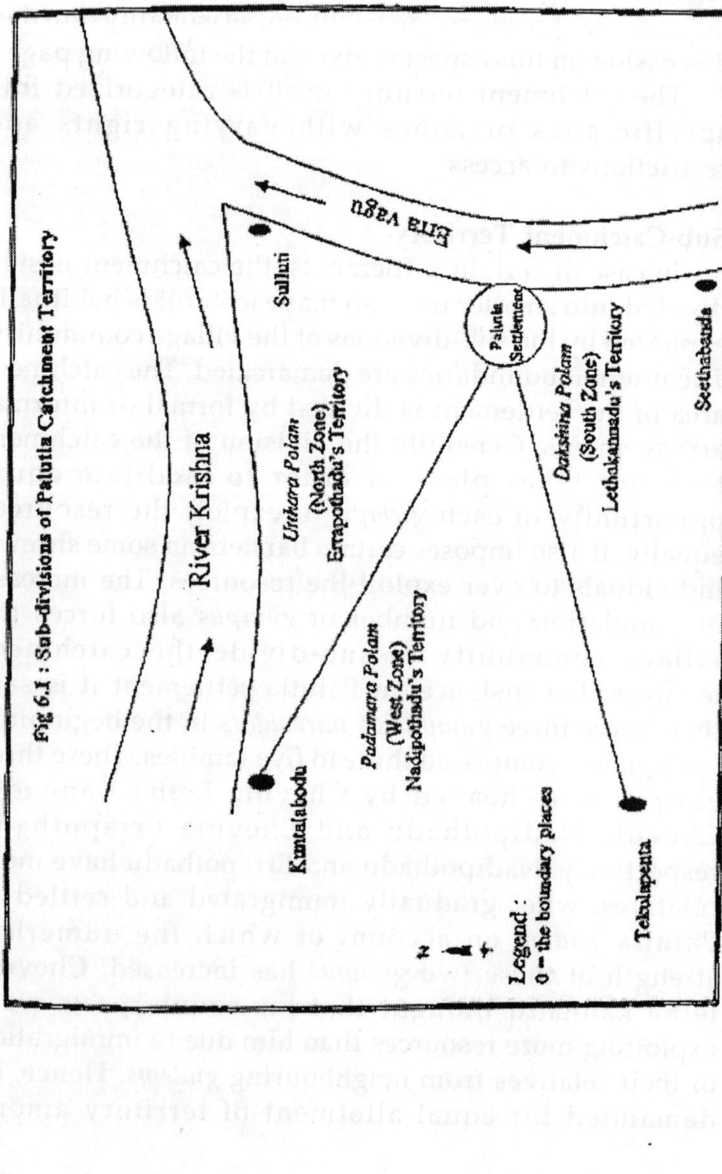

Fig 6.1 : Sub-divisions of Palutla Catchment Territory

mirasidars. The territory is sub-divided explicitly into three sub-territories like *utthàra polam* (north zone), *padamara polam* (west zone) and *dakshina polam* (south zone). Each sub-territory was allotted to single *gumpu* headed by a single elder man. North zone was allotted to Chevula Errapothadu's *gumpu,* west zone was allotted to Chevula Nadipothadu's *gumpu* and south zone was allotted to Chevula Lethakannadu *gumpu.*Figure 6.1 shows the division of Palutla territory.

As the size of the *gumpu* increases, it splits into sub-units under the leadership of a person. Each of such *sub-gumpu* gradually acquires other relatives and become an independent *gumpu.*

The informal sub-division of the catchment area is seen in Guttlachenu *gudem.* It is divided into two sub-catchments viz., *dakshina polam* (southern) and *utthara polam* (northern zones). There are two ego-centric groups *(gumpus)* in the *gudem* : Kudumula Gadasala's *gumpu* and Kudumuda Chinnapothadu's *gumpu.* The houses of each *gumpu* are clustered separately. Gadasala *gumpu* forages in the southern catchment and Chinna Pothadu's group confines itself to northern zone. But the honey collection *(serri* type) is executed communally in whole territory of the settlement. The territory of the studied settlements is formally or informally divided into sub-catchment areas. However, in Panthanala and Alatam this division has not occurred, as there is only one *gumpu* in each of these settlements.

Fugitive Resources Boundary Rules

Special rules apply to fugitive resources. In principle, all living resources belong to every one. Wild animals do not fall under the category of resources pertained to the catchment as long as they are alive and not hunted. Hence, for animal hunting, territorial rules are not reckoned. The hunters of one settlement can enter the catchment territory of another settlement while chasing a game or tracing a wounded animal. If an animal is shot at one's territory but it dies in another territory, it can be claimed by the shooter. However, some share of meat is invariably offered to the people of other *gudems* present on the spot in case the animal is a big one. Hunting should always begin within one's territory and comprising in other territories for ambush is not permitted.

Reserved Zones

Certain zones within the catchment area are proscribed to entry for normal exploitation. Such places are opened for exploitation during conditions of famine and scarcity of food. These zones are usually located far away from the *gudem,* and are intractable, located in deep gorges, ravines etc. The reserved zones in the catchment area of sample settlements are shown in the following Table 6.2.

Table - 6.2 Reserved Zones in Sample Settlements

Sl. No.	*Settlements*	*Names of Reserved Zones*
1.	Alatam	Musaldani banda
2.	Chinthala	Barakula guntha, Pullala dona
3.	Guttalachenu	Birruti, Boyalakota, Gadasala serri
4.	Marripalem	Nallamala cheruvu, Ootala dona, Mondoni revu
5.	Nekkanti	Revagani banda, Thambella madugu
6.	Palutla	Barla madugu, Mejjikonda, Malla gundam, Katthu madugu
7.	Panthanala	Jeribanda, Mulamaddi gundam
8.	Ponnalabailu	Thavisichettu kona

The reserved zones shall not be exploited by any individual or group till the resources are exhausted in allotted sub-zone. The sub-catchment boundary rules are not applicable in exploitation of reserved zones.

Buffer Zones

Buffer zones are patches of land, which overlap the other territories of adjoining settlements and are jointly exploited. Ownership rights exist with the *gudems* jointly exploiting the buffer zones. Buffer zones are usually localities for executing summer camps. Two or three neighbouring *gudems* jointly exploit the resources in the buffer zone. They establish camps at a waterhole combinedly. The zone is divided into small areas for each group such that, competition among the groups is mitigated. Each group comprises people of single settlements and confines to the allotted area. The buffer zones are to be exploited only after the resources in the territories of the respective adjacent settlements are exhausted. Entrance into the buffer zone stipulates prior information passed on to the settlement by the settlement which first intends to enter the buffer zone. Such stipulation ensures equity as well as protection of resources to the best advantage of the settlements falling adjacent to the buffer zone. The Table 6.3 shows the number of buffer zones exploited by the sample settlements.

Table - 6.3 Buffer Zones Exploited by the Sample Settlements

Sl. No.	*Name of settlements*	*Zones exploited*
1.	Alatam and Guttalaehenu	(1) Jenkulbonda
2.	Guttlachenu and Ponnalabailu	(2) Bakkachintha penta, (3) Peddabanda serri, (4) Chinnabanda serri, (5) Golloni sada serri.
3.	Guttalaehenu, Ponnalabailu and Palutla	(6) Sankella gundam
4.	Guttalaehenu and Palutla	(7) Ankamma kunta (8) Sulluti,
5.	Guttalachenu, Palutla, Ponnalabailu and Nekkanti	(9) Darabailu
6.	Palutla and Nekkanti	(10) Thathani penta,

7.	Chinthala and Marripalem	(11) Gangaram, (12) Garbà gundalu (13) Jangam middela, (14) Maddi gundam, (15) Devaluti and (16) Sakirevu
8.	Panthanala	Nil

The following Fig. 6.2 gives the details of exploitation of various buffer zones in the settlements.

Of all the sample settlements Panthanala does not share zones with the neighbouring settlements. The reason seems to be that a long distance of 12 miles separates Panthanala and its nearest neighbouring settlement Nekkanti. To a large extent the people of Panthanala depend on whatever resources available in the territory of Panthanala.

SacredPlaces/Spirit Invaded Zones

Several sites within the catchment territories of the sample *gudems* are deemed as sacred either due to presence of a local shrine or abode of deities, spirits. These are not visited frequently excepting during special occasions such as, conducting ceremonies like tonsure, fulfilling vows, offering, sacrifices etc. Menstruating women are not allowed into these areas. The prominent floral species are mango, *neredu, jammi,* bamboo, *thella maddi, sirumanu* and *kaljeevi*. Generally the exploitation does not take place in this zone.

The resources are not collected directly from the trees. But the fruits dropped on the ground are collected and consumed. Water is used only for drinking purpose. Fire-wood is also not gathered in the precincts of these localities. The usage of knife, axe and cutting of trees are strictly prohibited in these zones. The table 6.4 gives details of sacred groves, deities and ceremonies associated with the sacred groves.

Fig. 6.2 : Exploitation of Buffer Zones by Sample Settlements

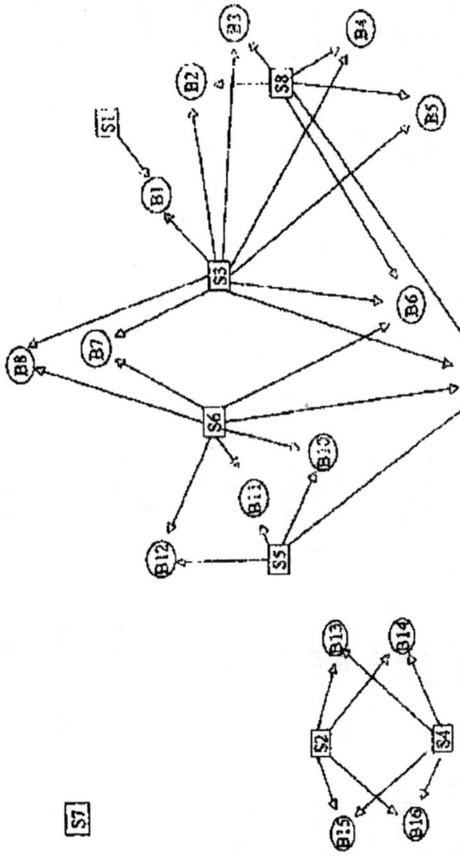

Legend :
(B) = Buffer Zone, (S) = Settlement,
S1 = Alatam, S2 = Chinthala, S3 = Guttalachenu, S4 = Marripalem,
S5 = Nekkanti, S6 = Palutla, S7 = Panthanala and S8 = Pnnnalabailu

Table - 6.4 The Sacred Groves, Associated Deities in the Catchment Territory of the Sample Settlements

Name of Settlement	*Name of sacred grove*	*Associated deity*	*Representation of deity*	*Extent of area (Acres)*	*Number of species*	*Ritual activities*
Alatam	Gundam penta	Pothuraju	Ant hill and stone slab	2	14	Tonsure, Naming
Chinthala	Maddi gundam	Bayvanna	Stone slab	2	16	Vowing
Guttalachenu	Palanka,	Veeraiah.	Sivalingam	3	18	Tonsure,
	Sankella gundam,	Divine cows,	Sacred pond	3	15	Sacrifying
	Gadasala serri	Pothuraju, Malalamma	Stone slab Stone slab	2	12	Tonsure
Marripalem	Jangala kona	Pothuraju	Stone slab	5	25	Sacrifying
	Vontimarribai penta	Lingamaiah	Stone slab	1	7	Naming
Nekkanti	Darabaiti vagu	Bayanna	Stone slab	5	23	Tonsure,
	Thambella madugu	Peddamma	Stone slab	1	6	Sacrifying
Palutla	Thota	Siva	Sivalingam	3	15	Naming,
	Kuntalabodu	Peddamma	Stone slab	2	10	Vowing, Sacrifying
Panthanala	Kamakshamma vagu	Lingamaiah	Stone slab	1	10	Vowing
Ponnalabailu	Challapidathala revu	Pothuraju	Stone slab	2	18	Naming, Tonsure, Sacrifying

Chenchus attribute some divine quality to the *serries*. At each *serri* a stone slab representing of Goddess *Malalamma* is present along with the other deities. For instance, at *Gadasala serri* in Gutlalachenu territory, a stone slab symbolizing *Gadasala Pothuraju* the deity is present along with goddess *Malalamma*. *Darabaiti serri* in Nekkanti territory is enshrined by goddess *Peddamma* and *Malalamma*. These *serries* are given utmost respect and are feared; transgression of the customary codes amounts to sacrilege and seriously dealt.

Proscribed Zones

Certain sites/places within the catchment territory are totally proscribed to human entry. Various beliefs are associated with these sites/places. The Chenchus believe that gods abode in certain areas and they should not be disturbed by human activity. The wild animals like tigers, pythons, cobras and demons/ghosts are believed to abode in certain areas. Due to fear of deities or animals or ghosts these places are never visited by the Chenchus. The Table 6.5 gives the details of proscribed zones in the territories of sample settlements.

Table - 6.5 Proscribed Zones in the Territories of the Sample Settlements

Sl. No.	*Settlements*	*Proscribed zones*	*Causes*
1.	Alatam	Peddarevu sela	Due to fear of ghosts
2.	Chinthala	Mudepala matta	Due to fear of ghosts
3.	Guttala chenu	Boyalakota sela	Due to fear of wild animals
		Pacchipalanka	Presence of divine trees
4.	Marripalem	Nil	-
5.	Nekkanti	Darabaiti vagu	Presence of divine spirits
6.	Palutla	Nil	-
7.	Panthanala	Nil	-
8.	Ponnalabailu	Thavisi chettu sela	Wild animals and divine spirits

Boundaries of Specified Resource Zones

Specific resources such as *serri* or honey deposits on some giant trees, water holes, salt-licks, tamarind topes etc., are defined by sharp boundaries. For instance, in Guttalachenu territory, some sites such as *Bakka chanthapenta, Kota, Ankamma kunta* etc. are demarcated with the tamarind topes ; *Palanka jede* and *Ankamma kunta jede* are demarcated as salt licks. *Palank serri, Gadasala serri* are the resource areas for honey collection. There are many perennial water holes like *Palanka gundam, Sankella gundam, Sulluti, Challapidathala revu* etc. The number of various resource zones in the sample settlements is shown in the Table 6.6.

Table - 6.6 Specified Resources Zones in the Sample Settlements

		Resource zone		
Sl. No.	*Settlements*	*Salt-licks*	*Tamarind topes*	*Serries*
1.	Alatam	Nil	2	1
2.	Chinthala	Nil	3	4
3.	Guttalachenu	8	7	4
4.	Marripalem	6	4	5
5.	Nekkanti	3	6	4
6.	Palutla	12	13	10
7.	Panthanala	4	5	3
8.	Ponnalabailu	5	4	5

Though the Chenchu settlements have an explicit notion of territorial boundaries of *polam,* the people move from one *polam* to other *polam*. It is not uncommon to notice a Chenchu working in a place quite far away from his native *gudem*. Boundary rules among the Chenchus are not rigid. Flouting of rules and contested disputes over boundaries, stealing, trespassing are reported to occur. While some boundaries belonging to some villages are non-overlapping, other *polams* are overlapping. In the same way some villages maintain their core areas, the rest of the area is jointly exploited.

Boundary marks do not remain constant forever; they are contested, arbitrated and refuted. Boundary rules assume a degree of strictness depending upon the type of resource, nutritional/commercial/sustainable value. Thus, boundary rules are also resource specific within the *polam* of a *gudem*. Boundary rules also exhibit different degrees of strictness and relaxation, which are resource specific. Some resources are clearly demarcated (e.g. *serri,* gum trees) and some are allocated to individuals (e.g. gum trees) while some are regulated by distributing them to segments of village community in order to preventing all groups to concentrate on a single patch. Some localities are opened seasonally, occasionally and some are totally proscribed to entry. The reasons behind the array of boundary rules are quite complex and not easy to unravel. Some of the rules reflect resource management oriented to achieve sustainability. They seem to arrest resource crashes.

Property Notions Among the Chenchus

Concept of property in indigenous societies has not been adequately understood by the concrete facts and conditions of use. Property in these societies is a sum total of the rights, duties, privileges and mutualities. It has been generally held that the 'property' sense is little developed among primitive people and that the concept of 'possession' rather than ownership is far more suitable in describing the primitive institution of property. Mere emphasis on legalistic and economic condition of surplus criteria for defining property can very well exclude property institutions among the indigenous communities. Cairns (Hallowell, 1955) stated that "property relation is triadic: 'A owns B against C' where C represents all other individuals". This includes not simply the objects owned by individuals but also "patterns of rights, duties, privileges, powers etc., which control the behaviour of individuals or groups in relation to one another and to the custody, possession, use, enjoyment, disposal etc., of various classes of objects" (quoted in Hallowell, 1955).

Absolute control on property does not exist among the Chenchu society. Even though certain objects are individually owned, there are numerous restrictions on the use and disposal of property. The Chenchus do not have a simple linguistic expression for 'ownership'. Terms like *sonthamu* (one's own) or *hakku* (ownership right) reflect a triadic relation than dyadic relation. These two terms are used only in a context of dispute. If a person is asked to name the owner of say, a patch of agricultural field, the answer is usually not in the sense of individualized affirmation. The most likely answer is *made* or *mavollade* meaning ours or our people's. They do not use the word *nadi* (mine). This indicates lack of concern for individualized ownership rights.

Among the Chenchus the notion of property can be perceived at different levels. In a generalized plane, the Chenchus say that there are no exclusive ownership rights on any resource. To them, any person by virtue of sheer necessity of that resource, usually for survival, just like any other human being or animal, can utilize a resource. By this, they mean to say that anybody, not necessarily a Chenchu, is free to exploit the resources of their country. It is incorrect to prevent a person from utilizing the resources for survival. It is not uncommon to see the non-Chenchus visiting these forests in search of some essential commodities like timber, bamboo, and food items like tamarind, amla, berries etc. The essence of this generalized notion is that the resources are to be shared for satisfying basic needs. A further probe reveals that the resources should not be squandered, and nobody should unduly appropriate or hoard resources for selfish ends. The Chenchus never object a stranger from entering their territory. On the other hand a stranger is soon treated as a guest and gradually accepted as a member of their village community. The researcher has encountered few alien persons living among the Chenchus. Thus, at a generalized level, the Chenchus hold that resources should be meaningfully utilized, and accessible to any person. In other words, the Chenchus have broad perspective and an altruistic outlook. Philosophically they quote repeatedly that "no person would carry all the wealth with him once expired". In their *Weltans chauung* (comprehensive image of universe and of man's relations to it) and *Weltansicht* (worldview), sharing is the fundamental essence of material resource and human existence.

From the above account it may appear that the Chenchus lack property notions and treat the forest as open access sources. However, the Chenchus become more and more specific as the question of property gets contextualized and comes to a situation of reality and practice. A complex web of property notions is under operations among the Chenchus.

Communal Ownership

The village community identifies the resources in its territory as communal property excepting a few specified resources. In principle all members of the village community have access to any resource available within the territory of the village community. The village community customarily exploits its territory and prevents others from exploitation of resources. In this sense a village community exercises its control on the territory to the extent that outsiders were denied ownership rights and counter any efforts of outsiders to confiscate resources. In other words an individual has no customary right to expropriate the territory of other village community. However, an individual can enter the territory of other village community as a guest or kin or in search of fugitive resources like animals.

In the same sense, the village community opposes any move by any of its own members claiming absolute ownership rights on resources except a few. No member of the village community can prevent other members from exploiting forest resources within the territorial limits of the village community. Thus, each member of the village community has equal rights over exploitation of forest resources. Equality of opportunity to exploit resources is the essence in the notion of communal ownership. Hence the notion of communal ownership ensures that (1) right of the village community over its village territory so that, resources can be exploited equally by all members and (2) prevents the outsiders from trespassing, confiscating the territory.

Many forest resources like game, grazing grounds, bamboo seed, mahuwa flowers and food resources are shared equally by everybody. If an animal is killed by a predator say, wild dogs and the same was found by an individual Chenchu(s), the dead animal belongs to the entire village community and each and every house gets a share. For instance, in 1997 in Chinthala settlement a *kanithi* (Indian elk) was killed by wild dogs at a place called *Peddakonda vagu.* Kudumula Venkataiah of Chinthala had identified the animal and informed to the village. Many of the villagers came to the spot and equally shared the game. Shares were given to all the households in the *gudem.* Those who could not visit the site were also given the equal share.

In the same way, bamboo seed and mahua flowers are collected by *gumpu* and shared equally by all the households in the *gumpu.* However sometimes, individuals form into groups to collect bamboo rice, jowar and mahua flowers. This rule does not apply to an animal killed by a hunter.

Mirasi

Mirasi is a customary right of enjoyment *(anubhavam)* over certain specific resources. Customarily a few resources having commercial importance are assigned to some persons evidently for protection, control and to ensure equity. It is likely that some outside agency bestowed these rights on some individuals. The Chenchus were in contact with the erstwhile kingdoms like *Vijayanagara* and were supposed to have functioned as sleuths, guides and guards, overseeing any intrusion from local enemies and Muslim rulers. Some of these Chenchus had also acted as 'informers' in tracing thieves who used to hide themselves in the Nallamalai forest. Some Chenchus and some *Vaddi* caste people have taken-up robbery as their profession. These out-laws used to hide grains or goats, or money and ornaments in the forest after stealing. The Chenchus were contacted by the government to know about the hideouts of these out-laws. The government or local chiefs might have conferred some rights on certain individuals or to village communities to exploit certain forest resources like honey, tamarind, soap-nuts etc., in lieu of their services.

Conversely, it is also possible that in the distant past each Chenchu *gudem* was inhabited by a dominant clan which either by virtue of its numerical preponderance or its claim as original settlers of the *gudem*, established customary rights over certain valuable resources like honey, tamarind, soap-nuts, etc.

A third possibility is that in the distant past, the first settlers of the Chenchu *gudems* might have assumed the role of trustees in order to safeguard the resources and to mitigate competitive claims in a situation of indeterminate membership in the village community given the semi-nomadic, fission and fusion life-style.

It is very difficult to prove the correctness of the above hypothesis. In food gathering and hunting societies, such exclusive property rights may be superfluous. The existing literature amply endorses presence of communal ownership on resources among the hunter-gatherers. Most of the examples of these communities like the Kalahari Bushmen, Eskimo etc., live in very harsh environments. The Nallamalai forests are neither extremely harsh nor abundantly rich in resources. While many resources are widely dispersed, a few tend to occur in definite restricted concentrated zones. Most of the *mirasi* rights are pertained to only these concentrated resources. A special variety of honey deposits on the sides of cliffs/gorges called *serris* fall under *mirasi* whereas the other types of honey combs *(junnu, musara, thondi* and *kannugulla)* are not included. In the same way, *mirasi* rights are bestowed in tamarind, gum trees, *morli pappu* trees that usually grow in clusters. However, soap-nut tree, which are dispersed also falls under the umbrella of *mirasi*. Dyson-Hudson and Smith (*op. cit.*) have indicated that exclusively maintained areas occur where critical resources are dense and predictable in time and location. *Mirasi* is one such arrangement. Further *mirasi* also facilitates easy trading activity. *Serri* ceremonies are symbolic means of communicating the *mirasi* rights to others.

To sum up, some resources are exclusively owned. These rights are inherited in the male line. It should also be mentioned that the *mirasi* rights are not manorial in nature. These rights stipulate a certain amount of share due to the *mirasidars*. The *mirasidars* have no right on the whole resource as such. In one sense, the *mirasi* rights reflect Indian feudalism. Shelvankar (1940) wrote that "Indian feudalism remained fiscal and military in character. It was not manorial". The *mirasidars* (claimants of resources) have ensured equity, protection from expropriation, over exploitation. In lieu of this, they extracted a share. They never ascertained manorial rights on the resources. The *mirasidars* used to invite the *non-mirasidars* of the village communities in the collection of honey or tamarind and they only extracted *bagam* (share of *mirasi). Mirasi* may be read as *ma* = mine or our, and *rasi* = share of the produce collected. A certain share is given to the *mirasidar* from the produce collected. Usually the original settlers of the *gudem* have *mirasi* rights in almost all *gudem* studied.

Allocated Property

Certain resources are allocated to individual members of the village community by the *kulapanchayathi.* In many sample settlements each adult member per household is allotted about 50-100 gum trees. Gum collection is beset with the problem of stealing. Besides there is a possibility for individuals to extract gum from more trees if he has big labour force in the family. In case of few other individuals, it may not be possible for them to collect gum during a particular time period in which case others would have collected more gum from trees. Because gum extraction is almost a perennial affair the gum trees located nearer to the settlement get quickly exploited causing the Chenchus to expand the area to search for trees which in turn cause more time for travel. The Chenchus also hold the view that if the gum trees are allocated to individuals, they would try to follow the correct procedure of collection more strictly because their claim on the yield is collectively ensured and safe guarded.

The *raju* or the head of *kulapanchayathi* in consultation with 'elders' or representatives of *gumpus,* has allotted gum trees. More trees were allotted to those families with more adults or working population. The owners of the gum trees can temporarily allow some kinsmen to collect gum but are not supposed to transfer full rights permanently to others. The right ceases to exist if the person dies. His children can share these trees but with the prior information to the *kulapanchayathi*. The latter tries to redistribute trees in order to ensure equity.

Group Rights

The catchment territory is divided into two or more sub-divisions each one is customarily gleaned by one or two groups of households. The village community divides the catchment territory between the households in order to mitigate conflict and ensure equity. Conflicts arise owing to inequity in resource procurement because some groups tend to exploit more because of large population size. If one group in the village exploits more resources because of its numerical strength, the other groups object. Several generations ago *Darabayulu, Alatam, Guttalachenu, Ponnalabailu, Burugundala, Nadathadikala* were under a single catchment territory. It is said that the descendant of one individual named Kudumula Namakannu Thatha migrated to the above places and established independent *gudems* each with an independent catchment territory. In Palutla, Guttalachenu and Chinthala settlements, the territory was divided into sub-territories and allocated to small groups, which are supposed to confine their foraging activities in these territories.

Joint Property

Resources like *serries* (honey deposits) and certain buffer locations are jointly owned or groups belonging either to a single *gudem* or different *gudems*. These groups or individuals may belong to two segments of a single *Kulam* or separate segments of two different *Kulams*. It is said that originally a single ancestor of the groups had ownership rights which subsequently was shared by his heirs. Both Guttalachenu and

Ponnalabayalu settlements jointly owned *serries* located in both the catchments till 1996 after which each *gudem* started collecting honey individually from the serries located in one's own catchment territory.

Combined summer campsites set up by two or more settlements are another example for joint property right. *Bakka chintha penta* is common summer campsite to Guttalachenu and Ponnalabailu settlements. *Thatani penta* is a summer campsite for Palutla and Nekkanti settlements. The *mirasi* share is also owned jointly by *mirasidars*.

Sometimes the resources like roots of *sugandapala theega* (Hemidesmus, indicus), are jointly exploited by the residents of two settlements. This generally occurs at the summer campsites at buffer zones. For instance in April 1998 Kudumula Anjaiah, Kudumula Venkataiah of Palutta and Chevula Edigadu, Chevula Pothadu and Edamma of Nekkanti together set up summer camp at *Thathani penta,* a border area between Nekkanti and Palutla. All stayed at this campsite for ten days and jointly exploited resources within allotted area. Another combined camp is established during February, 1998 to collect *sugandapala* roots at a place called Bakkachinthapenta, by Seelam Muttaiah, Kudumula Bayanna, Kudumula Chinnapothadu, Chevula Kondaiah, Chigulla Kanniah, Damsani Gantalu and Bhumani Ankanna of Guttalachenu and Kudumula Reddi Ankanna and Pothaiah of Ponnalabailu. They jointly stayed there for 15 days and collected roots. Firewood, fodder, CNTFP are all can be gathered together by several households especially those in the *gumpu* and can be jointly shared.

Tenurial Property

Certain resources are exploited for a stipulated time period. Extraction of honey from some *serri* is time-bound and alternated between joint owners. One group of owners exploits the *serri* for a period of two successive years and in the next two successive years, the other groups of owners take over exploitation. *Mirasi* rights are also alternated between the heirs every year or once in two years. Tamarind, soap-nuts, and other CNTFP fall under this right.

The income at *Palanka* shrine are claimed by people belonging to the *Kudumula kulam* in both Ponnalabailu and Guttalachenu settlements. There is a *Shiva* shrine in the *Palanka* valley in the catchment area of Guttalachenu and Ponnalabailu. The pilgrims visiting Srisailam pass through this shrine come on foot though forests. The *Kudumula* people of these two *gudems* clear the path to the shrine on alternate years and give protection to the pilgrims trekking in the forest. In lieu of these services they get the share in the income of the shrine. One year the share is given to Guttalachenu people and another year to Ponnalabailu people.

Most of the agricultural lands also fall in the purview of tenurial property. Generally the Chenchus are not much interested in cultivating their lands. In sample settlements like Palutla and Guttalachenu, it is seen that the Chenchus lease out their land to the *Sugalis* (a Scheduled Tribe) who are living in Palutla and Guttalachenu, for share cropping called *palu* or *bagamu*. The *Sugalis* bear the cost of inputs like seeds, manure, agricultural implements etc. The Chenchu landowners do not actually take part in agricultural operations excepting crop watching. The owner gets one part and the tenant gets two parts.

Adhoc Rights

Certain localities are also exploited for a defined period of time, usually one season by one group and the next year by another group. Honey combs found on trees, in the ant-hills or on any object other than *serri* can be claimed by a person who detects it first by simply keeping a fresh branch of a green tree by the side of the tree or ant hill or scraping the bark of tree. The installed green branch or scrapping mark indicates that the honeycomb has been already identified and no other person should claim or steal away the honey deposit. This is the right of the person who detected it first. For instance, Kudumula Bodeiah of Palutla settlement has detected a honeycomb on a bamboo tree at *Pedd vagu*. He kept a freshly cut branch of tree on the ground near the bamboo tree to indicate that the comb has been already identified. This adhoc right is respected by all members of his village community. After 10 days Bodeiah collected honey.

The adhoc rights are also observed at the hunting grounds. Certain suitable hunting sites are claimed by setting up for *motu* (ambush) or *kundetibonu* (a trap set up for rabbits). *Motu* is a watchtower with a platform on which the hunter hides himself and waits for animals. A Chenchu who sets up *motu* first either at a waterhole or *jede* (a salt-lick) has the right to prevent others from using the same site for hunting, till he kills at least one animal. The others also recognize this right.

Kundeti bonu is a trap for rabbit set up in winter in suitable sites. If a person sets up a *bonu* first at one site then it is treated as his property till the end of the winter. No other individual will enter this site. In December 1997, Damsani Pulla Guravadu of Guttalachenu had put up *kundetibonu* at a place called *Palanka jede*. He caught fifteen hares in that winter till February 1998. No other Chenchu put up a trap near that area. But this right is only for one season. It is not a permanent right forever.

Many forest produces collected by individual Chenchus are treated as adhoc individual property. All vegetable food items come under this class of corporeal property of individuals. Individuals who collected tubers, fruits, leaves, seeds etc., are entitled to consume them. The collected stuff belongs to the individual collector and the manner of its disposal is largely the affair of the collector. Though collected produce in the forest is brought home for consumption of family members, the collector is free to distribute to others. Prior permission is necessary to partake from such produce. In the same way fire-wood collected belongs to the individual and permission is secured by a person who wants to use some fire-wood collected by a different person. All the commercially valued forest produce is carefully retained as individual property to be sold in the market. For example, gum collected is carefully dried and stored in the house day-by-day till a substantial quantity is amassed for later disposal. In case of food, however, there is an obligation to partake with those who lack it.

Seasonal Property

Campsites fall under the category of seasonal property right. Many *gudems* maintain several areas within the catchment territory, for seasonal camps. Such areas are occupied during the summer. This right of seasonal occupation is respected by other *gudems*. During the other times, other villagers also glean these campsite areas. *Musaldani banda* area is a campsite recognized as the property of Alatam settlement. In summer, only Alatam people exploit *sugandapala* roots, soap-nuts and tamarind in this zone. The neighbouring villagers do not enter this place in this season. For hunting, food collection and grazing the Alatam people do not object the neighbours.

Apart from campsite, the catchment territory itself is sub-divided between the *gumpus* of one single settlement, each *gumpu* confines itself to its own sub-catchement area.

In Palutla settlement Chevula Lethakannadu does not allow the members other than his group to collect tamarind and soap-nuts at places like *Seetha banda, Janku madugu* and *Senjala* which are treated as the property of his *gumpu*. After the end of season he does not object the people going for food, fodder, fuel, grazing, etc.

Private Property

Private property notion among the Chenchus is of recent origin. Many personal belongings kept by the Chenchus are of recent trend. Individual property comprises the personal belongings of an individual like hunting implements like bow and arrow, hook, axe, knife, etc. Even the members of the family maintain individual implements and are not transferable without the permission of the holder. Some years ago, the hook, bow and arrow and knifes were not given to any individual even within the family.

Hut, domestic animals, agricultural land and agricultural implements are under the control of the head of the family. Members of the family are free to use this property and each member has right over this property. But it is under the nominal headship of the head of the family. The heirs can claim their right on the property after the death of head of the family.

From the above account, it can be deduced that the Chenchus have different mechanisms to control various resources. It appears various property rights ensured equity, protect resources, excludes outsiders, define rightful stake-holders minimizes expropriation and regulates equality of opportunity to resource exploitation. Thus, the institutions of property rights play a very crucial role in defining the resource boundaries and resource management.

Social Organization

In the previous pages institutions are portrayed as a set of rights and rules. Most of these rules are pertained to resource boundaries and rights and restriction over resource accessibility and exploitation. In this section an attempt is made to understand how the Chenchus organize themselves and exercise these rights and rules and go about exploiting the resources without prejudice to the norms.

As already pointed out each village community comprises groups locally called *gumpu* headed by a central person. This *gumpu* is the most viable unit that organized various activities. The group membership is determined by several strategic criteria such as age, skill, and leadership abilities.

Each *gumpu* member is skilled in a special activity. Though it is generally held that specialized tasks and skills are absent among the hunter-gatherers, specialized skills are noticed among the Chenchus. This arises due to division of labour in a few activities like hunting and sharing the game, honey collection from the *serries*, cutting of bamboo poles, collection of *beedi* leaves or platter leaves, etc. Group effort is required in order to accomplish these activities. Each activity comprises a series of tasks and each task is usually entrusted to a group member every time the activity is undertaken. Conversely, an individual habitually performs one single task and thereby specializes in that. It may be a matter of convenience on strategy that there is an explicit preference and cultural prescription that an individual should adhere to a single task in each of the activities listed above. This arrangement would ensure perfection in the execution of the task. Further, this practice is said to facilitate foresight and premonition of any danger or risk that may jeopardize the whole activity.

However, it does not mean that each Chenchu is an independent expert. Quite contrary, every adult Chenchu almost 'knows' what and how to perform a task in any activity cited above. It is not uncommon that the Chenchus interchange roles in the execution of an activity. In spite of this, the *gumpu* members habitually divide roles among them. This division of roles is an important criterion that underlies group membership. Redundancy is usually discouraged by which an additional expert, say chief honey collector, may have to settle for another role or leave the *gumpu*. Thus, each *gumpu* comprises members with different skills like hunting, tracing the wounded animal, making bow and arrow, sharing the game, detecting *musara*, *thondi* (honeycombs in hallow trunks of the tree), climbing down to the *serries* for honey collection, etc. In commensurate with various tasks or roles comprising each activity. Each *gudem* has multiple *gumpus*, the details of which are shown in the following Table 6.7.

Table - 6.7 The Number of *Gumpus* and Average Households in Each *Gumpu*

Sl. No.	*Settlements*	*Number of gumpus*	*Average household per gumpu*
1.	Alatam	1	6
2.	Chinthala	6	7
3.	Guttalachenu	2	10
4.	Marripalem	6	8
5.	Nekkanti	2	6
6.	Palutla	9	8
7.	Panthanala	1	4
8.	Ponnalabailu	2	5

It can be observed that each *gumpu* is small in size, the membership is not fixed, and is not constant. A member is free to dissociate with the *gumpu* and can join another *gumpu*. A member can leave his *gumpu* temporarily to join another for a specific duration and rejoin his parent *gumpu*. Food sharing and generalized reciprocal relations are seen within the *gumpus* members. The *gumpu* is sustained by a spirit of mutual common interests and cooperation. At any point of time, the *gumpu* contains 10-15 adults of both the sexes or 5-8 households. This small group size facilitates cooperative activities, reciprocal relations. As the *gumpu* enlarges due to birth or accumulation of relatives from neighbouring *gudems* it splits into small groups.

Thus, *gumpu* organisation divides the village community into smaller units, each unit tries to be self-sufficient. Each *gumpu* maintains its own resources and confines to its own territorial sub-division. This reduces the pressure on the land.

The *kulam* is mainly oriented to regulate marital relations. However, the *kulam* also had a role in the management of natural resources. As already pointed out certain members belonging to particular *kulam* groups have *mirasi* rights over resources like tamarind, honey (*serries* and giant trees type) soap-nuts. The *mirasi* rights are vested on these individuals for the duty of supervising the resources from over-exploitation, intrusion from outsiders, etc. The *mirasidars* receive an additional share for having performed the role of protecting the resources. The institution of *mirasi* might have been primarily intended to ensure a harmonious relation with the environment and sustainable resource use. *Mirasi* rights are restricted only to a few resources possibly because these resources occur in limited patches and subjected to excessive exploitation owing to their commercial value and demand from the outsiders. These goods have exchange value vis-a-vis essential requirements such as salt, chillies, iron, cloth etc., which the Chenchus need. In order to ensure regulated exploitation and equity, and to mitigate conflict situation from eruption, the Chenchus themselves would have devised or borrowed *mirasi*.

Kulam group itself is loosely organized. The members belonging to each *Kulam* are widely dispersed. What are seen in each settlement is only independent detached segments vis-a-vis other segments of the same *kulam* stationed elsewhere. This discrete feature is true only when *kulam* is conceptualized as a unit. In other words at the level of *kulam,* there is virtually not even a single occasion when the segments of *kutam(s),* dispersed in various settlements will all assemble together. Siblings tend to live away from each other. *Kulam* members are dispersed far and wide. But at the individual or household level kin connection are always remembered, activated in different permutations and combinations. Lineal and collateral connections through father and mother and connections through one's affines are all given equal importance. Loosely organised *kulam* facilitates and promotes development of a network of kin connections without any hurdles. Such an organization equally facilitates easy disassociation from the existing linkages. In effect a Chenchu can establish linkages with any other Chenchu in any other settlement. Such an organization is essential for a nomadic life style. There is no guarantee that food resources are available for everybody, given the pattern of plant distribution. As already indicated food resources as well as other floral species are dispersed in the Nallamalai barring a few. Just as floral species are dispersed, the Chenchu social organisation also facilitates dispersal of its own members. This mode of social system is developed in order to deal with the constraints imposed by the ecological system.

Seasonal Movements

The deciduous nature of the forest, seasonal flowering and fruiting and seasonal availability of various floral produce, dispersed distribution of floral species impose conditions of relative scarcity spatially. Accordingly the Chenchus indulge in seasonal movement that cause fission and fusion in the social group. The available literature indicates that the Chenchus of the olden days had led a pure nomadic life without any base. Haimendorf (1941) records seasonal nomadism among the Chenchus. The present day movement of the Chenchus is not the same as that in the past. Firstly, not everybody shifts his residence or indulge in seasonal movements. Secondly, there are now several types of movements. Now-a-days, the Chenchus live in 'permanent' huts in 'well established' settlements. One popular movement is daily trips, or at least 3 to 4 times a week, to the forest in search of food, CNTFP, fire wood, fibre, etc. The second type is a brief stays in the forest usually by a couple of days foraging or collecting CNTFP especially gum and soap-nuts. These trips do not involve any erection of hut and last for less than a week. The third type involves establishing a summer camp in definite named places, which have been campsites since the time that their memory can recall. Fourthly, a few individuals regularly stay in the forest itself collecting CNTFP and food materials. They visit the *gudem* once in a fortnight. This stay in the forest may not be prolonged forever. One or two couples may live in a particular place by erecting a small hut for about 6 to 8 months. Lastly, a group of individuals sets out into the forest for hunting. This hunting may last for a maximum period of five days. They subsist on plant food available in the forest and the animals they hunted. Small animals are eaten whereas big game is butchered and meat, is dried to be distributed among the kin back home.

Haimendorf (*ibid*) has portrayed the movement of the Chenchus as seasonal nomadism wherein the Chenchus camped in the forest by erecting small beehive huts during summer. In winter and rainy season, they stayed back in their permanent settlements from where they made daily visits to forest and returned back to settlement by evening. Presently the Chenchus temporarily shift to forest almost anytime in the year, though summer camps are still organised. The Chenchus have two terms, which they use to indicate visits to the forest. *Polam povadam* means going to the forest to carryout either food collection, hunting or collection of CNTFP. This term does not indicate whether an individual is going to stay in the forest for a few days or not. The second term *nidrapolam* or *kandava povadam* is more specific indicating night stay in the forest. The Chenchus show great interest in establishing camps and prefer to stay away from their permanent settlement as and when an opportunity arises.

The Chenchus establish seasonal camps in a named localities. These localities are usually quite far away from the permanent settlement. The distance would not be less than 8-10 kms. Geographically the locality must be suitable for easy traversing. The locality must be sufficiently rich in various resources and shall be able to support a small group of households for about a month or two. Besides, the water must be available throughout the year in the locality.

Each Chenchu settlement has several camp sites usually located within its own catchment territory. However, sometimes a campsite may either overlap with the territory of neighbouring settlements or fall outside one's catchment territory. A campsite may be usually visited by Chenchus belonging to a few Chenchu *gudems*. The Table 6.8 gives the details of campsites for the sample settlement.

Table - 6.8 Number of Camp Sites in the Sample Settlements

Sl. No.	*Sample Settlements*	*No. of gumpus*	*No. of exclusively owned camp sites*	*No. of camp sites jointly owned by more than one gudem*	*Total camp sites*
1.	Alatam	1	2	1	3
2.	Chinthala	5	5	4	9
3.	Guttalachenu	3	4	9	13
4.	Marripalem	6	5	4	9
5.	Nekkanti	2	2	4	6
6.	Palutla	9	12	7	19
7.	Panthanala	1	3	-	3
8.	Ponnalabailu	2	3	6	9

Each of the campsites is regularly and customarily visited by one group comprising 2 to 4 households. However, other households can also camp in consultation with the customary groups. There are certain campsites, which are visited by many people because certain resources are abundantly available. For instance, *Kuntalabodu* a campsite in Palutla territory is visited by about 20 households whereas other camp sites are gleaned by one to five households.

Movement results in dispersal of individuals to different places. The Chenchus explicitly recognize that crowding will disturb social interactions, do not ensure minimum food and CNTFP to each individual. The "Tragedy of Commons" is thus avoided by means of dispersal and seasonal movements. Several rules operate in order to ensure that a sufficient space is available to each group so that they could collect enough NTFP needed for their survival.

Elderly and incapacitated individuals, women with young children may stay back in the *gudem*. Women also accompany their men folk. The children below five years are also carried to the campsites. Children aged five years and above are usually left in the custody of the elderly or warden of the Ashram (residential) school run by Ministry of Tribal Welfare of Andhra Pradesh. The Chenchus start establishing camps from January. Gradually one by one leave the permanent settlement and reach their respective campsites. They would stay there till the end of hot season.

The population in the permanent settlement gradually decrease as summer season advances and this trend continues till the end of June. This trend suddenly reverses in July due to the onset of south-west monsoon in Nallamali. The Chenchus return to their permanent settlement. The seasonal changes act as centrifugal and centripetal forces.

The seasonal movements of the Chenchus and the !Kung Bushmen are oppositional to each other. While Chenchus are dispersed in summer, the !Kung Bushmen cluster together at waterholes in the same season. The Chenchus cluster in the settlement in rainy season, the !Kung Bushmen disperse to different places. In the Chenchus the food resources and CNTFP cause centrifugal effect whereas among the !Kung Bushmen water sources play the role of centripetal movement.

A brief account of the seasonal movements of the Chenchus of Ponnalabailu settlement is discussed in the following. Ponnalabailu settlement comprises ten households with the population of fifty three. There are two *gumpus,* headed by Kudumula Reddi Ankanna and Kudumula Peddankulu respectively. There are nine campsites out of which three are exclusively owned by Ponnalabailu people and the rest are shared by the neighbouring Chenchu settlements. *Dokutu* and *Samiserri* are the campsites which are exploited in normal conditions. *Thavisichettu kona* is a reserved zone, which is exploited in drought conditions. Kudumula Reddi Ankanna's *gumpu* exploits *Dokutu* campsite and Kudumula Peddankulu's *gumpu* exploits Sami serri area.

Both the *gumpus* jointly glean the reserved zone. The Ponnalabailu Chenchus also go for camps to the buffer zones.

Out of the ten families eight families involved in seasonal camps in 1998. Kudumula Pothaiah along with his wife and son (three members) went to *Dokutu* site in January for collection of gum and roots. He was followed by *Chevula Somaiah* and his wife (two members) who went to same place. In the beginning of February Reddi Ankanna and Pothuraju along with the other members of family joined with the earlier group. In Reddi Ankkanna's group, only Avulaiah's family remained in the settlement. In the other *gumpu* Peddankulu, Mallaiah, Chinnankanna along with members of family (seven members) went for *Sami serri* campsite for gum and root collection in February. These two *gumpus* stayed in their respective campsites till the end of February. The individuals in each *gumpu* used to visit the permanent settlement and stay three or four days and again go to the campsite. The gum yield had gradually decreased during the end of winter and starting of summer. By the end of February the collection of *sugandapala* roots was completed in the respective campsites. At the end of February Somaiah and Pothuraju of Reddi Ankanna's group came back to the settlement as the resources were not sufficient to all households and informed the villagers about their plan to go for the camp in the reserved zone for collection of *sugandapala* roots and *vippa pulu* (mahua flowers). The members of Peddankulu's *gumpu* who were staying in the village went to *Sami serri* camp site and informed about the plan of exploitation of buffer zones by the other *gumpu* to Peddankulu, who were staying there.

Mahua flowers blossom in March and April. The Chenchus are fond of collecting these flowers for eating and for liquor preparation. Reddi Ankanna, Somaiah and Pothaiah, along with the members of family went to reserved zone called *Thavisi chettu kona* for collection of mahua flowers and *sugandapala* roots. Pothuraju and his family remained in *Dokutu* campsite and collected mahuwa flowers and roots till the end of April. In Peddankulu's *gumpu,* Peddankulu and Mallaiah went to *Thavisichettu kona.* Chinnankanna and Darabayanna remained in *Sami serri* camp. In reserved zone both the groups set up two small separate huts and exploited the resources separately. Both the groups stayed in reserved zone till the end of April. During this period they exploited mahua flowers, tamarind, soap-nuts and *sugandapala* roots. By the end of April the resources are depleted in reserved zone and the season of above said resources is also over.

Honey, *sugandapala* roots and seeds of *morli, nekkara,* are available during May and June. When the resources exhausted in April 1998, they wanted to shift their campsites to buffer zones of *Bakkachintha penta* and *Sankella gundam.* The information is passed to the neighbouring *gudems* like Guttalachenu and Palutla. Out of five families staying at the reserved zone, four families left the zone. Reddi Ankanna and his *gumpu* member Pothaiah left for buffer zone called *Bakka chintha penta.* Peddankulu and Mallaiah left for another buffer zone called *Sankella gundam.* Only Somaiah and his wife remained in *Thavisichettu kona.* In buffer zones they collected *sugandapala* roots. These families stayed in the campsites till the end of June and the families started coming back to original settlement in late June due to the rainfall.

The large scale honey collection at *serries* and large trees takes place by the end of June and early July after the first showers. All the residents of Ponnalabailu sat together and decided to go for camp for collection of honey in the places like *Sami serri* and *Thavisi chettu*

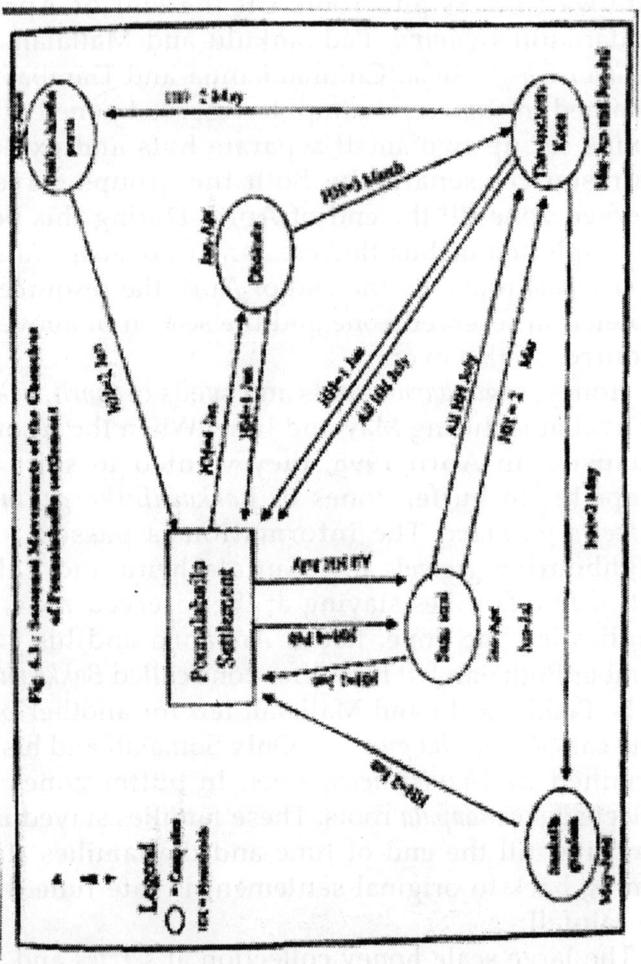

kona. During the early July all the heads of ten families and able adult male children went to *Sami serri* and stayed there one week and later on they went to *Thavisichettu kona* and stayed three days. Generally, the honey collection at *serries* takes place only in nights. All the residents returned to settlement by the mid July. Fig. 6.3 shows the seasonal movement of the Chenchus of Ponnalabailu settlement.

The population in the permanent settlement gradually decreases from January. Fission takes place in the settlement till the end of June. This trend suddenly reverses in June due to the onset of southwest monsoon in the Nallamalai. The population increases in the settlement. Again for few days the Chenchus left the *gudem* in July for honey collection and came back to the settlement. The population increased in the *gudem*. The following Fig. 6.4 shows the seasonal fluctuation of population in Ponnalabailu settlement.

Fig. - 6.4 Seasonal fluctuations in Population in Ponnalabailu settlement

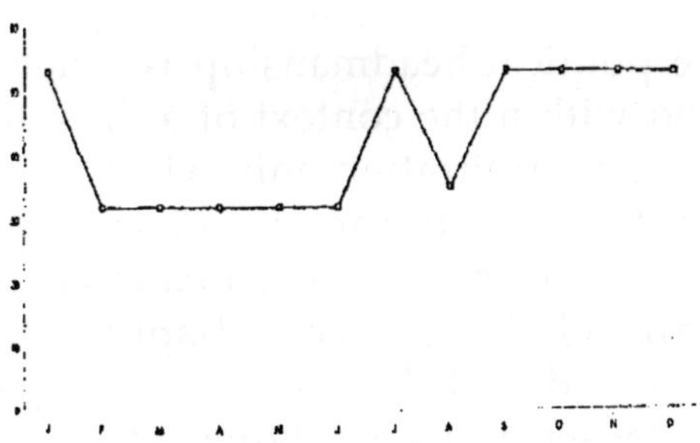

Note: The small trips (two/three days) for hunting and gum collection are not taken into consideration.

In this manner, residential shifts are organized in accordance with the seasonal availability of resources.

Leadership and Political Organization

The Chenchu community can be designated as egalitarian. No status groups or specialized political offices are reported to exist. Leadership roles are iterated between several persons. No single individual repeatedly assumes leadership roles. For each activity one individual assumes leadership role. In another activity this person assumes the role of a follower. Thus, leadership roles keep shifting from individual to individual according to a specific pattern. For many resources harvesting operations, the guidance of an expert is deemed as mandatory. Such an expert's role is said to facilitate to organize the harvest, control access, supervise local rules and act as a steward. Such a person may not participate in the actual operation. But the harvesting team may comprise several experts and thus leadership roles are iterated such that the group functions more democratically and efficiently. Thus, no person tries to assume a totalitarian power. Such a system ensures sustainability and equity. Further leadership role is not something that overrides other roles.

Even the political headmanship is strictly relevant and activated within the context of a dispute. Political leader enters into arbitration only when at least one of the disputants requests for his intervention. In the absence of such a petition, the headman would not volunteer himself to resolve a dispute. Further the headman should indulge, if at all requested, in generating a consensus by involving elders in the village community. The headman does not have any power vested in him. It is only the 'word' of all people that is implemented by the headman.

The village political body is confined to the village itself. There is no centralized authority. In case of inter-village disputes, political bodies of both the villages sit down to hear over the dispute. The village political units safeguard catchment territories. Allocate resources to the members, guide Chenchus in establishing camps, regulate equitable access to resources and resource sharing and conflict resolution.

Conflict Resolution

In spite of all the rules and rights concerning resource use, instances of breach of the accepted behaviour are reported. Disputes over ownership rights pertained to honeycombs *(serri* type), tamarind, gum and soap-nuts are quite frequent. Some of the disputes lead to homicides. Conflicts are resolved usually by three mechanisms: (1) voluntary physical separation by the disputants in which one disputant may choose to leave the settlement and settle in another *gudem;* (2) resorting to the intervention of the village political council ; and (3) use of force which involve direct attack with bow and arrows, arson, confiscating live-stock, etc. Recourse to the first mechanism is most popular. The Chenchus seem to visualize that physical separation would solve the problem and prevent further aggravation. In fact, by separating, the individuals are dispersed thereby the pressure on resources is reduced at a given location. Following case studies explain the conflict resolving mechanisms of the Chenchus :

Case -1

Kudumula Ankanna and his *gumpu* immigrated to Palutla *gudem* from Gandripenta *gudem* due to the clashes between him and his kinsmen. Gandripenta is a Chenchu settlement in Yerragonda palem mandalam. In Gandripenta settlement *Kudumula* surname group possesses the *mirasi* rights. There were two small *gumpus* in *Kudumula* surname group. One *gumpu* was headed by Kudumula Ankanna and the other by Kudumula Pothuraju. The latter *gumpu* possess many relatives and is numerically dominant. Owing to this numerical domination they used to exploit more resources than the former *gumpu.* Kudumula Ankanna objected Pothuraju and demanded for sub-division of catchment area, into two equal parts, so that equity of exploitation can be maintained. Pothuraju thought to physically eliminate Ankanna as he was objecting several times and was questioning his relatives. Pothuraju felt he was insulted by Ankanna. During same period two goats of Ankanna were killed by cheetah and he was attacked by a bear. Ankanna thought that Pothuraju was practicing black magic against him and he simply left the settlement along with his *gumpu* and settled in Palutla.

Case - 2

In 1995 Chevula Letha Edaiah of Palutla trespassed the boundary and collected soap-nuts in the catchment territory of Guttalachenu settlement. Edaiah broke the boundary rules. Knowing the fact Kudumula Gadasala and Bakkabayyana of Guttalachenu came to the spot and asked Edaiah to hand over the soap-nuts to them and leave the place. Edaih rejected to hand over the booty. They resorted to *kulapanchayathi* in Palutla and Guttalachenu. The two gudems conducted joint *kulapanchayathi* and asked Edaiah to hand over the soap-nuts to Guttalachenu people and warned him not to trespass the boundary.

Case - 3

Udathala Mallaih and his brother Guravadu are living in Palutla gudem. They immigrated from their native *gudem* called Thadigundala settlements in Mahboob-nagar distirct. There were eight families in Thadigundala settlement belonging to *Udathala* clan, which possessed *mirasi* rights. In May 1997, Udathala

Mallaiah and his brother Guravadu exploited honey in a small *serri* called *Kothula banda serri*, without informing other *mirasidars* of the settlement. The village community treated that they broke the rule of obtaining prior consent from other *mirasidars*. The other *mirasidars* called upon *kulapanchayathi* and asked Mallaiah and his brother to pay compensation for violating the rule of exploitation. But Mallaih and his brother rejected, saying that as they were also *mirasidars*, they exploited one *serri*. There was a clash between two parties. Mallaiah killed one of the opponents by shooting an arrow. Both Mallaiah and Guravadu left the settlement and migrated to Palutla due to fear of attack by opponents. The relatives of the deceased man confiscated the live-stock of Mallaiah and his brother and ablazed their huts. In this case the right to information is broken and the conflict was solved by deserting the settlement and maintaining physical separation.

To conclude, various institutional mechanisms discussed above serve to achieve sustainability. Foremost, equity is ensured by boundary rules, exclusion rights, reserved zones and proscribed zones. Within the village catchment all members have equal opportunity to resource consumption. This is ensured by various mechanisms: existence of separate catchment to each *gumpu*; sharing of resources; mutual exchange of labour, conditional entry into other territories (when resource crunch pervades in one's own territory).

The problem of 'assurance' (mutual obedience to rules) is tackled by means of various boundary rules and seasonal nomadism. The principle of sharing or sociability reduces unsustainable competition in the sense, that each individual would not flout to hoard away resources suspecting others might indulge in hoarding. Sharing mitigates such an eventuality. Sharing as a norm that is high ranked. The Chenchus are careful even in small matters that may endanger sociability. For example, the food is always eaten outside one's own hut such that any person can see what is being eaten. Food offering is an unavoidable social gesture. Sharing of pooled resources or income is done with a meticulous care, which involves a collective effort. Any extra share due to the working capital borne by an individual, specialized expertise rendered in an activity, or other conventional shares, is very transparent.

Sharing discourages exploitation of resources in excess quantities. Hunting is also restricted both in the number of animals killed and number of times hunting is carried out. The Chenchus are careful in preventing the animals from learning about their hunting practice. They do not scare away the animals. Hunting trips are usually confined to one's own territory unless an injured animal runs into other territories.

The Chenchus have been exploiting the forest resources since times immemorial. Until the recent times, forest was a chief and lonely source of their livelihood. Given the physiographic conditions and nature of floral distribution, the Chenchus have devised various organizational mechanisms for management of natural resources in which availability and utilization of resources are regulated through various institutional mechanisms discussed above. The most essential and significant organizational feature is the wide extension of kin relations and flexible *kulam* organization that facilitates movement across different territories.

Various forest policies have gradually alienated the Chenchus from exercising their rights. The Forest Department does not give due consideration to their traditional property rights and territoriality. The present day Chenchus find it difficult to ascertain their traditional customary rights even among themselves.

The institutions are all under a serious threat, which may erode soon under the influence of Forest Department.

7
Summary and Conclusions

Forests and forest dwelling tribal communities have attracted academic interest from anthropologists since a long time. However, the role of forest and its produce in the economic and socio-cultural life of forest dwelling communities is not addressed adequately. Currently, the environmental interests and forest resource management issues have once again necessitated a fresh look at the forest-tribe relationship. Looking at this relationship holistically is said to provide deeper insights and facilitate critical appraisal of forest-tribe relationship, which hitherto largely portrayed in a romantic or idealized dimension.

The present study is carried out among a tribal population called the Chenchu, traditionally inhabiting the Nallamalai forests in Andhra Pradesh. Originally they were food-gathering and hunting people. The study is confined to two Mandals in Prakasam District viz., Dornala and Yerragonda palem. In spite of a prolonged contact with the neighbouring agricultural communities in plain areas, their dependence on forest resources for subsistence needs has survived to the present day. The study is focussed on (1) a critical appraisal of ecological conditions and resource-base; (2) flow of NTFP at the household level; (3) cultural perception of forest resources and the traditional knowledge system; and

(4) institutional dimensions of resource management and utilization.

The field-work is conducted during 1997 and 1998. Participant observation was the chief method employed in the collection of data. Tools like interview guide, household schedule, case study, ecological survey are employed. The sample comprise eight Chenchu settlements in which all the households were taken into account.

The Nallamalai are the most prominent middle hill ranges of the Eastern Ghats of south India. The major portion of the Nallamalai lies on the borders of three districts viz., Kurnool, Prakasam and Mahboobnagar in the state of Andhra Pradesh. Geographically, this region is located between 15°10' and 16°30' northern latitude and 78°30' and 80°10' east longitude encompassing an area of 5161 km^2. Altitude ranges between 275 mt and 915 mts MSL. The forest is chiefly deciduous with scanty a few sporadically distributed ever-green belts. Important topographical and climatic features are as follows:

The Nallamalai is characterized by small mounds to big hills, flat plain areas to plateaux, narrow steep valleys to broad basins, tapering hill-slopes to deep narrow ravines/gorges/precipice etc. The Chenchus identify these topographical conditions and name them as *sarava* (flat stretches harbouring grass and scanty trees), *baraka* (open place devoid of tree growth), *madhugu* (thick forest area), *palugu* (gentle slopes), *bodu* (forest on hillocks), *sela* (narrow valley with dense stands), *penta* (cattle resting place), *serri* (cliffs), *jede* (salt-licks), *vagu matta* (forests on bank), *dona, chelma* (spring).

The Nallamalai falls under semi-arid zone. The Chenchus identify six seasons : *Nemmi pandla Kalam* (July and August); *Dadiri pandla Kalam* or *Chenchu gadda*

Kalam (September and October); *Thuniki pandla Kalam* (November and December); *Banka Kalam* (January and February); *Morli pandla kalam* or *Vippaputha Mam* (March and April) and *Jana pandla Kalam* or *Thenelu theese kalam* (May and June).

The Chenchus identify 284 floral species in the forest. Of these 284 species 256 species are used for various purposes. The rest of the species are branded as unused. Even though tree as a floral type registered maximum number of species, other floral types such as shrubs, herbs, creepers etc., together constitute a significant proportion (77%). A variety of needs are met from these 'lesser' floral types.

The floral species are put to 13 end-uses: food, fodder, fuel, fibre, medicine, construction material, liquor preparation, fishing, commercial sale, magico-religious, ornamental etc. A large number of species (121) are used as food though there is selectivity depending upon taste, digestibility and processing etc. Altogether 15 parts of plants are used : root, tuber, stem, bark, leaf, flower, pods, seeds, spikes etc. Each species may be used for multiple purposes.

Multiple uses of floral species can be related to the conservation practices such as restrained use, collection strictly confined to seasons, minimization of profligacy and wastage, etc. The overall value of floral species gets elevated due to multiplicity of uses. The Forest Department, on the other hand, entertains one single use of plants viz., revenue. Only in the recent past the Forest Department is viewing forest as having ecosystem services.

The Chenchus identify 33 mammals, 17 reptiles, 43 birds, 10 insects, 4 amphibians and 8 aquatic etc. Of these, 75 species are classified as edible, 22 species as having medicinal value and 21 species associated with magico-religious and symbolic connotations. Some species have multiple purposes. The faunal resources have food as well as medicinal values apart from symbolic associations.

Given the topographical, edaphic features and altitude of the Nallamalai, floral resources in the region exhibit differential distribution in terms of species density, richness of the plants, carrying capacity, seasonality etc. This is reflected in the catchment territories owned by each Chenchu gudem. Each of these territories can be divided into different zones with specific physiographical features. For instance, in Nekkanti gudem the following zones are seen : *kunta* (pond), *kondavalu* (hill slopes), *kondalu* (big hills), *gadda* (flat uplands), *serri* (gorges and cliffs), *sarava* (plain tract), *sela* (a narrow valley traversed by seasonal stream). These zones are visualized by the Chenchus in their native topographical terms mentioned above. These zones offer different possibilities for hunting, fishing, gathering, honey collection, plantation, collection of commercial forest produces and also agriculture.

Such physiographical conditions prevailing in the catchment territories of the Chenchu *gudems* influence the faunal and floral distribution, life-cycle patterns, quality and quantity of the produce. An overall assessment reveals : (a) existence of a wide variety of floral species with deciduous nature ; (b) wide distribution of more or less similar types of resources throughout the Nallamalai, with a few plant species endemic strictly confined to specific zones ; (c) absence of ecotonal formation ; (d) existence of superior and inferior vegetation, differential availability of food reserves and NTFP in terms of quality and quantity ; and (e) differential seasonal developmental cycle of various species.

The Chenchus depend upon various forest resources to meet various needs such as food, fodder, fuel, medicine, material for construction of hut, and other structures, making of implements and household equipment, etc. The elderly Chenchus reported that their quantum requirement of various types of forest produce has been increasing gradually. Their ancestors used much less forest produce compared to the present day Chenchus. Their ancestors did not have permanent big shelters, corrals, enclosures and did not depend on sale of forest produce. The situation has changed now.

An estimation has been made as to know the quantity of bio-mass that a typical Chenchu household utilizes for various end-uses such as food, fuel, fodder, fibre, medicine, shelters, instruments and equipment. A typical Chenchu household is defined here as a household which represent the Chenchu Community residing in the present study area of the Nallamalai; its dependence on agriculture or animal husbandry is minimal but dependence on the forest resources to meet its several needs is high ; its family size is also conforms to the average size of the Chenchu household viz., one adult couple with three unmarried children.

The quantity of forest produce utilized for various end-uses by the typical household per annum is as follows : food (335 kg); fodder (2044 kg); fibre (30 kg); fuel-wood (1800 kg) ; Structural material (2530 kg); CNTFP (460 kg) ; Instrumental and equipment (125 kg), Total 7324 kg.

There is a large gap between the quantity of minimum and maximum consumption of biomass at household level. The range of difference and the consumption of biomass at an average household (average for 25 households) is shown in the following Table 7.1

Table - 7.1 The Consumption of Biomass at Average Household Level and Range of Differences

End-Uses	*Food (kg)*	*Fodder (kg)*	*Fire-wood (kg)*	*Fibre (kg)*	*Structural (kg)*	*CNTFP (kg)*	*Instruments (kg)*
Range	100-400	175-16930	720-3600	10-45	1060-3000	120-700	20-460
Average	300	1780	1670	25	1360	284.50	100

Quantities of NTFP for various other end-uses were not estimated due to sporadic occasional utility in negligible amounts.

Some observations can be made based on the data regarding the flow of NTFP at the household level :

(1) The gap between the minimum quantity and maximum quantity utilized (range) appears to be very wide. This may be construed as an indication that quantum requirement of NTFP may exhibit an increasing trend in the days to come. However, the wide gap itself does not indicate steep skewness because the average quantum of NTFP is close to the minimum quantity utilized. In other words a majority of the Chenchu household's requirement or utilization of NTFP does not agree with the maximum quantity recorded for each end-use.

(2) The forest produce is very important to the Chenchus in view of the fact that a great many needs are satisfied without actually paid for the material that is availed.

(3) Forest produce contribution to the household economy is quite substantial compared to agriculture and wage labour.

(4) Collection of gum, *sugandapala* roots and grazing of livestock seem to result in causation of damage to the forest; the rest of the pursuits are harmless. The pressure on selected resource is mainly due to commercialization.

(5) The Chenchu exercise great selectivity among the various species of floral resources used for different

end-uses. The choice of preference to certain species does not indicate a rigidity. Selectivity should be regarded as an adaptation to the nature of resource, distribution and availability, namely, deciduous nature and seasonality and relative homogeneity in the distribution of diverse species wide across the Nallamalai.

(6) There is a shift in the emphasis given to the collection of certain species for commercial exchange. Before 1970 there were several species, which were being collected for commercial exchange. Relative consistency in demand is observed for honey and tamarind. Rest of the produce like nux-vomica, seeds of buchanania latifolia, *madapa* and *tendu* leaves, broom grass, pods of silk cotton, mahua seeds, soap-nuts, seeds of clearing nut, myrobalam etc., seem to have lost commercial value atleast in the area under study. Further the Chenchus themselves say that these produce are not available in sufficient quantity - because there are not many of these trees and also because of the rules and regulations imposed by the Forest Department. Presently gum, *sugandapala* roots, honey and tamarind have relative importance and the Chenchus show more interest to collect these produce than other produce.

(7) The Chenchus are increasingly realizing that the NTFP availability is slowly getting dearer, scarce and not worth the effort. They are increasingly realizing that commercial collection is not fetching them minimum income that satisfies their minimal essential needs. They have to walk for longer distance ; there are many people competing for the same resources; competition is getting aggravated as the non-tribal people from plain areas are also falling upon these produce.

(8) Comparatively speaking, quantum of NTFP utilized by the Chenchus for certain end-uses like fodder, fibre, structures like huts, corrals is less than the quantity utilized by the rural agricultural households in the plain regions. But the Chenchu requirement for food, CNTFP, medicine and such other end-uses are quite substantial. These requirements are almost absent among the rural agricultural households.

(9) The forest environment imposes certain constrains on the Chenchus in the exploitation of resources : (a) seasonality induced resource fluctuation ; (b) resource fluctuation in terms of quantity and quality in space and time ; (c) unpredictability and risk in the procurement of certain resources like fugitive game and honey deposits on the cliffs ; (d) more or less evenly dispersed resource base with a few concentrated resources (e.g., honey, game, gum, roots), such that resources in an extent of area is exhausted in a stipulated period of short intervals (less than 30 days) and necessitates shift to an other place ; this results in residential shifts ; (e) seasonal resource depletion (barring a few belts of evergreen forests) which also stipulates nomadism ; (f) uninterrupted, contiguous but diverse landscape with sparsely dotted ecotones facilitating movement of predators and prey populations including the Chenchus ; (g) existence of buffer areas, overlapping catchment territories, existence of unguarded areas which are like 'key-stone zones' to fall upon in case of food exhaustion in the immediate vicinity of habitations and usual camp sites.

The Chenchus understand the nature in terms of its predominant spatial or phenomenological manifestations. They do not simply view the forest as if it is an aggregate of spaces and species. It is not an abstracted inventory of its contents. The Chenchus do not conceptualize the resources in terms of morphological or functional criteria as enunciated in chapter 3 and 4. In those chapters, the researcher made an attempt to classify the resources under several parameters. The Chenchus on the other hand do not have an inventory of resources of a specified number classified in accordance with type of flora, number of end-uses, number of parts used etc. To them the resources exist in their respective habitats which form a part of a larger physical whole which again is enmeshed with symbolic and sentimental expressions. Thus, the physical environment and the resources are culturally perceived and constructed.

The Chenchus have myths and tales concerning the origin of the earth, the water bodies, the plants and the animals. The Supreme God is said to have created land, forest, animals and other beings. Forest forms the centre to their culture. The rain is viewed as given by *Vaana devatha* (rain goddess). Rain is equated as mother and earth as her child. The forest is also the child of rain mother. Its survival depends on the rain mother who in turn loves its child by showering rain. Certain localities or sites are said to be the abodes of the deities. These sites are given much respect and are prevented from polluted. These sites are symbolized by keeping a stone slab or identifying an ant-hill as a landmark of sacredness. For instance *Sankella gundam* and *Thota* in Palutla territory and Darabailu in Nekkanti territory are such sacred places in the area of present study.

The Chenchus view that rainfall is associated with sanctity and the ethics practiced by the people. Where people practice *dharma* (ethic) and righteous life the rainfall is said to be regular and adequate. The inadequate rainfall or the frequent droughts are conceived as the result of the human behaviour. Cutting the large trees, sacred trees, polluting the sacred places and failure of leading righteous life are believed to be the major causes for natural calamities. The Chenchus view that the calamities are created by the deities as punishment to the human beings, when they fail to lead a righteous life.

The Chenchus conceive no discrimination between the animals and themselves. They view that both are created by Supreme God called *Paramathmudu* or *Bagavathudu*. Animals, plants and human beings have to share the same environment without disturbing the other. They draw similarities between themselves and the animals. Frequently the Chenchus use the proverb saying "there is no permanent settlement to the Chenchu and honey bees. We move wherever the food resource are available". Their ancestors are reported to have developed the art of hut construction by observing the behaviour of wild boar, which thatches a shrub and prepares a type of conical hut at the time of breeding. It resembles with the most elementary type of hut erected by the Chenchus. Regarding family system there is a close relationship between the Chenchus and the birds like *gokiragadu, garibichuka* etc. The seasonal nomadism of some animals like *edupandi* (hedghog), *manutbothu* (nilgai) wild goat and birds like parrot, *gorinka* etc., is linked with the Chenchus seasonal nomadism.

The Chenchus are familiar with the spatial distribution of the plants and the seasonal behaviour like flowering, fruiting etc. They know the characteristics of the floral and faunal resources. For instance, the *musti* (nux-vomica) is used for snake bite. The leaves of *ari* and *dusara theega* are used to cool the body in summer. They use 97 plants and 27 animals for medical purpose.

They associate magico-religious and symbolic characteristics to the plants and animals. The neem, banian and *ari* trees are treated as sacred and they do not cut the branches of these trees except in certain occasions. The tiger, cheetah are revered as the symbols of tribal deities. *Dasaripamu* (a type of python) is regarded as divine snake and the region where it is present is believed to be prosperous.

The Chenchus have devised various ways of negotiating with their environment in the procurement of various forest resources for their survival. Their social organization of production has the following features.

The Chenchus are seen living in more or less permanent base or focal settlements, each one is separated from the other by considerable distance. Each settlement communally owns a catchment territory with known but loosely guarded boundaries. Each territory possesses several campsites. The neighbouring territories overlap. The Chenchus also identify neutral or buffer zones, which are not guarded. Such zones may be gleaned by Chenchus belonging to neighbouring settlements. In similar way some camp sites located in the territory of a Chenchus settlement, may also be visited by people belonging to other settlements. Such arrangements facilitate fission and fusion of the population in accordance with the availability of resources.

Selection of specific zones for establishing a temporary camp depends upon conscious choice or logistical decisions. Primary motives like grazing, hunting, honey-collection, CNTFP collection, collection of specialized food items like *chenchu gadda* (a tuber) influence this decision. The focal settlement groups tend to disperse rather than conglomerate at a few places. This type of spatial organization is thus characterized by the principle of flexibility in order to disperse the base settlement population in small groups during summer season.

The Chenchus perceive two types of forest resources: predictable, synchronous, seasonal floral resources and unpredictable asynchronous faunal resources. Floral resources are more or less evenly distributed whereas faunal resources are not. Certain resources like honey occur in large quantities confined to certain localities called *serries*. A few commercially valuable floral resources such as tamarind, gum trees occur in dense and predictable in location and time.

In principle, all resources are communally owned. However, certain traditional rights called *mirasi*, tenurial property rights, allocated property etc., exists. Honey, tamarind, soap-nuts fall under the category of *mirasi* ownership wherein a few families belonging to one *Kulam* or agnatically related clans exercise rights of protection and are entitled for ownership share. Collection of these resources however do not stipulate exclusion of members other than the *mirasidars*. Gum is one important commercially valued resource. Individuals have transitory usufruct rights on a certain number of gum trees. Agricultural land entails patrilineal succession but bequeathing to others (uterines or neighbours) is not uncommon.

In accordance with the topographical features and associated floral distribution, the Chenchus have adopted radiating mobility wherein keeping a focal (permanent) site as base, the neighbouring areas are exploited in day time to be returned to the base in the evening for rest. As the resources are exhausted, a fresh site is chosen, camp established and the surrounding area is exploited. This involves not only appropriate selection of sites and resources for exploitation but also fission into small groups to be dispersed in different directions. Radiating mobility is usually restricted to a definite area. It is characterized by logistical organization to acquire, store and distribute resources, and maintenance of connection between the base (focal) site and camp site. Food and other resources flow into the base site from the camp site. Camp sites are organized in such a fashion high quality goods are procured. In the same way, to hunt large to medium animals and to extract honey in *serri* (ravines, cliffs), the Chenchu organize special task groups so as to procure high quality resources. This rich food facilitates in turn, confinement to focal sites for longer period instead of executing a circulating movement from place to place in search of food. Diet selectivity assumes an important factor given the ecological features. Only those food items which cater to the nutritional requirements of their bodies, are selected. In the absence or depletion of these resources, do the Chenchus shift to the next class of species. It is the food resources and its availability that determine group mobility. The same kind of selection is exercised in meeting various requirements like fibre, fuel, medicine, structural material etc. However, in the case of CNTFP, broad-spectrum collection is exercised wherein no grading is done by the Chenchus.

The Chenchus are occasional hunters. Hunting involves rules regarding the membership of the hunting party, skill distribution, division of labour, distribution of the game, and hunting ethics embedded in observance of restraint regarding the number of animals to be killed in one hunting trip, gap between successive hunting trips, animals' physiological conditions (like mating, parturient, with young ones, non-season etc.), Meat is highly prized food. Usually the Chenchus prefer to kill small animals. Big animals are targeted only during group hunting.

In the preceding pages, an attempt was made to show how intimately, intricately and critically the Chenchus are linked with the forest and its resources.

The Chenchus are fairly well versed with the forest and its resources. They have devised institutions in order to manage these resources for equitable exploitation on a sustainable basis. In the past 50 years, the Chenchus are under pressure from the outsiders and government. The National Forest Policy discourages forest dwelling and life in forest. National Commission on Agriculture alleged that free supply of forest produce to the tribals brought distruction to the forest. The NCA recommended to curtailment of their rights.

In the recent past, the Chenchus are being evacuated from the core areas on account of establishing Nagarjuna Sagar - Srisailam Tiger Reserve in the Nallamalai. However, the Chenchus are determined to stay back and thwart the government attempts of displacement. Displacement certainly relegates them into a state of utter dependence and despondency. It is suggested that their knowledge of the forest is usefully utilized for the mutual benefit and welfare.

Appendix - I

Availability and Utilization of Floral Resources

Trees

Sl No.	Local Name	Available botonical Name	Habitat	End use	Actual use	Part used	Process of preparation and use
1.	Adavi Dirisena chettu	Albizzia lebbeck	H	- Instrument	- Axle spindle for cart wheel	S	- trimming
2.	Adavi madi chettu	Spondias mangifera	H	- Food	- Fruits are edible	P	- Collected and prepare chutney
3.	Anduga chettu	Boswellia serrata	H	- Fodder	- cattle graze	L	- Grazing in forest
				- Magico-religious	smoke to child to prevent evils	E	- Kept in Fire to emit smoke
4.	Ari chettu	Bauhinia racemosa	P	- Food	- pods are eaten	P	- Plucked and eaten
				- Magico-religious	- ward off devils and evils	*Baj*	- Kept in amulet
				- Medicine	- Cools body	L	- Mixed with water and drunk
5.	Banda jeevi chettu	Ficus infectoria	H	- Food	- fruits are edible	F	- Ripen fruits are eaten
6.	Battakara chettu	Stephegyne parvifolia	B	- fodder	- Goats browse	L	- Graze in forest
				- medicine	- Cure bums	L	- Soaked in goat's milk and kept on wounds
7.	Bonthada chettu	Not available	H	- fuel	- fire wood	Br	- Dried are collected
				- instrument	- yoke for plough	Br	- Yoke is made

8. Chali kunkudu	Lepisanthes tetra phylla	P	- Fodder	- Goats browse	L	- Graze in forest
			- Fuel	- Fire wood	T	- Dried are collected
9. Chedepa/ vepa chettu	Melia azadirach	P	- food	- Children eat fruits	F	- Ripen fruits are eaten
			- fodder	- Goat browse leaves	L	- Graze in forest
			- medicine	- Cure small pox, cough	B	- Pounded, mixed with hot water and drunk
10. Cheeki reni chettu		B	- Miscellaneous uses	- Bathing	L	- Pounded and used as shampoo
11. Chilla	Strychnos potatorum	H	- CNTFP	- Sold	Seeds	- Collected sold in GCC store
			- Miscellaneous	- Water filtering	Seeds	- Paste mixed with muddy water
			- Medicine	- Remove tumors in stomach	Seeds	- Eaten
12. Chintha chettu	Tamarindus indica	P	- Food	- Fruits & leaves edible	F, L	- Chutney is prepared
			- Fodder	- Goats browse leaves	L	- Browse in forest,Collect to lambs
			- Fuel	- Twigs used for fuel	T	- Dried twigs are collected
			- Medicine	- Cools the body heat	F	- Mixed water and apply to body
			- CNTFP	- Sold to GCC	F	- Sold to GCC
			- Instrumental	- Musical instrument	Br	- used as outer brand
13. Dela chettu		B	- Food	- Prepare, curry, chutney	L, N	- Cooked
			- Fuel	- Fire wood	T	- Dried twigs are

						collected
14. Gadda nelli chettu		P	- Food	- Fruits are edible	F	- Fruits are eaten
				- Prepared curry	L	- Boiled, prepared curry
15. Gara chettu	Balanites roxburghii	P	- Fodder	- Goats browse		- Browse in forest
			- Medicine	- Cure skin disease	N	- Roasted, pounded and smear
			- Fishing	- Fish fuddling	*Baj*	- Pounded and thrown into pond
			- Magico religious	- Ward off evil spirits	*Baj*	- Kept in amulet
16. Gumpani chettu	Odina wodier	H	- Fuel	- Fire wood	T	- Dried twigs are collected
			- Medicine	- Cure wounds	B	- Pounded and tied around the limb
			- CNTFP	- Exudate sold	E	- Sold in GCC store
17. Jammi chettu	Prosopis spicigera	P	- No use	-	-	-
18. Jeedi chettu	Semecarpus anacardium	P	- food	- fruits are edible	F	- Eaten
			- miscellaneous use	- welding the holes of *'dappu'*	N	- Pounded, pasted and heated
19. Jeeluga chettu	Aeschynomene aspera	H	- fodder	- cattle	L	- Cattle browse in forest
20. Jeevi chettu	Ficus retusa	P	- food	- fruits are eaten	F	- Ripen fruits are collected and eaten
			- fuel	- fire wood	T	- Dried twigs are collected
21. Jirra maddhi (Yerra maddhi)	Terminalia arjuna	B	- fuel	- fire wood	Br	- Dried branches are collected
			- structural	- poles and beam to hut	S	- Cut and dressed
			- instrumental	- bullock cart	S	- Used for cart

22. Jittegi	Dalbergia latifolia	H	- fuel	- fire-wood	Br	- Dried branches are collected
23. Kaljeevi		B	- food	- fruits are eaten	F	- Ripen fruits are plucked and eaten
24. Kaninga chettu	Pongamia glabra	B	- fishing	- fish fuddling	B	- Pounded and thrown into pond
25. Kanuga chettu		P	- CNTFP	- Seeds are sold	Seed	- Dried and sold in GCC store
26. Karaka chettu	Terminalia chebula	H	- fodder	- Goats browse	P	- Graze in forest
			- fuel	- Fire wood	Br	- Dried branches are collected
			- medicine	- Curing cough and cold	B	- Mixed with hot water and drunk
			- CNTFP	- Pods are sold	P	-Sold to people of plains
27. Karepaku chettu	Murraya koenigii	P	- Food	- Used in currv	L	-Used in curry
28. Katikari		H	- Food	- Fruits are edible	F	- Ripen fruits are plucked and eaten
29. Kola musti	Hollarrhena antidysenterica	H	- Medicine	- Cure cough	B	- Pounded and engulfed
30. Konda gogu	Cochlospermum gossypium	P	- Food	- Gum is eaten (rarely)	E	- Soaked in water and eaten
			- Fodder	- Cattle eat pods	P	- Goats browse in forest
			- CNTFP	- Gum is sold	E	- Dried and sold to GCC store
31. Kondangi thoka chettu		P	- Food	- Fruits are eaten	F	- Ripen fruits are eaten
			- Fodder	- Goats browse leaves	L	- Goats browse in forest
			- Instruments	- Used for cots	Br	- Cutting &. trimming
32. Konda ragi chettu	Balsamodendron caudatum	H	- Fodder	- Cattle browse	L	- Cattle browse in forest

33. Korivi chettu	Ixora parviflora	P	- Food	- Fruits are edible	F	- Eaten in forest
			- Fodder	- Cattle browse	F, L	- Goats browse in forest
			- Fuel	- Firewood	T	- Dried twigs are collected
			- Medicine	- Improve sight	F	- Fruits are eaten
34. Kunkudu	Sapindus emarginatus	B	- Food	- prepared curry	L	- Boiled and made currry
			- CNTFP	- sold	P	- Collected dried and sold
35. Maddi chettu	Terminalia arjuna	B	- Fuel	- Fire wood	T	- Dried twigs are collected
			- Instrumental	- yoke for bullock cart	S	- Cutting and trimming
36. Magalinga chettu		P	- Medicine	- Improve sexual potentiality	B	- Mixed with milk and drunk three days
37. Manchi neredu/Maredu	Aegle marmelos	P	- Fuel	- Fire wood	T	- Dried twigs are collected
			- Medicine	- blood motions	F	- Eaten
			- Magico-religious	- Protect cattle from evil spirits	*Baj*	- Mixed with milk and sprinkled on herds
38. Marri chettu	Ficus benghalensis	P	- Food	- Fruits are eaten	F	- Ripen fruits are eaten
			- Fibre	- Ropes	Ar	- Pounded and twined ropes
39. Morli chettu	Buchanania latifolia	H	- Food	- Fruits are edible	F,N	- Ripen fruits are collected and eaten
			- Fodder	- Cattle graze	L	- Goats browse in forest
			- Fuel	- Fire wood	T	- Dried twigs are collected
			- Medicine	- body pains	E	- Boiled and coated to body
			- CNTFP	- Commercial	E, N	- Dried and sold to GCC

				purpose		store
40. Muriki nimma chettu	Atalantia monophyila	B	- Fodder	- Cattle browse	L	- Goats Drowse in forest
			- Instrument	- *'guntaka'* (agricultural implement)	Br	- Cutting and trimming
41. Musti chettu	Strychnos nux-vomica	B	- Medicine	- snake bite	B	- Pounded, mixed with urine and -given orally
			- CNTFP	- Seeds are sold	Seed	- dried and sold in GCC store
			- Magico-religious	- Ward off evil spirits	*Baj*	- Kept in roof
42. Naga musti	Strychnos nux-vomica	B	- Medicine	- snake bite	B	- Pounded, mixed with urine and given orally
			- Magico-religious	- Ward off evils	*Baj*	- Kept in roof
43. Nalla balusa chettu	Canthium dicoccum	P	- Food	- Fruits are edible	F	- Eaten in forest
			- Fuel	- Fire wood	T	- Dried twigs are collected
44. Nalla maddhi chettu	Terminalia tomentosa	H	- Instrumental	- plough, gorru	S	- Cutting and trimming
			- Miscellaneous	- Ash is mixed with tamarind	Br	- Ash is mixed to reduce acidity
45. Nalla neredu chettu or Neredu	Eugenia jambolana	B	- Food	- Fruits are edible	F	- Ripen fruits are collected
			- Fuel	- Fire wood	T	- Dried twigs are collected
46. Neeru mamidi	Commiphora caudata	B	- Fuel	- Fire wood	T	- Dried twigs are collected
			- Medicine	- Cure motions	B	- Pounded, mixed with curd and drunk
47. Nemali chettu	Holoptelea integrifolia	P	- Food	- Prepare curry	L, Fl	- Boiled and made curry
			- Fuel	- Fire wood	Br	- Dried branches are collected
			- Medicine	- Cure body pains	B	- Wind at the pain area
			- Instrumental	- Use for bullock cart	S	- Cutting and trimming

48. Nemmi chettu		B	- Food	- Fruits are edible	F	- Collected in large quantities
			- Fuel	- Fire wood	T	- Dried twigs are collected
			- Instrument	- Use for plough	Br	- Cutting and trimming
49. Nerlinga	Albizia amara	P	- Medicine	- Cure eye irritation	L	- Juice applied to eye
			- Instrumental	- Plough	S	- Cutting and trimming
50. Pachha botika chettu or botuku	Trewia nodiflora	B	- Food	- Fruits are edible	F	- Eaten in the forest
			- Fodder	- Cattle browse	L	- Goats browse in forest
			- Fuel	- Fire wood	T	- Dried twigs are collected
			- Instrumental	- Used for cots	Br	- Cutting and trimming
51. Pachhara chettu	Albizia procera	H	- Fuel	- Firewood	T	- Dried twigs are collected
			- Medicine	- Cools body heat	B	- Soaked in water and drunk
52. Palapariga chettu		H	- Fodder	- Goats browse leaves	L	- Browse in forest
			- Medicine	- Cure boils	E	- Smeared on boils
			- Instrumental	- Hand grinder	B	- Cutting and trimming
53. Peddha chitimiti		P	- food	- fruits are eaten	F	- Collected in large quantities
			- miscellaneous use	- used as tumbler to drink water	L	- folded like tumbler
54. Peethiri chettu		P	- medicine	- cure headache and consecutive fever	L	- Wind on head and warmed
55. Pichhi chettu		P	- fodder	- goats browse pods	P	- Goats browse in rarest
			- medicine	- as anti infectant	L	- Fried with kerosene and applied
			- miscellaneous use	- fencing to fields	Br	-Kept around field

56. Poliki chettu	Givotia rottalariformis	B	- food	- nuts are edible	N	- Collected and eaten
			- fodder	- cattle eat fruits	F	- Cattle graze in forest
			- fuel	- fire wood	T	- Dried twigs are collected
			- Magico-religious	- sacred foods	N	- Used in sacred food
57. Pulchera chettu	Phyllanthus reticulatus	P	- Fuel	- fire wood	Br	- Dried branches are collected
			- Medicine	- fever, snake bite	R	- Pounded, boiled and given orally
			- Fishing	- fish fuddle	B	- Pounded and thrown in to pond
			- Magico-religious	- ward off devil	*Baj*	- Kept in amulets
58. Puli chintha chettu	Bauhinia malabarica	B	- Food	- prepare Chutney	L	- Boiled and ground (to paste)
			- Fuel	- fire wood	T	- Dried twigs are collected
59. Ragi Chettu	Ficus religiosa	P	- Food	- fruits are edible	F	- Eaten in forest
60. Regu Chettu	Zizyphus jujuba	P	- Food	- fruits are edible	F	- Collected and eaten
			- Fodder	- goats browse leaves	L	- Browse in forest
			- Miscellaneous	- fencing	Br	- Kept around field
61. Rella chettu	Cassia fistula	P	- No use	-	-	-
62. Reppadi chettu	Wrightia tinctoria	B	- food	- fruits are edible	F	- Eaten in forest
			- fodder	- goats browse leaves	L, F	- Grazed in forest
			- medicine	- cure eye irritation	F	- Fruits are eaten
63. Sandra chettu	Acacia chandra	P	- fuel	- firewood	S	- Dried stems are collected
			- structural	- use as poles for huts	S	- Cut and dressed

			- instrumental	- for *'gorrii'*, *dappu*	T	- Cut and trimmed
64. Seema thumma	Acacia planiformis	B	- medicine	- used for sting of scorpion	L	- Pounded and wound on the spot
65. Seethapalam chettu	Annona squamosa	P	- food	- fruits are edible	F	- Ripen fruits are eaten
66. Sirijaviri		B	- food	- fruits are eaten	F	- Eaten in forest
			- fodder	- cattle browse leaves	L	- Browse in forest
67. Sirimanu/ Tirumanu	Anogeissus latifolia	H	- Food	- gum is eaten (rarely)	E	- Soaked in water and eaten
			- Fodder	- cattle browse	L	- Browse in forest
			- Structural	- used as poles for huts	Br	- Dressed and erected
			- CNTFP	- gum is sold	E	- Sold in GCC Store
			- Instrument	- used for *'gorru'*	S	- Cut and trimmed
68. Somi chettu	Soymida febrifuga	B	- Fuel	- fire wood	Br	- Dried branches are collected
			- Medicine	- post-parturitional use	B	- Pounded, boiled and drunk
			- Liquor	- liquor preparation	B	- Soaked for many days and boiled
			- Fish	- fish fuddling	B	- Pounded, thrown into pond
69. Surugudu pala chettu		B	- Medicine	- improve sexual potentiality	E	- A drop mixed with jaggary and *korra* and engulfed
70. Thabisi	Sterculia urens	H	- food	- eating gum and nuts	N	- Soaked in water and eaten
			- CNTFP	- gum is sold	E	- Dried, cleaned and sold to GCC store
			- Instrumental	- rolling board	S	- Cutting and trimming

71. Thada chettu	Grewia tiliaefolia	B	- instrumental	- used to make cots	s	- Cutting and trimming
			- Miscellaneous use	- used as leaf plates	L	- Plucked and used
72. Thadi chettu	Borassus flabillifer	P	- Food	- Prepare chutney	N	- Pounded to paste
			- Fodder	- cattle browsing	L	- Browse in forest
			- Fuel	- fire wood	T	- Dried twigs are collected
			- Medicine	- cure Jaundice	B	- Soaked in water and drunk
			- CNTFP	- pods are sold	P	- Dried and sold in GCC store
73. Thalati chettu		B	- No use	-		
74. Thaluku chettu		H	- instrumental	- vessel/dish	Br	- Cutting and trimming
75. Thandra chettu	Terminalia bellirica	B	- food	- seeds are edible	Seed	- Eaten in forest
			- medicine	- cure tonsils	Seed	- Tied around neck
76. Thella billudu chettu	Chloroxylon swietenia	P	- fodder	- browsing	P	- Goats browsing in the forest
			- fuel	- fire wood	T	- Dried twigs are collected
			- structural	- used as poles for huts	S	- Cut and dressed
			- instrumental	- used for plough	Br	- Cutting and trimming
77. Thella kommi chettu	Webera corymbosa	P	- food	- fruits are edible	F	- Eaten in forest
			- fuel	- fire wood	T	- Dried twigs are collected
			- medicine	- cure fever, stomach pain	R	- Pounded, boiled and drunk
78. Thella maddhi chettu	Terminalia arjuna	P	- fuel	- Fire wood	T	- Dried twigs are collected
			- Miscellaneous	- For bathing	L	- Pounded and applied as shampoo

79. Thella thumma	Acacia Ieaucophloea	P	- fodder	- Goats browse	L	- Goats browsing in the forest
			- Liquor	- Prepare liquor	B	- Soaked for many days and boiled
80. Thene pachhara chettu	Dalbergia sissoo	H	- Fuel	- Firewood	T	- Dried twigs are collected
			- Medicine	- Cools body heat	B	- Soaked in water and drunk
81. Thunki chettu	Diospyros melanoxylon	B	- Food	- Fruits are edible	F	- Collected and eaten
			- CNTFP	- leaves are sold	L	- Collected and sold in GCC store
82. Usiri		B	- food	- fruits are edible	F	- Eaten in forest
83. Varagogu chettu	Salvadora persica	B	- Food	- Fruits are edible	F	- Eaten in forest
			- Medicine	- Digestive to baby	R	- Pounded, mixed with water oral use
84. Velaga chettu	Feronia limonia	B	- Food	- Fruits are edible	F	- Collected and eaten
			- Fodder	- Cattle eat leaves	L	- Browse in forest
85. Vippa/Ippa	Bassia latifolia	P	- Food	- Flowers are edible	Fl	- Collected in large quantities
			- Fodder	- Cattle browse	L	- Graze in forest
			- Fuel	- Firewood	T	- Dried twigs are collected.
			- Liquor	- Prepare liquor	Fl	- Soaked, mixed with jaggery and boiled
			- CNTFP	- Seeds are sold	Seeds	- Dried and sold in GCC store
86. Yegi/egi	Petrocarpus marsupium	B	- Fodder	- Cattle browse	L, F	- Browse in forest
			- Instruments	- used for bullock	S, Br	- Cutting and trimming

				cart parapat		
87. Yepi chettu	Hardwickia binata	P	- fodder	- cattle browse	L	- Browse in forest
			- fuel	- fire wood	T	- Dried twigs are collected
			- fibre	- rope making	Bar	- Fibre is extracted and trimmed
			- structural	- poles used for hut	Br	- Cut and tressed
			- instrumental	- used for plough, *guntaka* and music	Br	- Cutting and trimming

SHURB

Sl. No. *Local Name*	*Available Botanical Name*	*Habitat*	*End-use*	*Actual use*	*Parts used*	*Process of preparation and usage*
1. Alii chettu	Maba buxifolia	P	- Food	- Fruits are edible	F	- Eaten in the forest
			- Fodder	- Cattle browse fruits	F	- Cattle browse in forest
			- Fuel	- Fire wood	F	- Dried stems are collected
2. Balusa chettu	Canthium parviflorum	P	- Food	- Fruits are edible	F	- Eaten in the forest
			- Fodder	- goats browse	L	- Goats browse in forest
3. Bandharu chettu	Dodonaea viscosa	P	- medicine	- cure boils	L	- Roasted in castor oil and kept on boils
				- sets the broken parts of animals	L	- Placed on broken part and wind
			- structural	- wattle walls	S	- Wattles are made
4. Beera chettu		H	- food	- fruits are edible	F	- Eaten in the forest
			- fuel	- fire wood	S	- Dried stems are collected
5. Bocchu butta chettu		B	- food	- Fruits are edible	F	- Collected in large quantities
			- fuel	- Fire wood	S	- Dried stems are collected

6. Chakali chunnapa chetai		B	- No use	-	-	-
7. Chitimiti	Gardenia gummifera	P	- food	- fruits are edible	F	- Collected in large quantities
			- fuel	- fire wood	T	- Dried twigs are collected
8. Dadiri chettu	Erythroxylon monogynum	P	- food	- fruits and leaves are edible	F L	- Collected to home - Collected and prepared curry
			- fodder	- goats browse	L	- Goats browse in forest
			- fuel	- firewood	T	- Dried twigs are collected
			- medicine	- cure stomach pain	B	- Boiled with water and drunk
9. Dhanthi chettu	Celastrus senegalensis	P	- fodder	- goats browse	L	- Goats browse in forest
10. Eatha chettu	Phoenix sylvestris	P	- Food	- Fruits are edible	F	- Collected and eaten
			- Instrument	- Prepare mats	L	- Mats are woven
11. Erra guruvindha chettu	Abrus precatorious	P	- No use	-	-	-
12. Erra nelajammi		B	- fodder	- cattle browse	W	- Cattle browse in forest
			- medicine	- stops bleeding for women	W	- Juice is mixed with sugar and drunk
13. Gacchaka chettu	Caesalpinia bonducella	B	- medicine	- Used for hernia	L	- Ash mixed with caster oil and applied
14. Gajji manga	Randia dumatorum	P	- Fodder	- Goats browse	L	- Browse in forest
			- Medicine	- Cure wounds	E	- Smear on wounds
15. Gandu manga	Randia malabarica	P	- Medicine	- Good health for children	F	- Pounded and given orally
16. Gotti chettu	Zizyphus xylopyros	B	- Food	- nuts are edible	N	- Eaten in forest
			- Fuel	- fire wood	Br	- Dried branch are collected

			- Medicine	- used for snake bite	B	- Pounded, mixed with urine and given orally
17. Gummudi chettu	Gmelina asiatica	B	- fodder	- Goats browse	F, L	- Browse in forest
			- medicine	- Dandruff	P	- Pounded and used as shampoo
			- fuel	- Fire wood	T	- Dried twigs are collected
18. Jana chettu	Grewia populmifolia	P	- Food	- Fruits are edible	F	- Collected in large quantities
			- Fodder	- Cattle browse	L	- Browse in forest
			- Fibre	- bind faggots etc.	B	- Bark is used as fibre
19. Kaleva chettu	Carissa carandas	P	- Food	- Fruits are edible	F	- Collected in large quantities
			- Fodder	- Goats browse	L	- Browse in forest
			- Fuel	- Fire wood	S	- Dried stems are collected
20. Kattakanthri butta		H	- food	- fruits are edible	F	- Eaten in the forest
			- fodder	- goats browse	L	- Browse in forest
			- fuel	- firewood	S	- Used as fire wood
21. Kondabikki chettu	Gardenia latifoha	B	- food	- fruits are edible	F	- Eaten in the forest
			- fodder	- goats browse leaves	L	- Browse in forest
22. Konda butta chettu		H	- Food	- Fruits are edible	F	- Collected to home and eaten
			- Fuel	- Fire wood	T	- Dried twigs are collected
			- Fishing	- Fish fuddling	P	- Pounded and thrown into pond
23. Kondeetha chettu	Phoenix humilis	H	- Food	- Fruits are edible	F	- Collected and eaten
24. Manga chettu	Randia dumetorum	P	- Medicine	- post parturition use	R	- Pounded, boiled and drunk
			- Fishing	- fish fuddling	P	- Pounded and thrown intc pond

			- CNTFP	- sold	P	- Sold in GCC store	
			- Misc. purpose	- bathing and washing	P	- Pounded and used as soap	
25. Naga jenku chettu		p	- food	- fruits are edible	F	- Eaten in forest	
			- medicine	- scabies	E	- Applied on spot	
			- fishing	- fish fuddling	S	- Pounded and thrown into water	
			- magico-religious	- ward off devils	*Baj*	- Kept in roof	
26. Nalikiri butta chettu		P	- food	- fruits are edible	F	- Eaten in forest	
			- fodder	- cattle browse	L	- Browse in forest	
			- fuel	- fire wood	S	- Dried stems are collected	
			- structural	- wattle for huts	S	- Wattles are owven	
27. Nalla kommi	Webera corymbosa	H	- food	- fruits are edible	F	- Eaten in forest	″
			- fuel	- fire wood	T	- Dried twigs are collected	
			- medicine	- cure fever, stomach pain	R	- Pounded, boiled and given orally	
28. Nalla papidi chettu	Pavetta indica	B	- food	- fruits are edible	F	- Eaten in the forest	
			- fodder	- goats browse	L	- Browse in forest	
			- fuel	- firewood	S	- Dried stems are collected	
			- medicine	- post parturitional use	R	- Pounded, boiled and given orally	
29. Nalla ustha chettu		B	- food	- pods are edible	P	- Boiled and eaten	
			- medicine	- used for snake bite	R	- Pounded, boiled and given orally	

30. Nekkara chettu	Xemenia americana	P	- food	- Fruits are edible	F	- Eaten in the forest
			- fuel	- Firewood	S	- Dried stems are collected
			- CNTFP	- Seeds are sold	Seed	- Dried and sold in GCC store
31. Nela manga		P	- Fodder	- Goats browse	L	- Browse in forest
32. Pala chettu	Cryptolepsis buchanani	H	- Food	- Edible	Fl, P	- Eaten in the forest
33. Pala pariga		P	- Food	- Fruits	F	- Eaten in the forest
34. Paramalla chettu		B	- Medicine	- Cure wounds	L	- Pounded and kept on wounds
35. Polimera chettu		P	- Instrument	- Handle of axe, prongs	T	- Leaves are used as plates in forest
			- Misc. purpose	- leaf plates	L	- Used as Leaf plates
36. Sanyasi mundla chettu		B	- medicine	- cure night blindness	E	- Two drops are kept in eyes for two days
37. Shyagalu	Agave americana	P	- fibre	- fibre is ex' acted	W	- Soaked for 15 days
			- medicine	- cure jaundice	T	- Tied around neck
38. Thangedu chettu	Cassia auriculata	P	- medicine	- Cure motions	L	- Pounded, mixed with curd and eaten
			- ornamental	- Keep in hair	F	- Women adorn in hair
39. Thella Kalabandha	Agave americana	P	- Food	- Prepare chutney	S	- Boiled and prepare chutney
			- Fodder	- Goats browse flowers	F	- Browse in forest
			- Medicine	- Cools body heat	S	- Inner layer is kept on fore head
40. Thella nelajammi		H	- Fodder	- Cattle browse	w	- Browse in the forest
			- Medicine	- Stops bleeding for women	w	- Juice is mixed with sugar and drunk

41. Thella papidi chettu	Pavetta indica	B	- Food	- Fruits are edible	F	- Eaten in forest
			- Fodder	- Goats browse	L	- Browse in forest
			- Fuel	- Fire wood	S	- Collected dried stems
			- Medicine	- Post parturitional use	R	- Pounded, boiled and drunk
42. Thella ustha chettu		B	- food	- fruits are edible	F	- Boiled and eaten
			- medicine	- Post parturitional use		- Pounded, boiled and drunk
				- Scorpion sting		- Pounded and kept on the spot
43. Thutthera chettu		P	- structural	- thatching	T	- Dried and used for thatching
44. Ulcha chettu		P	- structural	- wattles for huts	S	- Wattle are woven
			- instrumental	- used for arrows	S	- Made arrows
45. Ulinda	Dispyrus chloroxylon	P	- food	- fruits are edible	F	- Eaten in the forest
46. Veduru	Dendrocalamus strictus	B	- food	- eaten	Seed	- Collected, stored and cooked
			- fuel	- fire wood	S	- Dried bamboos are used
			- structural	- wattles for hut	S	- Wattles are woven
			- instrumental	- agriculture, bow	S	- Used for implements
47. Yalthuri chettu	Dicbrostachys cinerea	P	- fodder	- goats browse	L	- Browse in forest
			- medicine	- cure cough	B	- Tide around neck
			- magico religious	- ward off devils	*Baj*	- Kept in amulet

HERBS

Sl. No.	Local Name	Available Botanical Name	Habitat	End-use	Actual use	Parts used	Process of preparation and usage
1.	Adavi Affiudharrm	Jotropha glandulifera	H	- No use	-	-	-
2.	Adavi janumu	Crotalariajuncea	P	- fodder	- goats browse	L Spi	Goats browse in forest
3.	Adavi Thangedu	Cassia obovata	H	- no use	-	-	-
4.	Adavi thulasi		P	- fodder	- goats browse	L	Goats browse in forest
5.	Adavi vankaya	Salamim malongena	P	- food	- pod are edible	P	Cooked and eaten
6.	Aditha chettu		B	- no use	- -	-	
7.	Aku manga		P	- fodder	- goats browse	L	Goats browse in forest
8.	Allapaku		P	- fodder	- goats browse	L	Goats browse in forest
9.	Balintha chettu		P	- medicine	- post parturitional use	L	Pounded, boiled and drunk
10.	Baljawa	B. kankda	P	- food	- edible	Tu	Cleaned with water and eaten
11.	Banda baianika	Stefflera stellata	H	- magico-religious	- ward off evil spirits	*Baj*	Kept in amulets
12.	Bankakura		P	- food	- edible	L	Boiled and made curry
13.	Bedula chettu		B	- medicine	- cure motions	W	Pounded, mixed curd and eaten
14.	Bodagadda		P	- food	- edible	Tu	Cleaned with water and eaten
15.	Buragakura		P	- food	- edible	L, Spi	Boiled, mixed salt and eaten
16.	Buthankamu	Elaeodendron roxburghii	P	- medicine - magico-religious	- cure fever - scare devils	R L	Cut and tide around neck Tucked in roof

17. Chamakura	Colocasia antiquonim	P	- food	- edible	L	Boiled and eaten
18. Chencbalaku		P	- food	- prepare soup	L	Boiled, mixed chilli powder and eaten
19. Chetla kindha kura		P	- food	- prepare soup	L	Boiled and eaten
20. Chittmkarulu		H	- food	- fruits are edible	F	Eaten in the forest
21. Chukka kura	Rumex vesicarius	P	- food	- edible	L	Eaten in the forest
22. Doggalaku		P	- food	- edible	L, Spi	Boiled and made curry
23. Dundiga chettu	Oroxylum indicum	P	- medicine	- free motions	E	Smear for three days
24. Eddu banthi		P	- medicine	- cure frequent sneezes to cattle	L	Juice is applied through nose
25. Erra chithramala	Plumbago rosea	P	- medicine	- cure pain in legs	R	Pounded, boiled and drunk
			- magico-religious	- scare evil eyes on cattle	L	Pounded, mixed with goat's milk and sprinkled on herd.
26. Erra dundiga chettu	Oroxylum indicum	P	- medicine	- free medicine	E	Smear for three days
27. Erra gunugu	Abrus prectorius	P	- food	- eaten	Spi	Ground, roasted and make *roti*
			- fodder	- cattle grazing	S	Graze in forest
28. Erra nelemi	Andrographis paniculata	H	- medicine	- used for snake bite	R	Pounded, mixed with urine and given orally.
29. Gaddi vemplai		B	- fodder	- goats browse	L	Goats browse in forest
30. Gayapaku	Sida cordata	P	- medicine	- heal wounds	L	Pounded and kept on wounds
31. Goddu kanithi		P	- medicine	- healing pain in ear	P	Tied to ear
32. Goddu mulaka		P	- fodder	- goats browse	*L*, F	Goats browse in the forest
33. Goggera patthi		P	- Medicine	- Heals pain in ear	Seed	Mixed with water and drink

				and cools body heat	Seed	Juice is applied
			- Ornamental	- Keep in hair	L	Kept in hair
34. Golagondi	Tragia involucrata	H	- No use	-	-	-
35. Guddawa		P	- food	- edible	Tu	Boiled and eaten
36. Konda muchhu thoka		H	- food	- edible	Tu	Boiled and eaten
37. Kukka jeeluga		B	- medicine	- cure eye irritation	L	Juice is applied to eyes.
38. Kundeti chewu	Caraluma umbellata	B	- no use	-	-	-
39. Lukki		P	- fodder	- Cattle graze	L	Cattle graze in the forest
			- Misc. Purpose	- Fire making	S	Create friction with dried twigs
40. Mundlakura		P	- Food	- Edible	L	Boiled and made curry
41. Nakka peechu gadda		P	- medicine	- cure hernia	Wh	Burnt and ash is applied
42. Nalla jilledu chettu	Calotropis gigantea	P	- medicine	- used for snake bite	R	Pounded, mixed with urine and given orally
				- scorpion sting	R	Pounded, kept at stung place
			- magico religious	- scare away devils	R	Made in thread and tied to neck
43. Nela bajanika		B	- no use	-	-	–
44. Nela etha		P	- no use	-	-	–
45. Nela maddhi		B	- fodder	- goats browse	L	Goats browse in forest
47. Nela mukkadi		H	- no use	-	-	–
48. Nela usiri	Phyllanthus amarus	P	- medicine	- cure jaundice	L	Dried, pounded, mixed butter milk and drunk.
49. Neia vempali	Tephrosia purpurea	P	- no use	-	-	
50. Nelemi	Andrographis	H	- medicine	- used for snake bite	R	Pounded, mixed with urine and given orally

	paniculata			- scorpion sting	R	Pounded, kept at stung place
51. Nidhra rani chettu	Mimosa pudica	P	- medicine	- stops over sleeping	L	Juice smeared on face
52. Panchodi	Bridelia hamiltoniana	P	- fodder	- Goats browse	L	Browse in the forest
			- Misc. purpose	- Fire making	S	Produce friction with dried sticks.
53. Pandi boda gadda/ Erra boda gadda		P	- food	- edible	Tu	Boiled and eaten
54. Pedda vempali		P	- fibre	- make ropes	B	Pounded and twined ropes
55. Penta janumu		P	- medicine	- cure boils	L	Pounded to paste and applied
56. Pichhi bangi		P	- medicine	- scorpion sting	L	Pounded and kept at singed place
57. Poga podi		P	- magico-	- emit smoke to scare evil spirits from child	W	Kept on fire, divert smoke towards child.
58. Ponnaganti kura	Alternanthera triandra	P	- food	- edible	L	Boiled and prepared curry
59. Purudaku chettu		P	- medicine	- cure motions to children	L	Pounded with garlic and given orally
60. Sunnapu katte		P	- Oranamental	- kept in hair	F	Women kept in hair
			- Misc. use	- Used as *killi* (pan)	L	Chewed as betel leaf
61. Thella boda gadda		P	- No use	-	-	
62. Thella chithramala	Plumbago zeylanica	P	- medicine	- cure pains in legs	R	Boiled with red gram and eaten
			- magico-religious	- scare evil eyes on cattle	L	Pounded, mixed with goats milk and sprinkled on the herd.

Sl. No.	Local Name	Available Botanical Name	Habitat	End-use	Actual use	Parts used	Process of preparation and use
63.	Thella jilledu chettu	Calotropis gigantea	P	- medicine	- used for snake bite	R	Pounded, mixed with urine and given orally
					- scorpion sting	R	Pounded, and kept at stung place
				- magico-	- scare away devils	B	Made into thread and tide around neck
64.	Thella mulla chettu	Flugea monophylla	P	- medicine	- healing wounds	L	Pounded and applied on wounds
65.	Thella thulasi		B	- no use	- _		
66.	Thella ulava		P	- fodder	- cattle graze	W	Cattle graze in forest
67.	Thummukuxa		P	- food	- edible	L	Boiled and prepared curry
68.	Udumu sulli		B	- Misc. purpose	- Make dogs active	Tu	Dried powder is fed to does
69.	Vedureima	Commelina benghalensis	B	- no use	-	-	-

CLIMBERS

Sl. No.	Local Name	Available Botanical Name	Habitat	End-use	Actual use	Parts used	Process of preparation and use
1.	Adavi anapa		H	- food	- seeds are edible	S	Boiled and eaten
				- fodder	- cattle graze	L	Cattle graze in forest
2.	Adavi chikkudu	Vicia faba	B	- food	- seeds are edible	Seed	Boiled and eaten
				- fodder	- oats browse leaves	L	Goats graze in forest
3.	Alavara gadda		B	- food	- tubers are edible	Tu	Cleaned with water and eaten
4.	Alikiri theega		B	- fodder	- goats browse	L	Goats browse in forest
5.	Bocchu bontha		B	- food	- fruits are edible	F	Eaten in the forest

6. Boddu kura	Rivea ornata	B	- food	- prepare curry	L	Boiled and made curry
			- fodder	- cattle browse	L	Cattle graze in forest
7. Chenchu donda	Coccinia grandis	P	- food	- fruits are edible	F	Eaten in the forest
8. Chenchu gadda		B	- food	- tubers are edible	Tu	Boiled and eaten
9. Chilaka duddera		P	- food	- fruits are edible	F	Eaten in the forest
10. Erraboddi		P	- fodder	- goats browse	L	Goats browse in forest
11. Koteru theega		H	- medicine	- curing cough	E	Mixed turmeric and given orally
12. Kukkabiddi chettu		B	- food	- fruits are edible	F	Eaten in the forest
			- fodder	- goats browse	L	Goats browse in forest
13. Mallakura		P	- food	- prepare curry	L	Boiled and made curry
			- medicine	- increase eye sight	L	Boiled and eaten
14. Meka chanukattu gadda		P	- medicine	- improve sexual potentiality	Tu	Dried, pounded and eaten with dried coconut for three days
15. Movanchi chuwa		B	- fodder	- goats browse	L	Goats browse in forest
			- structural	- wattle walls	S	Wattles are woven
16. Nalleru kadalu	Cissus quadragularis	P	- medicine	- cure wounds of cattle	S	Pounded and applied
17. Nulu gadda		B	- food	- tubers are edible	Tu	Boiled and eaten
18. Pala chettu		P	- food	- fruits are eaten	F	Eaten in the forest
19. Palatthri theega chappidi theega		H	- no use	-	-	-
20. Pamu donda		P	- fodder	- goats browse	F,L	Goats browse in forest
21. Pendli boddu kura		F	- food	- prepare curry	L	Boiled and made cuiry
22. Pillipisuru gadda		B	- food	- tubers are edible	Tu	Cleaned with water and eaten
23. Pilli vattakayala chettu		B	- food	- fruits are eaten	F	Eaten in the forest
			- medicine	- provide good health	F	Eaten

Sl. No. Local Name	Scientific Name	Habitat	End-use	Actual use	Parts used	Process of preparation and use
24. Podapathri theega	Gymnema sylssestre	P	- fodder	- goats browse	L	Goats browse in forest
			- medicine	- cure eye irritation	L	Juice is applied
25. Revagani gadda		K	- Misc. uses	- hair growth	Tu	Pounded, mixed with goat's milk and applied to hair
26. Suganda pala gadda or Netnatheega gadda	Hemidesmus jndicus	B	- Medicine	- Cure chest pain	R	Pounded, boiled and applied
			- CNTFP	- sold in GCC store	R	Dried and sold in GCC store
27. Velaka nekkara		P	- Fodder	- Goats browse	L	Goats browse in forest
28. Yade theega	Combretum albidum	B	- Instrumental	- prepare *'dappu'* (musical instrument)	S	Used as outer band
			- Misc. purpose	- beedi	L	Scrolled as beedi

CREEPERS

Sl. No.	Local Name	Scientific Name	Habitat	End-use	Actual use	Parts used	Process of preparation and use
1.	Adavi kandi	Alylosia scarabaeoides	H	- food	- edible	Seeds	Boiled and eaten
				- fodder	- cattle graze	L	Cattle graze in forest
2.	Adavi pesara	Phaseolus aconitifoloius	H	- food	- edible	Seeds	Boiled and eaten
				- fodder	- cattle graze	L	Cattle graze in forest
3.	Adavi vulava	Cassia absus	P	- food	- edible	Seeds	Boiled and eaten
				- fodder	- cattle graze	L	Cattle graze in forest
4.	Baccharawa	Spinacia oleracea	P	- food	- tubers are edible	Tu	Cleaned with water and eaten
5.	Banda nelemi		B	- medicine	- cure fever	W	Pounded, mixed with hot water and drunk
6.	Dusara theega	Cocculus hisutus	B	- food	- fruits are edible	F	Eaten in the forest

			- fibre	- tying	W	Binding
			- medicine	- reduce body heat	L	Mixed with water and drunk
7. Juttapala theega	Pergularia daemia	P	- medicine	- keeps good health	R	boiled and drunk —
8. Kamma potha-		P	- no use	-	-	–
9. Korinda kampa		H	- no use	-	-	–
10. Nalla gummadi		P	- food	- fruits are edible	F	Eaten in the forest
			- medicine	- cure boils	B	Pounded, mixed salt and urine and applied
11. Neelamari		B	- medicine	- fever, stomach pain	R	Pounded, mixed with hot water and drunk
12. Nela aditha		P	- no use	-	-	-
13. Nela alumu		B	- fodder	- cattle graze	L	Cattle graze in forest
14. Nela kandi		H	- no use	-	-	
15. Nela usiri	Phyllasthus amarus	B	- medicine	- cure jaundice	L	Pounded and swallowed
16. Pamu theega		P	- fodder	- goats browse	W	Goats browse in forest
			- magico-religious	- protect cattle from evil spirits	W	Pounded, mixed with milk and sprinkled on cattle
17. Payala kura		P	- food	- prepare curry	w	Boiled and made curry
18. Peeka thumma		P	- fodder	- goats browse	L	Goats browse in forest
19. Sirrukura	Amaranthus polygonoides	P	- food	- eaten	L	Boiled and made curry
20. Theega amada		P	- no use	-	-	-
21. Theendra theega	Ipomoea stapalina	B	- food	- tubers and new leaves are edible	L Tu	Eaten forest Cleaned and eaten
			- fibre	- used to bind foggots	W	Binding
22. Thella Kavarika		H	- no use	-	-	-
23. Thippa theega	Tinospora cordifolla	B	- fodder	- goats browse	L	Goats browse in forest

Sl. No.	Local Name	Available Botanical Name	Habitat	End-use	Actual use	Parts used	Process of preparation and use
24.	Uppu kampa	Azima tetracantha	B	- medicine	- post parturitional	R	Pounded, boiled and drunk
25.	Uska Pavali kura		P	- food	- prepare curry	L	Boiled and made curry
26.	Varasa jaram chettu		B	- medicine	- cure consecutive fever	S	Tied to hand

GRASS

Sl. No.	Local Name	Available Botanical Name	Habitat	End-use	Actual use	Parts used	Process of preparation and use
1.	Adavi korra		H	- food	- prepare food	Spi	Grains are cooked
				- fodder	- cattle graze	W	Cattle graze in forest
2.	Aditha gaddi		B	- fodder	- animals graze	W	Cattle graze in forest
				- medicine	- cure wounds	Spi	Pounded and applied
3.	Chedu boda		B	- structural	- thatching hut	W	Dried grass used for thatching
4.	Chigurintha		P	- Food	- food is prepared	Spi	grains are cooked
				- Fodder	- cattle graze	W	Cattle graze in forest
5.	Edumulla gaddi		B	- Fodder	- Cattle graze	W	Cattle graze in forest
6.	Gadidha aditha		H	- Fodder	- Cattle graze	W	Cattle graze in forest
7.	Golla savarm	Chloris barbata	B	- Fodder	- goats browse	W	Goats graze in forest
8.	Gundu mukkarai		P	- Food	- tubers are edible	Tu	Cleaned and eaten
9.	Gunthanakka gaddi	Perotis indica	P	- No use	-	-	-
10.	Kamsa gaddi		B	- fodder	- cattle graze	W	Cattle graze in forest
11.	Karu gaddi/ duda gaddi	Aristida hystrix	B	- fodder	- cattle graze	W	Collected and stacked
12.	Kasi gaddi		H	- fodder	- cattle graze	W	Cattle graze in forest

Sl. No. Local Name	Scientific Name	Habitat	End-use	Actual use	Parts used	Process of preparation and use
13. Katterra gaddi / gudisa gaddi		B	- structural	- thatching hut	W	Dried grass used for thatching
14. Pala gadda		B	- medicine	- give milch animals for more milk	Tu	Dried powder, mixed with water and given orally
15. Pusikapulla/ Porakapulla	Aristida depressa	P	- CNTFP - Instrumental	- Sold - used as brooms	W	Dried and sold Used as brooms
16. Vupa chetta		B	- fodder	- cattle graze	W	Cattle graze in forest

FUNGI

Sl. No. Local Name	Scientific Name	Habitat	End-use	Actual use	Parts used	Process of preparation and use
1. Bumi putta kokku	Agaricus	B	- food	- edible	W	Prepared soup
2. Manu putta kokku		B	- medicine	- used for sting of scorpion	W	Pounded and kept on the place of sting
3. Nemitadugu putta kokku		B	- food	- edible	W	Prepared soup / sauce
4. Putta kokku		B	- food - medicine	- edible - cure motions and vomitings	W	Prepare sauce
5. Putta putha		B	- food	- edible	W	Boiled and made curry

AQUATIC PLANTS

SI. No. Local Name	Scientific Name	Habitat	End-use	Actual use	Parts used	Process of preparation and use
1. Adavi pavali kura		B	No use	_	_	_

2. Gurram dekkala chettu	Eichhornia crassipus	B	- no use	-	-	-
3. Kaluva gadda	Nymphoea stellata	B	- food	- tubers are edible	Tu	Cut into pieces and boiled
4. Mudda thunga	Cyperus rotandus	B	- fodder	- cattle graze	W	Cattle graze in forest
5. Thamara gadda	Nelumbo nucifera	B	- food	- tubers are edible	Tu	Cut into pieces and boiled
6. Vaeu aditha		B	- no use	-	-	-

Note: Expansion of abbreviations

Habitat: H = Hill forest, P = Plain forest, B = Both forest

Part : S = Stem, F = Fruit, P = Pod, L= Leaves, E = Exudate
Baj = Bajanika (Unshapped art on branch or leaves). Br =Branch, B = Bark
Seed = Seed, N = Nut, Tu = Tuber, T = Twigs, W= Whole.

Appendix -II

Availability and Utilization of Faunal Resources

ANIMALS

Mammals

Sl. No.	Local Name	English Name	Habitation	Living Pattern	Utilization	Actual utilization	Process of using	Remarks
1.	Aku elaka	Mouse	B	G	- Food	- Eaten	Prepare soup	-
2.	Bandeluka	Mouse	B	G	- Food	- Eaten	Prepare soup	-
3.	Betududha	Wild squirrel	B	S	- food - medicine	- Eaten - Cures head ache	skin is made into form of cap and worn on head	It lives on trees
4.	Burra jinka	Deer	P	G	- Food	- Meat is edible	Meat is cooked	It lives in sparse forest
5.	Chirupuli	Cheetah	H	S	- Symbolic - Food provider	- God Bayyanna - Scavenging	Incarnation of god Left animals half eaten	It confines to the sacred places
6.	Chitteluka	Small mouse	B	G	- Symbolic	- Food grains	If it present in home food grains are believed to be available	–
7.	Duppi	Spotted deer	P	G	- Food - Musical instrument - CNTFP	- Meat eaten - Membrane to musical instrument - horns are sold	Cooked and eaten Skin is tanned and covered to band Fallen horns are sold	–
8.	Duvvu	A kind of panther	H	S	- food provider	- scavenging	Leave dead game after eaten few parts	It hides the dead game on the tree

9.	Edu pandi	Hedgehog	H	P	- food	- Meat eaten	Cooked and eaten	It takes bath two times in every night
					- symbolic	- ward off evil spirits	Thorns are tied around neck of children	
10.	Elugu	Bear	H	P	- Food	- Eaten	Cooked and eaten	Most dangerous animal attacks on human beings
					- Medicine	- cures paralysis	Smearing its blood	
						- improve sexual potentiality to men.	Eating its testicles	
					- Symbolic	- Incarnation of god	Incarnation of god Pothuraju	
11.	Entava	Mungoose	B	P	- Food	- Meat is eaten	Roasted on fire /	It gives milk to squirrel also along its offspring.
					- Medicine	- gives good health	Cooked and eaten	
12.	Gadda pilli/ punugu pilli	Wildcat	B	S	- food	- eaten	Meat is cooked and eaten	–
					- symbolic	- Scare poisonous animals	Testicles dried and kept in home by mixing turmeric	–
13.	Gaddi nakka	Jackal	P	G	- Food	- Eaten	Meat is cooked and eaten	–
14.	Kanithi	Indian elk	B	G	- food	- Eaten	Meat is cooked and eaten	–
					- medicine	- Sets the broken parts	Bone marrow smear on the broken parts	
					- instrument	- Membrane	Taned and covered the *dappu*	
						- Rope	Skin is cut into pieces and used for ploughing	
					- CNTFP	- Sold	Fallen horns are sold	
15.	Konda gorre	Wild sheep	B	G	- Food	- Eaten	Meat is cooked and eaten	It excretes at the place where nilgai does so.
					- Instrument	- Musical	Dried and used as membrane	
16.	Konda mucchu	Wild monkey	H	G	- Food	- Eaten	Meat is cooked and eaten	It does not

No.	Name	English name			Use	Purpose	Method	Remarks
					- Medicine	- Provide health to children	Mixed one drop of urine with water and given daily	have sniffing capacity
17.	Kondrigadu/ kondrapothu		H	S	- Food	- Eaten	Meat is cooked and eaten	
					- Medicine	- Cure body pains	Eating meat	
					- Symbolic	- Eat unlimited	By smelling snout	
18.	Konka nakka	Fox	P	G	- Food	- Eaten	Meat is cooked and eaten	–
					- Medicine	- Cures head ache	Prepare a cap out of skin and wear	
19.	Kothi	Monkey	B	G	- no use	–	–	–
20.	Kundelu	Hare	P	S	- food	- eaten	Meat is cooked and eaten	–
					- medicine	- Cures cough	Eating intestines	
21.	Kura pandi		H	G	- Food	- Eaten	Meat is cooked and eaten	–
22.	Manne garudu		H	P	- Food	- Eaten	Meat is cooked and eaten	–
23.	Manubothu/nall apothu	Nilgai	P	S	- Food	- Eaten	Meat is cooked and eaten	
					- Instrument	- Rope	Skin is cut into pieces and made rope	
24.	Pandi	Boar	H	G	- Food	- Eaten	Meat is cooked and eaten	Build a hut at the time of breeding.
					- Symbolic	- Goddess	Treated as goddess *Nallamysamma*	
25.	Pandi kokku	Bandicoot	B	G	- Food	- Eaten	Meat is cooked and eaten	–
26.	Pedda jinka	Dear	P	S	- Food	- Eaten	Meat is cooked and eaten	–
27.	Pedda nakka	Fox	P	G	- Food	- Eaten	Meat is cooked and eaten	–
28.	Pedda puli	Tiger	H	S	- Symbolic	- goddess	Treated as goddess *Peddamma*	It does not attack on human beings until it is disturbed.
					- Scavenging	- provides meat	Kill the animal and leave some parts	
29.	Pudoka eluka	Mouse	B	P	- food	- Eaten	Meat is cooked and eaten	–
30.	Resulu	Wild dogs	B	G	- Symbolic	- Divine dogs	Treated as divine dogs	–
					- Scavenging	- Provide meat	Kill the animal and leave	

							half eaten	
31.	Revulu elugu		H	P	- Symbolic	- scare evils	Meat is cooked and eaten	
					- Food	- eaten	Meat is cooked and eaten	–
32.	Sarudutha	Squirrel	B	P	- Food	- Eaten	Meat is cooked and eaten	–
33.	Sundeluka	Rat	B	G	- Food	- Eaten	Meat is cooked and eaten	–

Reptiles

Sl. No.	Local Name	English Name	Habitation	Living Pattern	Utilization	Actual utilization	Process of using	Remarks
1.	Battala pothu	A kind of python	H	S	- No use	-	-	Sexual intercourse with iguana
2.	Billi bikkiri	Small snake	B	S	- No use	-	-	-
3.	Dasari pamu	A kind of python	H	S	- Symbolic	Divine snake	Its presence in believed to be prosperous in living area	If it moves from one place to other, the rain will fall very soon.
4.	Dodlankadu	Chameleon	B	S	- No use	-	-	-
5.	Erralu	Earthworm	B		- Fishing	Used as entice	Attached to hook as an entice fish	
6.	Gotti siddadu	Small snake	B	S	- No use	-	-	Sexual intercourse with iguana
7.	Konda chiluva	Python	H	S	- No use	-	-	-
8.	Jerri pothu	Snake	B	S	- No use	-	-	-
9.	Matti pinjara	A big snake	B	S	- No use	-	-	-
10.	Nalikira binda	A kind of chameleon	B	p	- No use	-	-	-
11.	Nattha	Snail	B	S	- No use	-	-	-

12.	Raktha penjara	A kind of python	B	S	- No use	-	-	-
13.	Ralla gotham	A small snake	B	S	- No use	-	-	-
14.	Thrachu pamu	Cobra	B	S	- No use	-	-	-
15.	Udumu	Iguana	B	S	- Food	eaten bow & arrow	Meat is cooked and eaten	
					- Instrument		Skin wrapped round to broken part of bow	
16.	Usiregu	Chameleon	B	p	- Symbolic	ward of evils	tail is kept in amulet to scare away evils	-
17.	Vana kokila	A kind of snake	H	S	- Symbolic	Divine snake	If it chips rain would fall soon	-

Insects

Sl. No.	*Local Name*	*English Name*	*Habitation*	*Living Pattern*	*Utilization*	*Actual utilization*	*Process*
1.	Chali cheemalu	Black ants	B	G	- No use	-	-
2.	Chedulu	White ants	B	G	- Symbolic	- help to grow earth	Deposits soil in the form of ant hill
3.	Erra cheemalu	Red ants	B	G	No use	-	-
4.	Domalu	Mosquito	B	G	No use	-	-
5.	Eagalu	Fly	B	G	No Use	-	-
6.	Nalla cheemalu	Black ants	B	G	Symbolic	- Rain fall	If they carry eggs frequently the rain would fall soon
7.	Pasari	Spider	B	S	Misc.	Web	Kept web in houses to arrests mosquitoe
8.	Theneega	Honey bee	B	G	- Food - CNTFP	- Eaten - Sold	Honey is eaten Honey and wax are sold
9.	Thuneega	Dragon fly	B	G	- Symbolic	- Rainfall	If frequently moves in group rain fall is expected soon
10.	Usullu	A kind of flies	B	G	- Food	- Eaten	After first showers they came out of ant hills and attracted by light or fire, roasted and eaten.

Aquatic

Sl. No.	Local Name	English Name	Living Pattern	Utilization	Actual utilization	Process
1.	Arjalu	A kind of fish	G	- Food	- Eaten	Cooked soup and eaten
2.	Budda pakki	A Kind of fish	G	- Food	- Eaten	Cooked soup and eaten
3.	Endrakaya	Crab	G	- Food	- Eaten	Cooked soup and eaten
				- Medicine	- Cures Fever	Eating soup cures fever
4.	Goggirai	A kind of fish	G	- Food	- Eaten	Cooked soup and eaten
5.	Jalla	A kind of fish	G	- Food	- Eaten	Cooked soup and eaten
				- Medicine	- Cures cough	Eating soup cures cough
6.	Korra menu	A kind of fish	G	- Food	- Eaten	Cooked soup and eaten
7.	Muggu purugulu	An insect	G	- No use	-	-
8.	Valaga	A kind of fish	G	- Food	- Eaten	Cooked soup and eaten

Amphibians

Sl. No.	Local Name	English Name	Living Pattern	Utilization	Actual utilization	Process
1.	Kappa	A kind of frog	G	- No use	-	-
2.	Pedda kappa	Toad	G	- No use	-	-
3.	Thabelu	Tortoise	S	- Food	- Eaten	Cooked soup and eaten
4.	Thala kappa	A kind of frog		- No use	-	-

BIRDS

Sl. No.	Local Name	Place of nest	Living pattering	Utilization	Actual use Pattern	Parts used	Process of preparation and use	Remakrs
1.	Aku chiluka	Holes of tree	G	- Food	- Eaten	- Meat	Roasted on fire or cooked soup	Habit of nomadism for food

2.	Anagogu pitta	Niches of cliffs/ gorges	P	- No use	-	-		It's legs, look like human beings, it chirps like humans
3.	Bedaguvva	On ground	P	- Food	- Eaten	- Meat	Roasted on fire or cooked soup	-
4.	Burrakamju	Ontrees/shurbs	P	- Food	- Eaten	- Meat	Roasted on fire or cooked soup	-
5.	Chakali pitta	On trees	P	- Food	- Eaten	- Meat	Roasted on fire or cooked soup	-
6.	Chekumuki pitta	On trees	P	- Food	- Eaten	- Meat	Roasted on fire or cooked soup	-
7,	Chiluka Odureeka	On ground	G	- Food	- Eaten	- Meat	Prepare soup/roasted	It eats stones
				- Medicine	- Improves digestion	- Meat	Eating meat improves digestive system	
8.	Dega	On trees	S	- Food	- Eaten	- Meat	Roasted on fire or cooked soup.	Snakes are scared away by listening the chirp of this bird
				- Medicine	- Cures poison	-Meat	If eaten the poison does not affect	
9.	Erraburaka	On ground	G	- Food	- Eaten	- Meat	Roasted on fire or cooked soup	-
10.	Erra jilla maya pitta	On trees	G	- Food	- Eaten	- Meat	Roasted on fire or cooked soup	-
				- Medicine	- Sexual potentiality	- Meat	Improves sexual potentiality to man	
11.	Erra jemudu kaki	Shurbs	P	- Food	- Eaten	- Meat	Roasted on fire or cooked soup	-
				- Medicine	- Fever	- Meat	Soup is eaten	
12.	Gada pitta/ sumpana pitta	Holes of tree	G	- Food	- Eaten	- Meat	Roasted on fire or cooked soup	If one is killed in pair the other feeds the young
13.	Garibichuka	On trees	G	- Food	-Eaten	- Meat	Roasted on fire and eaten	-
				- Medicine	- Cures cough	- Meat	Eating cures cough	

14.	Gokiri gadu	On trees	G	- food	- eaten	- Meat	Roasted/soup is eaten	
				- medicine	- fever, body pains, cough	- Meat	Eating cures body pains, cough, fever	-
15.	Gorinka	Holes of tree	P	- food	- eaten	- Meat	Roasted/soap is eaten	Kills the snakes to protect off springs
				- medicine	- head ache, - body pains, - fever	- Meat	Eating cures	
16.	Guba	On trees	P	- No use	-	-	-	Its chirp is treated as bad omen.
17.	Jigi pitta	Holes of tree, cliffs	G	- Food	- Eaten	- Meat	Roasted or prepare soup	They hang inverted
				- Medicine	- Fever, cough	- Meat	Eating cures	
				- Magico-religious	- Scare evil spirits	- Bones	Cut in to pieces and tied to neck of children	
18.	Jittaguwa	On shurbs	P	- Food	- Eaten	- Meat	Roasted on fire	
19.	Juttu gadda	On trees, cliffs	S	- Instruments	- Arrow	- Feathers	Tied at the free end of arrow	-
20.	Kaki bolaka	On trees	G	- Food	- Eaten	- Meat	Roasted in fire or cooked soup	Both feed off springs
21.	Kamju	On ground	G	- Food	- Eaten	- Meat	Roasted in fire or cooked soup	-
22.	Kandiledi pitta	On ground	G	- Food	- Eaten	- Meat	Roasted/prepared soap	The birds feed orphan off springs in the pack
				- Medicine	- Digestion	- Meat	Eating	
				- Magico-religious	- Scare evil eyes, spirit	- Meat	Eating cures fever, or illness caused by the evil eyes/spirits	
21.	Kappara gadu	On ground	P	- food	- eaten	- Meat	Roasted in fire	The pregnant women does not eat as the child will be borne with large mouth as the bird
23.	Kaviri gadu	In holes of trees	P	- food	- eaten	- Meat	Roasted in fire	-
24.	Karukodi	On ground	P	- food	- eaten	- Meat	Roasted in fire or cooked soup	-

25.	Kundeti salava	On trees	S	- No use	-	-	-	
26.	Nalla keechu gadu	On ground	P	- food	- eaten	- Meat	Roasted in fire	If one bird dies other in pair will feed the young
27.	Nemali	On ground	P	- food	- eaten	- Meat	Cooked and eaten	Lay eggs on ground but perch on trees in normal time
				- symbolic	- rainfall		If it frequently chirps rain would fall soon	
28.	Odureeka	On ground	G	- food	- eaten	- Meat	Roasted in fire or cooked soup	It eats small stones and tamarind seeds
				- medicine	- digestion	- Meat	Eating improves digestion	
29.	Pasala poligadu	On trees	S	- Food	- eaten	- Meat	Roasted in fire or cooked soup	It follows cattle throughout day
30.	Pasupu mudda	On trees	S	- food	- eaten	- Meat	Roasted in fire or cooked soup	It contains much fat contents.
31.	Pikkalawa	On trees	p	- food	- eaten	- Meat	Roasted in fire	If one in the pair dies other will join with new bird
32.	Pureli	On ground	p	- food	- eaten	- Meat	Roasted in fire or cooked soup	It never climb up tree or shurb
33.	Ragi guwa	On shurbs	G	- food	- eaten	- Meat	Roasted in fire	If one dies in the pair other will join with new one.
34.	Rama chiluka	In holes of trees	G	- food	- eaten	- Meat	Roasted in fire or cooked soup	Practice seasonal nomadism for food
35.	Sompitta	In holes of tree	P	- symbolic	- fore teller	-	It chirps and fly across the path of Chenchus in forest to prevent the danger to them	This is not killed by Chenchus. If one dies the other also will die.
36.	Thabisi pakshi	On trees/cliffs, gorges	G	- Food	- eaten	- Meat	Roasted and eaten	
				- Magico-religious	- scare evil spirits	- Bones	Tied around neck	
37.	Theethawa	On shurb	P	- No use	-	-	-	

38.	Thella jalla maya pitta	On trees	G	- food	- eaten	- Meat	Roasted in fire	
				- medicine	- increase sexual potentiality	- Meat	Eating	
39.	Thella jamudu kaki	On shurb	P	- food	- eaten	- Meat	Roasted in fire or cooked soup	
				- medicine	- cures fever	- Meat	Eating cures fever	
40.	Thikka theethi	On ground	P	- Misc. purpose	- Provide dogs to make active	- Eggs	Eggs are given to dogs in food.	It does not climb trees
41.	Tiktik gadu	On shurbs	P	- Food	- eaten	- Meat	Roasted	
42.	Thondala thochu gadu	On shurb	S	- no use	-	-		Kills snakes for food

Note : Abbreviations

Habitat	H = Hill forest	P = Plain Forest	B = Both forests
Living Pattern	G = Gregarious	S = Single.	

Bibliography

ADHIKARY, A.K. 1984. Hunters and Gatherers in India: A Preliminary Appraisal of their structure and Transformation. *Journal of India Anthropological Society* 19(1): 8-16.

ANDREWS, ELIZABETH. F.1993. "Territoriality and Land Use Among the Akulmiut of Western Alaska", in *Key Issues in Hunter-Gatherers Research.* Edited by Ernest S. Burch, Jr., and Linda J. Ellanna, pp. 65-95. Oxford: Berg Publishing Co. Ltd.

ANEETA, S.1974. Ethno-Medical Studies Among the Indigenous Groups. *Journal of Anthropological Research* 12: 155-166.

AREE PARAMPIL, MATHEW. 1992. "Forest Policy and Denial of Tribal Rights", in *National Development and Tribal Deprivation.* Edited by Walter Fernandes, pp. 148-173. New Delhi: Indian Social Institute.

ARORA, S.1993. Ethno-Medical Studies: A Research Potential. *Man in India* 73(4): 401-405.

BAXI, UPENDRA. 1983. "Towards a Design of Counter Veiling People's Power in Forest Law and Administration: Agendum for Democratic Law making", in *Towards a New Forest Policy: People's Rights and Environmental Needs.* Edited by Walter Fernandes and Sharad Kulkarni, pp. 102-107. New Delhi: Indian Social Institute.

BEHERA, SRICHARAN. 2000 "Forests, Tribes and Resources", in *Man in the Forest.* Edited by Klaus

Seeland and Franz Schmithusen, pp. 291-305. New Delhi: D.K. Print-world (P) Ltd.

BERNDT, RONALD. M. 1972. "The Walmadjeri and Gugadi", in *Hunters and Gatherers Today.* Edited by M. G. Bicchieri, pp. 177 - 213. New York: Halt, Rinehart and Winston.

BHANU, B. ANANDA. 1982. "The Nomadic Cholanaickan of Kerala: An Analysis of their Movement", in *Nomads in India.* Edited by P.K. Mishra and K.C. Malhotra, pp. 215-226. Calcutta: Anthropological Survey of India.

______________, 1992. "Boundaries, Obligations and Reciprocity: Levels of Territoriality Among the Cholanàickans of South India", in *Mobility and Territoriality.* Edited by Kasimer, M.J. and Aparna Rao, pp. 29-54. Oxford: Berg Publishing Co. Ltd.

BHATT, S.C. (eds.) 1997. The Encyclopaedic District Gazetteers of India. South Zone, (Vol.1) : 291. New Delhi : Gyan Publishing House.

BHOWMICK, P.K. 1989. *The Chenchus of the Forest and Plateaux: A Hunting -Gathering Tribe in Transition.* Calcutta: Institute of Social Research and Applied Anthropology.

BHUSHAN, B. 1997. *Dictionary of Sociology.* New Delhi: Anmol Publications Pvt. Ltd.

BIRD-DAVID, N. 1990. The Giving Environment : Another Perspective on the Economic System of Gatherer-Hunters. *Current Anthropology* 31(2): 189-196.

BOSE, N.K. 1969. The Tribal Situation. *Man in India* 49(3): 217-223.

______________, 1971. *Tribal Life in India.* New Delhi: National Book Trust of India.

BOSE, SARADINDU. 1964. Economy of the Onge of Little Andaman. *Man in India* 44(4): 298-310.

BRODT, SONJA. 1997. *Knowledge Creation in Central*

India: Rethinking the Indigenous Knowledge Debate. Paper Presented at the International Conference on Creativity at Grassroots for Sustainable Natural Resource Management, IIM, Ahmedabad, Jan. 11-14, 1997.

BROUWER, JAN. 2000. "Trees for Timber and Trees for the Forest - Aspects of Indigenous Knowledge of Wood and Stone in Karnataka, India", in *Man in the Forest.* Edited by Klaus Seeland and Franz Schmithusen, pp. 345-360. New Delhi: D.K. Printworld (P) Ltd.

BRUMBAY, F. 1983. "Traditional Ecological Knowledge in Perspective Concepts and Cases", in *Canadian Museum of Nature.* Edited by J.T. Indus. IDRC.

BRUUN, O. and KALLAND, A. 1995. *Asian Perception of Nature: A Critical Approach.* London: Curzon Press.

CHAKRABARTHI, K. 1989. Environmental Hazards in Tribal Life vis-a-vis Forest Policy. *Man and Life,* 15 (3-4) : 151-169.

CHAMBERS, R. 1983. *Rural Development: Putting the Last First.* Essex: Longman Scientific and Technical.

CHAMPION, H.G. and S.K. SETH. 1968. *A Revised Survey of the Forest Types of India.* Government of India, Delhi.

CHANDRA, RAMESH, 1981. "Ecology and Religion of the Kinner: Mountain Dwellers of North Western Himalayas", in *Nature-Man-Spirit Complex in Tribal India.* Edited by R.S. Mann and Vijoy S. Sahay, pp. 269-294. New Delhi: Concept Publishing Company.

CHATTOPADHYAY, SRIKUMAR. 1984. Deforestation in Parts of the Western Ghats Region (Kerala), India. Trivendrum : Centre of Earth Science Studies.

CHAUDHURI, H.N. RAI and D.C. PAL. 1975. Notes on the Magico-Religious Beliefs About Plants Among the Lodhas. *Vanyajathi* XXIII (2): 20-22.

CLARKE, W.C. 1994. "Learning from Ngirapo: Indigenous Knowledge and Sustainable Agricultural Development", in *The Margin Fades: Geographical Itineraries in a World of Islands.* Edited by E. Waddell and P.D. Nunn, pp. 231-266. Suva, Fiji: Institute of Pacific Studies.

CLASTERS, PIERRE. 1972. "The Guayanki", in *Hunters and Gatherers Today.* Edited by M.G. Bicchieri, pp. 138-173. New York: Holt, Rinehart and Winston.

COHEN, ERIK. 1976. Environmental Orientation: A Multidimensional Approach to Social Ecology. *Current Anthropology* 17(1): 49-61.

DALZIEL, J. Mc EWEN. 1937. *The Useful Plants of West Tropical Africa.* London: The Crown Agents for the Colonies.

DAMAS, DAVID. 1972. "The Copper Eskimos", in *Hunters and Gatherers Today.* Edited by M. G. Bicchieri, pp. 3-50. New York: Holt, Rinehart and Winston.

DAS, HARISH CHANDRA, 2000. "Man's Relationship with Forest - Deification of Trees and Plants", in *Man in the Forest.* Edited by Klaus Seeland and Franz Schmithusen, pp. 215-247. New Delhi. D.K. Printworld (P) Ltd.

DASH, JAGANNATHA. 1998. *Human Ecology of Forazers : A Study of the Kharia (Savara), Uja (Savara) and Birhor in Similipal Hills.* New Delhi: Common Wealth.

DEENEY, JOHN., and WALTER FERNANDES. 1992. "Tribals: Their Traditions and Management Systems," in *National Development* and *Tribal Deprivation.* Edited by Walter Fernandes, pp. 49-75. New Delhi: Indian Social Institute.

DIAMOND, J. 1993. "New Guineans and their Natural World", in *The Biophilia Hypothesis.* Edited by S. Kellert and E.O. Wilson, pp. 251-271. Washington

DC: Island Press.

DYSON - HUDSON, RADA and SMITH, ERIC A. 1978. Human Territoriality A Technological Reassessment. *American Anthropologist* 80(1) : 21-41.

EDER, K. 1996. *The Social Construction of Nature.* London: Sage Publications.

ELLIS, J.L. 1982. *Wild-Plant Resources of Nallamalais on the Eastern Ghats.* Proceedings of the Seminar on Resources Development and Environment in the Eastern Ghats. March, 24-27. Waltair, Visakhapatnam : Andhra University Press and Publications.

ESCOBAR, A. 1996. "Constructing Nature: Elements for a Post Structural Political Ecology", in *Liberation Ecologies: Environment, Development Social Movements.* Edited by R. Peet and M. Watts, p. 49. New York and London: Routledge.

FERNANDES. WALTER. 1983. "Towards a New Forest Policy: An Introduction," in *Towards a New Forest Policy: Peoples Rights and Environmental Needs.* Edited by Walter Femandes and Sharad Kulkarani, pp. 1-22. New Delhi: Indian Social Institute.

__________________, 1984. *Forest, Forest Dweller's Economy and Environment,* MAB Projects. Annual Reports. New Delhi: Man and Biosphere Programme, GOI Department of Environment.

__________________, 1990. Forest Policy: A Solution to Tribal Deprivation. *The Indian Journal of Social Work* L (1) : 35-56.

__________________, And GEETA MENON. 1987. *Tribal Women* and *Forest Economy: Deforestation Exploitation and States Change.* New Delhi: Indian Social Institute.

__________________, GEETA MENON, PHILIP VIEGAS. 1988. *Forests, Environment and Tribal Economy : Deforestation Impoverishment* and *Marginalization in Orissa,* New Delhi: Indian Social Institute.

FOX, RICHARD G. 1969. Professional Primitives: Hunters and Gatherers of Nuclear South Asia. *Man in India* 49(2) : 139-160.

FREEMAN, RICH, 1998. "Folk-Models of the Forest Environment in Highland Malabar", in *The Social Construction of Indian Forest.* Edited by Roger Jeffery, pp. 55-78. New Delhi: Manohar.

GADGIL, M. and V.D. VARTAK. 1976. *Sacred Groves of Westerns Ghats of India.* Economic Botany, 30.

GADGIL, MADHAV. 1985. Cultural Evolutions of Ecological Prudence. *Landscape Planning.* 12.

________________, BERKES, F. and C. FOLKE. 1993. *Indigenous Knowledge for Biodiversity Conservation.* Ambio 22(2-3) : 151-156.

________________, and P.R. SESHAGIRI RAO. 1995. Nature, Health and, Learning. For Power with Human Face. *The Hindu Survey of Environment,* pp. 37-41.

GANGADHARAM, V. 1997. *Indigenous Ecological Institutions: A Case Study of the Chenchu Tribe of Andhra Pradesh.* Paper presented in the International Conference on Creativity and Innovation at Grass roots. January, Ahmedabad: Indian Institute of Management.

________________. 1999. *Fertility' Behaviour in Tribal World: Anthropological Perspective.* New Delhi: Reliance Publishing House.

GANGWAR, A.K. 1990. Tribals and Forests of Northeastern India-Strategies for Sustainable Development. *Vanyajati* XXXVIII (2) : 14.21.

GARDNER, PETER. M. 1972. "The Paliyans," in *Hunters and Gatherers Today.* Edited by M.G. Bicchieri, pp. 404-447. New York. Holt, Rinchart and Winter.

GEELANI, G.M. 1986. The Role of Minor Forest Produce in the Tribal economy. *Vanyajati* XXXIV (4): 22-25.

GOKHALE, YOGESH., RAGHUNANDAN VELAHKAR., M.D. SUBHASH CHANDHARAN and MADHAV

GADGIL. 1977. *Sacred Woods, Grass lands and Water bodies as Self Organized Systems of Conservation in India.* A paper Presented to Regional Work shop on the Role of Sacred Groves in Conservation and Management of Biological Diversity, KFRI Peechi.

GOVERNMENT OF INDIA. 1987. *Seeds and Farms.* Dairy Seeds and Farms Corporation, Government of India.

GUHA, B.S. 1931. Census of India 1931. Vol. I. Part III. pp. XLIX. Government Publication.

GUPTA, AMITAYA DAS. 1981. "A Study in Nature-Man-Spirit Complex", in *Nature-Man-Spirit Complex in Tribal India.* Edited by R.S. Mann and Vijoy S. Sahay, pp. 41-56. New Delhi: Concept Publishing Company.

GUPTA, RANJIT, PRAVA, BANERJEE and AMAR GULERIA. 1981. *Tribal Unrest and Forest Management in Bihar.* Ahmedabad: Indian Institute of Management.

HAIMENDORF, CHRISTOPH VON-FURER. 1941. Seasonal Nomadism and Economics of the Chenchu of Hyderabad *Journal of Royal Asiatic Society of Bengal,* 175-196

________________________, 1982. Tribes of India : The Struggle for Survival. Delhi : Oxford University Press.

HALLOWELL, IRVING. A. 1955. *Culture and Experience.* Pennsylvania : University of Pennsylvania Press.

HART, T.B. and J.A. HART. 1986. The Ecological Basins of Hunter-Gatherer Subsistence in African Forest: The Mbuti of Eastern Zaire. *Human Ecology* 14 : 29-56.

HASNAIN, NADEEM.1983. *Tribal India Today.* New Delhi: Harnam Publications.

HELM, JUNE. 1968." The Nature of Dogrib Socio-Territorial groups," in *Man the Hunter.* Edited by

Richard B.Lee and lrven De Vore, pp.118-125. Chicago: Aldine Publishing Company.

_______________. 1972. "The Dogrib Indians" in *Hunters and Gatherers Today*. Edited by M.G. Bicchieri, pp. 51-89. New York: Holt, Rinehart and Winston.

HOWEL, SIGNE. 1996. Nature in Culture or Culture in Nature" in *Nature and Culture: Anthropological Perspectives*. Edited by P. Descola and G. Palsson. pp. 127-144. London: Routledge.

HOWES. MICHAEL AND CHAMBERS. R. 1980. "Indigenous Technical Knowledge: Analysis, Implications and Issues", in *Indigenous Knowledge System and Development*. Edited by D.W. Broken Sha and O. Werner, pp. 329-340. Lanham. MD : University Press of America.

HUSAIN, SYED KHAJA MAHABOOB. 1950. Medicines among Gonds, Kolams and Chenchus. *Man in India* 30(1): 23-31.

INGOLD, T. 1993. *Building, Dwelling, Living: How Animals and People Make themselves at Home in the World*. Paper delivered at ASA Decennial conference.

JANAH, SUNIL.1993. *The Tribals of India*. Calcutta : Oxford University Press.

JEFFERY, ROGE. 1984. *Indigenous Medicine and the State Before 1947. The Politics of Health in India*, pp. 42-52. Berkley: University of California Press.

JENA, MIHIR KUMAR. 2000." Forest and Tribal Sacred Complex - A Comparison of Three Tribes of Orissa," in *Man in the Forest*. Edited by Klaus Seeland and Franz Schmitusen, pp. 269-289 New Delhi: D.K. Print-world (P) Ltd.

JOSHI, GOPA. 1983."Forest Policy and Tribal Development Problems of Implementation, Ecology and Exploitation," in *Towards a New Forest Policy:*

People's Rights and Environmental Needs. Edited by Walter Fernandes and Sharad Kulkarni, pp. 25-46, New Delhi: Indian Social Institute.

KAKALI, CHAKRABARTHY, and DIGVIJAY NADH PANDAY. 1985. The Shompens - A Hunting-Collecting Nomadic Tribe of Great Nicobar. *Vanyajathi* XXXVIII.(4): 19-21.

KALAM, M.A. 1998. "Sacred Groves in Coorg, Karnataka," in *The Social Construction of Indian Forests.* Edited by Roger Jeffery, pp. 41-54. New Delhi : Manohar.

KANT, S. 1997. Integration of Biodiversity Conservation in Tropical Forests and Economic Development of Local Communities. *Journal of Sustainable Forestry* 4(1/2): 33-61.

___________________. 2000."Forest and Tribal Economy," in *Man in the Forest.* Edited by Klaus Seeland and Franz Schmithuscn, pp. 249-268. New Delhi: D.K. Print-world (P) Ltd.

_____________., and N.G. MEHTA. 1993. Forest Based Tribal Economy; A Case Study of Motisingloti Village. *Forests, Trees and People* 20. April 1993: 34-39.

_____________ , J.C. NAUTIYAL and R.A. BERRY. 1996. Forest and Economic Welfare. *Journal of Economic Studies* 23(2) : 31-43.

KARUPPAIYAN. V. 1990. *Kinship and Polity : A Study in Socio-Political Organization . Among the Upland Kallars of Thanjavur District in Tamilnadu.* Madras : Arulvel Achagam.

KEAY, R.W.J. 1989. *Trees of Nigeria.* Oxford: Clarendon Press.

KHIEWTAM RAMESH. S. and R.S. RAMAKRISHNAN. 1989. Socio-Cultural Studies of the Sacred Groves at Cherrapunji and Adjoining Area in North Eastern India. *Man in India* 69(1): 64-71.

KHOSLA. P.K. 1992. Why Farmers Dislike Forest Officials. *Tribune,* March-19.

KLOPPENBURG, JACK Jr. 1991. Social Theory and the De/reconstruction of Agricultural Science: Local Knowledge for an Alternation Agriculture. *Rural Sociology* 56(4) : 519-548.

KOTHARI, ASHISH. 1995, Forest Bill: Old Wine in New Bottle. *The Hindu Survey of Environment,* Madras : 51-54.

________________. 1996. Conserving Bio-Diversity: Doomed Without People. *The Hindu. Survey of Environment* 129- 135.

KULKARNI, SHARAD, 1983. The Forest Policy and the Forest Bill. A Critique and Suggestions for Change." In *Towards a New Forest Policy People Rights and Environmental Needs.* Edited By Walter Fernandes and Sharad Kulkarni. pp. 84-101, New Delhi: Indian Social Institute.

____________________. 1990. Indigenous Peoples - A World View. *Tribal Research Bulletin,* Sep XII(II): 5-10.

KUMARI, P. 1990. Forest and the Tribals of Bihar: Certain Basic Considerations. *Man and Life,* 16-3-4. July-Dec : 137-144.

LEE., RICHARD. B. 1968." What Hunters Do for Living or How to Make out on Scarce Resource," in *Man the Hunter.* Edited by Richard B. Lee, and Irven DeVore, pp. 30-48. Chicago: Aldine Publishing House.

________________. 1972. The Kung Bushmen", in *Hunters and Gatherers Today.* Edited by M.G. Bicchicri, pp. 327-368. New York: Holt, Rinehart and Winston.

________________., and IRVEN De VORE (eds.), 1968. *Man the Hunter.* Chicago: Aldine Publishing Company.

LINKENBACH, ANBTJE. 1998. "Forests in Garhwal and the Construction of Space," *In the Social*

Construction of Indian Forests. Edited by Roger Jeffery, pp. 79-106. New Delhi: Manohar.

MADAN, S.N. 1989. *Dictionary of Anthropology*, New Delhi: Anmol Publications.

MAHAPATHRA, L.K. 1994. Parameters of Forest Policy for Tribal Development. *Social Action* 44(4) : 91-104.

MALAMOUD, C. 1996. Ritual and Thought in Ancient India. Delhi : Oxford University Press.

MALHOTRA, K.C., DEBAL DEB., M. DUTTA., T.S. VASULU., G. YADAV and M. ADHIKARI. n.d. *Role of Non-Timber Forest Produce in Village Economy : Household Survey in Jamboni Range, Midnapore District, West Bengal*. Working Paper, Calcutta: IBRAD.

MALHOTRA, K.C., S.B. KHOMNE and MADHAV GADGIL. 1983. Hunting Strategies Among Three Non-Pastoral Nomadic Groups of Maharashtra. *Man in India* 63(1): 21-39.

MALINOWSKI, 1944. *A Scientific Theory of Culture*. Chapel Hill : University of North Carolina Press.

MANN, R.S. 1981. "Cultural Ecological Approach to the Study of the Bhil", in *Nature-Man-Spirit Complex in Tribal India* Edited by R.S. Mann and Vijoy S. Sahay, pp. 117-126. New Delhi: Concept Publishing House.

MC NETTING, R.C. 1971. *The Ecological Approach in Cultural Study*. Philippines: Addision Wesley. Pub. Co. Inc.

MEHAN; P. 1980. "Science, Ethnoscience and Agricultural Knowledge Utilization", in *Indigenous Knowledge Systems and Development*. Edited by D.W. Brokenshaw., D.M Warren and O. Werner, pp. 383-392. Lanham, MD: University Press of America.

MEHRA, J.D. 1977. "The Worldview of Indian Tribes", in *Tribal Heritage of India*. Edited by S.C. Dube, 58-84. New Delhi: Vikas Publishing House Pvt. Ltd.

MELKANIA, N.P. 2000. "Indigenous Knowledge in Traditional Modes of Forest and Tree Management in the Central Himalaya, India," in *Man in the Forest*. Edited by Klaus Seeland and Franz Schmithusen, pp. 173-193. New Delhi: D.K. Print-world (P) Ltd.

MISRA, K.K. 1998. Tree in the Religion and Folklore of the Konda Reddi of South India. *Journal of Human Ecology* (3): 257-262.

MISRA, P.K. 1992. Oral Strategies Among the Nomadic People. *The Eastern Anthropologist* 45(3): 215-225.

_______________. and B.A. BHANU, 1980. "Boundary Maintenance Among the Cholanaikan Cave-men of Kerala. *Man in India* 60(1-2) : 51-59.

MORAB, S.G. 1981. "The Soliga : A Study in Ecology, Society and Religion of a Hill Tribe in South India", in *Nature-Man-Spirit Complex in Tribal India*. Edited by R.S. Mann and Vijoy S. Sahay, pp. 127-178. New Delhi: Concept Publishing Company.

MURDOCK, GEORGE PETER. 1965. *Social Structure*. New York : The Free Press.

MURTY, M.L.K. 1985. *Ethnoarcheology of the Kurnool Cave Areas, South India*. World Archeology 17(2): 192-205.

_______________. 2000. *Tribal Heritage in the Eastern Ghats (South India) : A Historical Perspective*. Paper presented in Indira Gandhi Memorial Seminar ANADI-II. Tribal Heritage of South India. New Delhi : Indira Gandhi National Centre for the Arts.

NAMIHIRA, A.E. 1987. The Folk Belief System. An Analysis. *Human Organization* 90(1) Spring: 135-141.

NEW BOLD. 1846. The Chenchuwars: A Wild Tribe Inhabiting the Forests of Eastern Ghats. *Journal of Royal Asiatic Society Great Britain and Ireland*. Vol. 8: 271-278.

NORTH, DOUGLAS. 1990. *Institutions, Institutional Change and Economic Performance*. Cambridge : Cambridge University Press.

NOTES and QUERIES ON ANTHROPOLOGY. 1971. London : Routledge and Kegan Paul Ltd.

OOSTING, H.J. 1958. *The Study of Plant Communities.* Sanfrancisco: Freeman.

PAL, D.C. and R.SEN. 1986. Samidauk A Poisonous Plant of the Tribals. *Vanyajati* XXXIV(3) : 8.

PANT, ROUCHI 2000 "Conflicts, Resolution and Institutions in Forest Resource Management Experiences from the Traditional Mountain Communities of Arunachal Pradesh," in *Man in the Forest.* Edited by Klaus Seeland and Franz Schmithusen, pp.131-172. New Delhi : D.K. Printworld (P) Ltd.

PARTHASARATHY, V. 1978. *Andhra Pradesh Forest Souvenir,* Forest Department, Andhra Pradesh, pp. 1-107.

PATHI, PADMINI. 2000."Symbolic Representation of being in the Sacred Art of the Soara of Orissa," in *Man in the Forest.* Edited by Klaus Seeland and Franz Schmithusen, pp. 307-330. New Delhi: D.K. Printworld (P) Ltd.

PATNAIK, KAMALA KUMAR. 2000 "Folk Medicines and Plants Used by Tribals of Phulbani and Koraput Districts of Orissa and Their Future," in *Man in the Forest.* Edited by Klaus Seeland and Franz Schmithusen, pp. 331-344. New Delhi: D.K. Printworld (P) Ltd.

PATNAIK, NITYANANDA. 2000." Eco-Diversity and Indigenous Knowledge of Forests," in *Man in the Forest.* Edited by Klaus Seeland and Franz Schmithusen, pp. 89-111. New Delhi: D.K. Printworld (P) Ltd.

PETERS, CHARLES. M. 1996. *The Ecology and Management of Non-Timber Forest Resources.* Washington DC: World Bank. World Bank Technical Paper. Number 322.

PRASAD, R.K. 1981. "The Parahiyas: A Study in Nature Man-Script Complex," in *Nature-Man-Spirit Complex in Tribal India*. Edited by R.S. Mann and Vijoy S. Sahay, pp. 57-65. New Delhi: Concept Publishing Company.

PRATAP, D.R. 1973. *The Dietary Habits and Nutrition, states of the Chenchus*. Hyderabad.

RAJGOPAL, M.V. 1974. Andhra Pradesh District Gazetteers, Kurnool. The Government of Andhra Pradesh. Hyderabad : Sripada Art Printers, Andhra Pradesh. Government Text-book Press, pp. 17-23 and 27-28.

RAO. K. MOHAN. 1988. Towards Understanding Culture of Tribal Communities in India. *Man in India* 78 (1&2) : 103-118.

________________ . 1993. *Socio-cultural Profile of Tribes of Andhra Pradesh*. Tribal Cultural Research and Training Institute, Hyderabad. Tribal Welfare Department, Andhra Pradesh.

REDDY, G.P. 1972. *The Chenchus : A Scheduled Tribe of Andhra Pradesh*, Vol. I, Part-V, BIV, New Delhi : Government of India Press.

________________ . 1982. *The Tribal Communities of Eastern Ghats: Culture and Ecology*. National Seminar on Resources Development and Environment of the Eastern Ghats. March. Waltair, Visakhapatnam: The Andhra University Press and Publications.

________________. 1984. *Availability and Utilization of Food Resources : An Anthropoecological Study of Andaman Nicobar Islands*. MAB Projects. Annual Reports. New Delhi: Man and Biosphere Programme, GOI, Department of Environment.

________________. 1988. Socialization for Modernisation in the Tribals. *Social Change* 18(1): 32-40.

________________ . 1999. Ours and the Rest: Differential

Perception and Behaviour towards the Utilization of Natural Resources of an Indigenous Population in Nicobar Archipelago. *South Asian Anthropologist* 20(2) : 67-71.

_______________. V. SUDARSEN and RAJESH PATNAIK, 1987. Foraging: A Study of a Shompen Band of Great Nicobar Islands. *South Asian Social Scientist* Vol. III. (1): 31-46.

REDFIELD, R. 1962. "The Primitive Worldview", in *Human Nature and the Study of the Society: The Papers of Robert Redfield.* Edited by Margaret Park Redfield, pp. 280-281. Chicago: University of Chicago Press.

ROGERS, EDWARD, S. 1972. "The Mistassini", in *Hunters and Gatherers Today.* Edited by M.G. Bicchieri, pp. 90-137. New York: Holt, Rinehart and Winston.

ROY, A. RAPPAPORT, 1971. "Nature, Culture and Ecological Anthropology", in *Man, Culture and Society.* Edited by Harry Shapiro, New York : Galaxy Book, Oxford University Press.

ROY, BURMAN. B.K. 1994. *Economic Development of Tribal Communities on Forests.* Outline of Talk on Forest Development vis-a-vis Tribal Ecology. IIFM, Bhopal.

ROY, BURMAN. J.J. 1990. The Needs for Reappraisal of Minor Forest Produce Policies. *The Indian Journal of Social Work* LI(4): 649-658.

ROY, G.P. and K.K. CHATURVEDI. 1986. Plant Used as Tonic by the Tribes of Abujh - Marh Reserve Area, Baster District of Madhya Pradesh. *Vanyajati* XXXIV (3): 27-32.

SAHAY, VIJOY S. 1981. "The Nicobarese: A Study in Nature-Man-Spirit Complex", in *Nature-Man-Spirit Complex in Tribal India.* Edited by R.S. Mann and Vijoy Sahay, pp. 209-218. New Delhi: Concept Publishing Company.

SARKAR, R.M. 1986. Sedentarization of Nomadic Birhors - A Case Study. *Vanyajathi* XXXIV(I): 17-22.

SASTRY, V.N.V.K. 1993. Chenchu Food-gatherers and Hunters of Nallamalai Forest : Problems of Transitions. *Man and Life.* 19(1-2).

SCHLAGER, E. and E. OSTRUM. 1993. "Property Rights Regime and Coastal Fisheries: An Empirical Analysis", in *The Political Economy of Customs of Culture: Informal Solutions to the common problems.* Edited by T.L. Anderson and R.T. Simmons, pp. 13-41. Lanham, Maryland: Rowman and Little field.

SEKHAR, A. CHANDRA, 1965. *A Monograph on Byrlutigudem.* New Delhi. Census of India, 1961. Vol.11 : Part VI, Village Survey Monograph, Serial No. 33.

SERVICE, ELMAN R. 1962. *Primitive Social Organization: An Evolutionary Perspective.* New York: Random House.

SHELVANKAR. 1940. *Problems of India.* London.

SHIVA, VANDANA. 1988. *Staying Alive: Women. Ecology and Survival in India.* New Delhi: Kali for Women.

SHUKLA, BRIJESH KUMAR., and BRIJ. 1991. Ethnobotanical Study Among the Baigas of Mandla District of Madhya Pradesh, India. *Vanyajathi* XXXIX(3):21-30.

SHUKLA, ROHIT, AMBUBHAI, T. DESK, R.B. LAL, A.B. VORA and K.M. KULKARN1. 1990. *Forest and Tribal Life: A Study of Micro-Region.* New Delhi: Concept Publishing Company.

SILBERBAUER, GEORGE B. 1972. "The G/wi Bushmen", in *Hunters and Gatherers Today.* Edited by M.G. Bicchieri. pp. 271-326. New York: Holt, Rinehart and Winston. Inc.

SINGH, P. 1989. Focus on High Yielding Varieties: *The Hindu Survey of Indian Agriculture.* The Hindu. Madras, pp. 236-237.

SINHA, D.P. 1972. "The Bihors", in *Hunters and Gatherers Today.* Edited by M.G. Bicchieri, pp. 371-400. New York: Holt, Rinehart and Winston. Inc.

SINHA, R.K. 1979. Pandos and the Forest - A Study of Nature and Man Interaction. *Vanyajati* XXVIII (2): 30-34.

_______________ . 1981. "A Note on the Nature-Man-Spirit Complex of a Tribe (Pando)". in *Nature-Man-Spirit Complex in Tribai India.* Edited by R.S. Mann and Vijoy S. Sahay, pp. 69-116. New Delhi: Concept Publishing Company.

SINHA, S.C. 1957. The Media and Nature of Hindu Bhumij Interaction. *Journal of Asiatic Society of Bengal.* Letters and Science, 23(1): 23-37.

_______________. 1958. Tribal Cultures of Peninsular India as a Dimension of Little Tradition in the Study of Indian Civilization: A Preliminary Statement. *Journal of American Folklore* 71(281): 504-518.

TARAFDAR. 1984. Less Known Ten Medical Plants used by the Tribals for Bringing Taste to a Sick Person in Hazaribagh District, Bihar. *Vanyajati* XXXII (3): 9-12.

THRUPP, L.A. 1989. *Legitimizing Local Knowledge: from Displacement to Empowerment for Third World People: Agriculture and Human values:* Summer.

THURSTON, E. 1909. *Castes and Tribes of Southern India.* Vol.1 (VIII). Madras: Madras Govt. Press.

TINDALE, NORMAN, B. 1972. "The Pitjandjara", in *Hunters and Gatherers Today.* Edited by M.G. Bicchieri, pp. 217-268. New York: Holt, Rinehart and Winston. Inc.

TURNBUL, COLIN, M. 1968. "The Importance of Flux in two Hunting Societies", in *Man the Hunter.* Edited by Richard B. Lee and Irven DeVore, pp. 132-137. Chicago: Aldine Publishing House.

VIDYARTHI, L.P. 1963. *The Maler: A Study in Nature-Man-Spirit Complex of Hill Tribe in Bihar.* Calcutta; Patna, Allahabad; Bookland Private Limited.

WILSON, EDWARD O. 1975. *Sociobiology : The New Synthesis.* Cambridge : Harward University Press.

WINICK, CHARLES. 1964. *Dictionary of Anthropology London:* Peter Owen Limited.

Photos

Ponnalabailu settlement

The *Chenchu* with his children

Women carrying water from rivulet

Making wattle walls

Chenchu family eating Tamarind

Chenchus eating *nunni* fruits

Plucking and eating *Nekkara* fruits

Wife and husband digging *Suganda pala* roots

Drying *sugandpala* roots

Hunters observering foot prints of animals at salt ticks

Hunting by ambush

Hunters skinning the rabbit

Rope made of the skin of Nilgai

Sucking water from the trunk

making bow

Village deity under banyan tree

Data collection from chenchu *gudem*

The author

Index

G